Johnson in Japan

Johnson in Japan

EDITED BY KIMIYO OGAWA AND MIKA SUZUKI

FOREWORD BY GREG CLINGHAM

Bucknell University | University Press

Lewisburg, Pennsylvania

LCCN 2019058944

A British Cataloging-in-Publication record for this book is available from the British Library.

♾ The paper used in this publication meets the requirements of the American National Standard for Information Sciences—Permanence of Paper for Printed Library Materials, ANSI Z39.48-1992.

www.bucknelluniversitypress.org

Distributed worldwide by Rutgers University Press

Manufactured in the United States of America

For the members of the Johnson Society of Japan who share the values of *an interchange of help and communication of intelligence.*

Contents

Foreword

Global Johnson

GREG CLINGHAM

1

Eighteenth-century studies have undergone several transformations over the last thirty years, to some extent traced—and even shaped by—the book series in eighteenth-century studies published by Bucknell University Press.[1] Scholars of the "period" have intelligently absorbed critical and theoretical ways of reading texts, both present and past, that has made the study of the long eighteenth century as vibrant, exciting, and relevant to current concerns as it has ever been. In particular, paradigms articulated by such scholars as Felicity Nussbaum, Srinivas Aravamudan, and David Porter[2] have helped open the study of eighteenth-century literature and history to the relevance of trans-Atlantic and global networks and experience, including matters relating to gender and sexuality, race and slavery, trade and commerce, natural science and discovery, travel and colonial expansion, and religious and philosophical thought, as well as to the diverse abundance of human and cultural behavior offered by the world beyond Europe. In the new global orientation characterizing eighteenth-century studies, Europe's cultural relation to the Orient has become central. Generated mostly by anglophone and francophone critics, the interest in the Orient has been largely shaped by Western perspectives, although scholarly work reflecting the perspectives of non-Western cultures—especially those of the Ottomans and the Qing—has begun to revise and reorient our historical understanding of early-modern Europe and the Enlightenment.[3]

In this context Japan is anomalous. Ancient as Japanese art and culture is, the process of westernization in Japan, dating back to the Meiji in the mid-nineteenth century, to some extent explains the deep familiarity of Japanese readers with English and American literatures. If the Japan we find in literary histories or art histories was, like China, a product of the British and American cultural imagination, we might remind ourselves that Japanese scholars and readers have likewise been busy recuperating Western literatures according to their own lights for generations. A long tradition of studying, teaching, and appropriating works of English and American writers—most obviously the plays of Shakespeare—has produced a substantial, multiplicitous body of artistic, critical, and cultural thought in Japan. That there exists a "Japanese Johnson," who is, in the contours of his writing and personality, necessarily and significantly a product of the history and culture of Japan, has hardly been recognized in the United States and Britain. We read occasionally of the activities of the Johnson Society of Japan, or hear papers at conferences by Japanese scholars, or read essays or books on English literary topics by Japanese critics. But have we understood how deeply embedded in Japanese history the reception of Johnson has been in that culture? There has been little incentive or opportunity in Western academia to reflect on these phenomena, to consider whether a "Japanese Johnson," and the critical thought that phenomenon represents, might offer opportunities to reconceptualize our objects of study. *Johnson in Japan* provides such an opportunity.

2

In 1972 Earl Miner wrote as follows of a collection of essays by Japanese scholars on English literature: "The essays collected here take root in an educational heritage markedly different from that familiar to the personal experience of any but a Japanese reader. No doubt many Western readers will think they find Japanese traits in these essays. But what seems more immediately remarkable to me is that an educational system with a history and practice so much its own should have become so international in so short a period of time."[4]

What was true for Earl Miner in 1972 remains true today. Having gone to Japan in 1947 on a mission of cultural healing, Miner was won over by the people, language, and literature of Japan. He published books on Japanese poetry before becoming the distinguished scholar of Dryden and the English Restoration for which he is mainly known in the academy. One feature of Miner's collection of essays is its range: Johnson is absent, but it covers literature from Chaucer and Shakespeare and his contemporaries to Milton and Restoration comedy to the Romantics, Victorian fiction, and the poetry of Whitman and Eliot. Notably, however, the essays were felt to be both very like the critical idiom of those being published in anglophone countries at the time, and quite different.

On my first visiting lecture tour of Japan in 2009, I noted a similar hybridity. While the educational and social realities of Japan were obviously quite different from my British and American expectations, I was struck by how integral the study of English and American literature were to Japanese school and university curricula. In contrast to the studied insouciance of the undergraduates with whom I was familiar (at Cambridge, New York, Fordham, and Bucknell universities), the deliberateness and conscientiousness with which both undergraduate and postgraduate students in Japan tackled English literature took me by surprise. I knew the work of Daisuke Nagashima, whose *Johnson the Philologist* (1988) had initiated a small wave of scholarship on Johnson from Japanese scholars.[5] But I learned that the thriving Samuel Johnson Society of Japan (founded in 1964) was a serious scholarly enterprise, officially recognized by the government, organizing conferences, sponsoring publications, and energizing the larger Literary Society of Japan. This society, in its turn, hosts an annual conference and publishes a biannual journal, *Poetica: An International Journal of Linguistic-Literary Studies* (founded 1974, and now in its ninetieth volume).[6] *Poetica* was founded to encourage Japanese scholars to publish in English on English and American literature. By the turn of the century, it had begun to stimulate a substantial scholarship on Johnson, which has since flourished in response to international opportunities for participation and collaboration.

Works by Johnson are not only taught in schools and universities, they have also been widely translated and published by reputable houses (see the appendix to the present volume for a list of translations). Works by Johnson have, of course, been translated into several other languages, starting in the eighteenth century, including Italian, French, Spanish, Catalan, German, Russian, Swedish, Danish, Norwegian, Dutch, Vietnamese, and Mandarin Chinese.[7] In Japanese, one finds versions of the *Lives of the Poets*, *A Journey to the Western Islands of Scotland*, *Rasselas*, the *Life of Savage*, and the *Preface to Shakespeare*, as well as Boswell's *Life of Johnson* and *Journal of a Tour to the Hebrides*—all for sale to general readers in commercial bookshops. Other impressive scholarly projects support this widespread interest in Johnson, including a one-volume facsimile reprint of the first edition of Johnson's *Dictionary* (1983), a translation of Pat Rogers's *Samuel Johnson Encyclopedia* (1999), a collection of essays on the tercentenary of Johnson's birth, *A Goliath of British Culture; Samuel Johnson* (2009), and Japanese translations of Defoe, Swift, Richardson, and other eighteenth-century writers.

What, one might ask, sustains this interest in the works and the figure of Johnson, beyond the possibility that he has simply been scooped up in the larger process of westernization and modernization? Why Johnson in Japan? What might the Johnson found in the pages of this volume have to offer anglophone readers and Johnson scholars elsewhere? What might it have to say to the institution of eighteenth-century studies? While detailed answers to these questions are to be found in the essays themselves, I would briefly offer three responses, a personal reflection and two general thoughts on the significance of the essays specially commissioned for inclusion in this book.

3

First, the personal reflection. While the Japanese professoriate and student body are as professionally interested in critical, historical and theoretical aspects of Johnson's life and writing as any American or British professor, it is obvious that their engagement with Johnson is personal. Johnson matters to Japanese scholars and students because life matters. There is a sense—one hesitates to formulate the impression in this way, but it seems to be accurate—that Japan is *bound* to Johnson, if not by a wheel of fire, then by a more benign but still difficult logic, by a love of language, experience, and knowledge that Johnson's writings and literary presence produce in abundance. As Noriyuki Harada has written to me in an email, "details of Johnson's political and religious attitude are of course not always known well among Japanese readers, but I think his stable image based on his sincere consistency concerning 'moral backbone' evokes a favorable response among Japanese readers and students, even if some of his views seem to be narrow or prejudicial."

4

Second, factors addressing Johnson's prominence in Japan can more readily be described in literary-critical terms. Emerging in the nineteenth century from a long period of feudal isolation and then undergoing the trauma of World War II so closely linked to a grandiose nationalism, Japan is uniquely placed to recognize the dangers of a resurgent nationalism in the United States, Britain, and Europe. The Johnson we find in the essays in this book and in the Japanese classroom is a cosmopolitan, even global, figure, the moral force of whose writings is centrifugal, not one that fosters isolationism and triumphalism. Globalism, however, is not unproblematic. What, one asks, gives meaning to local, personal experience amid the centrifugal forces of global capital that seem to threaten the economic and cultural identity of nation states? For Arjun Appadurai it is the emancipatory force of the imagination working *within* the realm of the literal and the named.[8] Appadurai's "imagination" is not the instrument of romantic ideology or transcendental aesthetics, nor is it the sentimental or "fake" plaything of the privileged, but a force that informs the daily lives of ordinary people, working from within *and* across national boundaries to develop locality as a spatial fact and experience. The structural idea of space—of place imbued with more than literal meaning, such as we find on virtually every page of Johnson's oeuvre—has positive implications for humanistic methodology because it challenges the idea that critical and scientific inquiry and knowledge are static. The academic privileging of value-free and replicable knowledge, at the expense of what Appadurai calls "moral voice or vision" underlies the difference between "researchers in the strict academic sense and such modern thinkers as Goethe, Kant, and Locke" (13)—a group to which I would add Johnson. Though Johnson's epistemology might embody the idea that people "more frequently require to be reminded than informed,"[9] real knowledge for Johnson specifically *cannot* be replicated. His prose everywhere demonstrates the irreducibility of real knowledge. What he writes of Dryden's prose is true of his own, its truth being exemplified by the writing itself, in which "the author proves his right to judgment, by his power of performance."[10] While effective thinking for Johnson is clearly rooted in and nurtured by traditions and structures—formal, legal, social, and political—the force of what he calls "nature" lies in the intellectual shock and the newness of experience and thought, and consequently in their critical and even subversive force *as* knowledge.

Central to that orientation of mind is Johnson's characteristic (and extraordinary) ability of simultaneously inhabiting the local and the global, the particular and the universal. For Edward Said, such comprehensiveness is a mark of the public intellectual committed to "globalizing" literature in the modern world *without* replicating the old imperialistic pressures, by transcending the idea of culture as national identity. "Can one," Said asks, "formulate a theory of connection between part and whole that denies neither the specificity of the individual experience nor the validity of a projected, putative, or imputed whole?"[11] The question describes Johnson's cultural critique among which one would include his consideration of the dangers of imperial overreach in *Rasselas* (written at the height of the Seven Years War, the war for empire), the forged and provisional nature of national identity and culture as revealed by the Ossian controversy,[12] and his analysis of political power and the transnational movement of money and people in the aftermath of the 1745 rebellion, in his observations on the economics of luxury and trade in the life of a complex society.[13]

Several interlinked moments in Johnson's *Journey to the Western Islands of Scotland* (1775) articulate a global vision of history and culture that remains attentive to both the specifics and the universals of the situation, within Said's terms. Although Johnson may have set out to visit the Highlands with Boswell in the hope of seeing "a people of peculiar appearance, and a system of antiquated life,"[14] his anthropological account actually provides a more complex analysis of the impact of law, commerce, and manners on a culture significantly different from his own. In some ways, visiting the Highlands of Scotland in 1773 was not unlike visiting China or Japan, countries to which Johnson longed to travel. Clearly, his attitude toward the crushing of the various rebellions in Scotland since the English Civil War is a mixed one. He recognizes (even celebrates) one outcome: "what the Romans did to other nations, was in great degree done by Cromwell to the Scots; he civilized them by conquest, and introduced by useful violence the arts of peace" (27). Yet in remarking that "there was perhaps never any change of national manners so quick, so great, and so general, as that which has operated in the Highlands, by the last conquest, and the subsequent laws" (57), Johnson registers only a partial mitigation of the destruction of Highland culture by the introduction of money: "that their poverty is gradually abated, cannot be mentioned among the unpleasing consequences of subjection. They are now acquainted with money, and the possibility of gain will by degrees make them industrious" (58).

"Industriousness," with its relation to labor and with commercial and economic outcomes, is essential to Johnson's broader sociological understanding of modern civil society. In Aberdeen he was told that Cromwell's soldiers taught people how to make shoes and to plant kale (28). This prompts him to speculate on one of the anomalies of Scottish culture: "I know not whether it be not peculiar to the Scots to have attained the liberal, without the manual arts, to have excelled in ornamental knowledge, and to have wanted not only the elegancies, but the conveniences of common life" (28). This observation questions the logic of the argument by Adam Smith (in economics) and Lord Monboddo (in anthropology) for the stadial development of human beings and civil institutions. Their historiography necessarily places the mechanical *before* the intellectual arts and technology *before* aesthetics. The reverse may have been true for Scotland. Johnson observes the absence of shoes in Scotland as a cultural rather than as a social or purely economic phenomenon, for even the sons of gentlemen might be without them. Yet in the sixteenth century the Scots produced Latin poetry that was the envy of every educated European: "Yet men thus ingenious and inquisitive were content to live in total ignorance of the trades by which human wants are supplied, and to supply them by the grossest means. Till the Union made them acquainted with English manners, the culture of their lands was unskillful, and their domestick life unformed; their tables were coarse as the feasts of Eskimeaux, and their houses filthy as the cottages of Hottentots" (28).

This comparison sounds harsh, yet it contains two thoughts sympathetic to the plight of the Highland Scots: it asserts the necessity of technological competence for human dignity on a basic level; and it associates Scotland with Alaska and southern Africa as underdeveloped nations afflicted by poverty and neglect. If the geographical sweep of the "Eskimeaux" and the "Hottentots" seems merely rhetorical, no more than a theoretical point about economic underdevelopment and undercapitalization, it is important to notice the turn Johnson's narrative takes toward the end of this chapter on Inverness. The cleanliness or otherwise of the Khoi cottages is, of course, relative. More important is the sense that Johnson sees the force of material and social circumstances in the lives of real Highlanders.

For example, he finds a nature in the Highlands that is not only indifferent to the liberal arts of the Scots themselves, but which confronts the visitor with a daunting scene of undistinguished barrenness, seemingly insusceptible to humane cultivation: "An eye accustomed to the flowery pastures and waving harvests is astonished and repelled by this wide extent of hopeless sterility. The appearance is that of matter incapable of form or usefulness, dismissed by nature from her care and disinherited in her favours, left in its original elemental state, or quickened only with one sullen power of useless vegetation" (39–40).

As the looking "eye" of the passage is repelled, so the perceiving "I" feels cut off from a nature that nurtures civil and familiar sentiments. This may sound like an easy gesture of nationalistic superiority, lauding the pastoral felicities of an English landscape over the barren ruggedness of the Scottish, especially since Johnson extends the "uselessness" of the landscape from agriculture to the imagination: "it is easy to sit at home and conceive rocks and heath, and waterfalls . . . useless labours, which neither impregnate the imagination, nor enlarge the understanding" (40). But as in other moments of apparent cultural obtuseness in the *Journey*, this assertion marks an opening, a turn from the self to the nominal other, from the familiar to the new, that complicates and enlarges Johnson's perspective by incorporating a knowledge only derived from the particularities of place. For he recognizes that to "conceive" nature and, indeed, other cultures from the privileged position of "home"—natural though that may seem—is to feel that "these ideas are always incomplete, and that at least, till we have compared them with realities, we do not know them to be just. As we see more, we become possessed of more certainties, and consequently gain more principles of reasoning, and found a wider basis of analogy" (40).

In experiencing the Highlands and the Hebrides, Johnson implicates himself in the material circumstances underlying Scotland's poverty, and articulates an ameliorating awareness, a calculus of different modes and degrees of social and personal convenience. What is commonplace in cosmopolitan London is an almost inconceivable luxury in the Highlands. Yet the difference between London and Inverness or Fort William is framed by a consciousness of the claim of the English and the Scots to a commensurate human nature, if not to a common polity. To fail to see that Johnson's account of Highland technology links Scottish culture to their poverty and geography is to be blind to the social evils of warlikeness, lawlessness, nationalism, and a passionate, violent devotion to ethnic identity (e.g., chapter on "The Highlands," 43–49) by which they are afflicted. It is also to mistake a global analysis for a colonial one.

5

Authoritative as *Johnson in Japan* will be on current Japanese–English Johnsonian relations, and in introducing the work of the principal Japanese scholars and translators (past and present) to an anglophone readership, it will also raise larger questions. Might the volume occasion the introduction of a greater comparative fluidity and communication between cultures, American and Japanese, which are certainly already linked, but which also stand far apart, at opposite ends of the earth? Will the critical attention given to Johnson in this volume provide a model for other non-anglophone readers to flesh out their sense of Johnson and his works? Could we develop a Chinese Johnson on the basis of Tian Ming Cai's translations and Xiang Li's monograph on the *Dictionary*?[15] What are the chances of a Spanish Johnson?[16] Might *Johnson in Japan* play a role in the current "orientalizing" of eighteenth-century studies—that is, the growing interest in acquiring critical and historical perspectives *from the Orient* in order to open eighteenth-century studies and our educational paradigms themselves to a more comparative, global consciousness? Oddly, one criticism of *Johnson in Japan* might be that it is not Japanese enough, in that the contributors have so well mastered the scholarship and critical idiom of the West that, as Miner noted of his 1972 volume, it will be taken for a local production. One hopes not. For it is the *difference* of the Japanese perspective, within the context of its cosmopolitanism, that will contribute most toward the making of new knowledge about Johnson and eighteenth-century studies.

Notes

1 See Anthony W. Lee, "Bucknell University Press, 1996–2016: Two Decades of Eighteenth-Century Scholarship," *Eighteenth-Century Life* 42, no. 3 (September 2018): 1–28.

2 See, for example, Felicity Nussbaum, ed., *The Global Eighteenth Century* (Baltimore: Johns Hopkins University Press, 2003); Srinivas Aravamudam, *Enlightenment Orientalism: Resisting the Rise of the Novel* (Chicago: University of Chicago Press, 2012); and David Porter, "Sinicizing Early Modernity: The Imperatives of Historical Cosmopolitanism," *Eighteenth-Century Studies* 43, no. 3 (2010): 299–306.

3 See, for example, Kumkum Chatterjee and Clement Hawes, eds., *Europe Observed: Multiple Gazes in Early Modern Encounters* (Lewisburg, PA: Bucknell University Press, 2008); Nabil Matar, *Europe through Arab Eyes, 1578–1727* (New York: Columbia University Press, 2009); and Peter J. Kirsten and Robert Markley, eds., *Writing China: Essays on the Amherst Embassy (1816) and Sino-British Relations* (Cambridge, UK: D. S. Brewer, 2016).

4 Earl Miner, ed., *English Criticism in Japan: Essays by Younger Japanese Scholars on English and American Literature* (Princeton, NJ: Princeton University Press, 1972), xxiii.

5 See Greg Clingham, "A Johnsonian in Japan," *Johnsonian News Letter* 60, no. 2 (September 2009): 37–40; also, Daisuke Nagashima, "Johnson in Japan: A Fragmentary Sketch," *Transactions of the Johnson Society (Lichfield)* (1993): 14–19.

6 For *Poetica*, see https://myrp.maruzen.co.jp/ibd/intl_9244/. While the Johnson Society was founded in 1964, a separate but related entity, the Samuel Johnson Club of Japan, was founded in 1989; see Mami Sano and Shigeru Shibagaki, "The Samuel Johnson Club of Japan," *Johnsonian News Letter* 62, no. 2 (September 2012): 36–39.

7 John Stone, "Translations," in *Samuel Johnson in Context*, ed. Jack Lynch (Cambridge: Cambridge University Press, 2012), 38–44.

8 Arjun Appadurai, *Globalization* (Durham, NC: Duke University Press, 2001). Subsequent citations included parenthetically.

9 *The Rambler* no. 2, in Samuel Johnson, *The Rambler*, ed. W. J. Bate and Albrecht B. Strauss, 3 vols. (New Haven, CT: Yale University Press, 1969), 1:14.

10 Samuel Johnson, *The Lives of the Most Eminent English Poets; with Critical Observations on their Works*, ed. Roger Lonsdale, 4 vols. (Oxford, UK: Clarendon Press, 2006), II:120.

11 Edward W. Said, "Globalizing Literary Study," *PMLA* 116, no. 1 (January 2001): 68. See also Robert E. Livingston, "Global Knowledges: Agency and Place in Literary Studies," *PMLA* 116, no. 1 (January 2001): 146.

12 See Clement Hawes, "Johnson's Immanent Critique of Imperial Nationalism," chap. 7 in *The British Eighteenth Century and Global Critique* (New York: Palgrave Macmillan, 2005).

13 See Greg Clingham, "Johnson and China: Culture, Commerce, and the Dream of the Orient in Mid-Eighteenth-Century England," *1650–1850: Ideas, Issues, & Aesthetics in the Early Modern Era* 24 (2019): 178–242.

14 Samuel Johnson, *A Journey to the Western Islands of Scotland*, ed. Mary Lascelles (New Haven, CT: Yale University Press, 1971), 73. Subsequent citations included parenthetically.

15 See Tian Ming Cai's translations, *The History of Rasselas, Prince of Abissinia* (Beijing: International Culture Publishing, 2006) and *Limitations of Humanity: Samuel Johnson's Works* (Beijing: International Culture Publishing, 2009); and Xiang Li, *Li Lun Yu Yan Jiu (A Study of Samuel Johnson's Dictionary of the English Language [1755])* (Tian Jin, China: Nankai University Press, 2014). See also Xiang Li, "Qian Zhongshu and Samuel Johnson: Two Literary Figures in Different Times," *Johnsonian News Letter* 64, no. 1 (March 2013): 48–51; and Tian Ming Cai, "A Reflection on Johnson's Shakespeare in China," *Johnsonian News Letter* 66, no. 1 (March 2015): 48–52.

16 The silhouette of a Spanish Johnson already exists in the fragments of early translations identified and discussed by John Stone. See, "On the Trail of Early Rambler and Idler Translations in France and Spain," *Johnsonian News Letter* 57, no. 1 (2006): 34–41; "An Early Spanish Translation of *Rasselas*," *Johnsonian News Letter* 59, no. 2 (September 2008): 24–27; and "Johnson on Shakespeare in Spain: A New Document," *Johnsonian News Letter* 65, no. 2 (September 2014): 6–17. The lineaments of that Johnson would be much filled in if we could locate

the unpublished manuscript translations of Johnson's works by Jorge Luis Borges and Adolfo Bioy Casares to supplement the Johnson already present in their printed conversations and Borges's essays; see Greg Clingham, "Johnson and Borges: Some Reflections," in *Samuel Johnson Among the Modernists*, ed. Anthony W. Lee (Clemson, SC: Clemson University Press, 2019), 189–212, 272–275.

Notes on the Text

Boswell's Life of Johnson is an abbreviation for James Boswell, *The Life of Johnson: Together with Boswell's Journal of a Tour to the Hebrides and Johnson's Diary of a Journey into North Wales*, ed. George Birkbeck Hill, rev. L. F. Powell. 6 vols. (Oxford, UK: Clarendon Press, 1934–1964).

Sōseki Natsume is a pen name of Kinnosuke Natsume (1867–1916), a Japanese writer, critic, and scholar. His name could be represented as Natsume Sōseki, Sōseki Natsume, or just Soseki (with or without the macron). Just for convenience, in this volume we use Sōseki Natsume.

The authors' names, book titles, and other information in Japanese are added in the bibliography.

Johnson in Japan

Introduction

KIMIYO OGAWA AND MIKA SUZUKI

The Beginning of Johnson Studies in Japan

For Samuel Johnson (1709–1784) and James Boswell (1740–1795), Japan represented something extremely remote and strange, or something extraordinary and hard to bear. Johnson refers to Japan when he speaks of receiving what he held to be too warm a welcome in Edinburgh after a supposedly difficult journey along the coasts of Scotland, visiting the various islands of the Hebrides: "We are addressed as if we had made a voyage to Nova Zembla, and suffered five persecutions in Japan." [1] Elsewhere in Boswell's records of his conversation with Johnson Japan is imagined to be the farthest and most unfamiliar end of the earth, more an imagined place than a physical locale. As a result, in Johnson's view, the French philosophe Montesquieu used Japan purely as a means of justifying concepts or attitudes he knew his readers would find outlandish or unsustainable: "whenever he wants to support a strange opinion, he quotes you the practice of Japan or of some other distant country, of which he knows nothing." [2] The information that was available about Japan in eighteenth-century Britain was limited and the few goods that were able to be imported from the faraway country that remained under a seclusion policy probably encouraged a sense of wonder. When the term *Japan* is used in his *Dictionary* (1755), in entries such as *japan*, *to japan*, and even *japanner*, they are explicitly about lacquerware and, from the association of its color of the craftwork, it also means shoe blacking.[3] Johnson would have been surprised to learn that the Japanese government in the Meiji era (1868–1912), after abolishing a policy of seclusion, would introduce *The History of Rasselas* as a textbook for schools in order to teach Japanese children English. In fact, no fewer than twenty translations and editions of *Rasselas* were published in the Meiji era. In 1894, Mitsugi Uchida, or Roan Uchida, a scholarly writer of the time, published the first detailed biography of Johnson, simply entitled *Johnson*. In this book he informs us that "Many schools in Tokyo adopt *Rasselas* as an English textbook so fervently now that this work is known more widely than the Nine Chinese Classics."[4]

Extraordinary as this phenomenon is, it may not have been the real beginning of Johnson studies in Japan. In the Taisho era (1912–1926) not a single scholarly book that dealt mainly with Johnson was published. The early Showa era (1926–1989), however, saw a breakthrough in the interest in Johnson in the academic world of English literature in Japan with the 1933 publication of Kenji Ishida's *Johnson and His Circle*.[5] Ishida was a renowned professor of English literature at Kyoto Imperial University. This book, based on Ishida's PhD dissertation at Kyoto Imperial University, also discusses Goldsmith, Gibbon, Reynolds, Burke, Richard Sheridan, and Frances Burney. Studying Johnson's works in detail, with a deep sense of pioneering mission, it signaled the beginning of Johnson studies in Japan.

Ishida was followed in his interest in Johnson by many scholars, most notably Rintaro Fukuhara, who published *Great Dr Johnson* (1969), and by Daisuke Nagashima, honored by the American Society for Eighteenth-Century Studies (ASECS) as a great teacher and author of *A Critical Biography of Samuel Johnson* (which was distributed on a floppy disk in 1999 because its great length meant no one would publish it as a printed book) and of *Johnson the Philologist* (1988), among other studies of Johnson in both English and Japanese. This upsurge in Johnson scholarship coincided with the visit to Japan by James L. Clifford in 1964, which in turn inspired the formation of the Johnson Society of Japan (JSJ) in 1966.

The Johnson Society of Japan[6]

The Johnson Society of Japan's main event is an annual conference, an all-day gathering that features a plenary lecture, a panel of four speakers, and an annual general meeting. Since 1968 the annual meeting of the JSJ has been the locus of serious academic discussion; in addition to Johnson himself, the lecturer and the speakers usually address major eighteenth-century topics such as literary criticism, satire, and scholarly methods of philosophical enquiry during the period. Regionals have also thrived in Kyoto and Tokyo, where eighteenth-century researchers gather to hold regular seminar meetings. The society distributes three newsletters a year with occasional additions and an annual bulletin.

The main purpose of the Johnson Society of Japan in recent years may be characterized by its efforts to expand its membership, especially among the younger generation. By creating awards in 2011 and introducing individual paper sessions at the annual conference in 2014, the society has sought to encourage younger speakers to share their concerns, interests, and new research methods. In 1996 the society published *Studies in Eighteenth-Century English Literature*, which featured essays covering the century from Defoe to Austen with an emphasis on Johnson. Since 2002, several edited volumes, mostly in Japanese, have been sponsored and published by the society. One notable feature of the volumes published in 1996, 2002, 2006, 2010, 2014, and 2018 is that the individual names of editors are not present on the title pages. Instead, five or six scholars are chosen to form the editorial committee in each case, and all volumes are thus offered as the work of the Johnson Society of Japan as a whole.

The Johnson Society of Japan is distinctive in that it represents scholars of eighteenth-century literature in general, not just Johnson specialists. While the identity and the very name of the society has been the subject of periodic debate, its openness has made it possible to entertain occasional speakers from abroad, including Maynard Mack in 1984 and Greg Clingham in 2009.[7] The result of this receptivity to international perspectives has been to confirm the importance of Johnson in the context of eighteenth-century literature, and of the Johnson Society of Japan in furthering an understanding of that nexus.

By undertaking the challenge of clarifying the continued significance of Johnson, the society aims to improve the dialogue among the academic community, the general public, and its own officials. After years of preparation, in 2008 the society decided to apply for membership to the Science Council of Japan, necessitating the clarification of its name and purpose to the satisfaction of government bureaucrats. Over a period of five years, paired officers of the society—Masaaki Takeda and Noriyuki Harada, Toru Nishiyama and Tadayuki Fukumoto, and Yoichi Kuno and Wataru Nakajima—were called on for interviews to argue for Johnson's relevance and for the importance of the study of eighteenth-century English literature for Japanese academia.

On 22 August 2013, the Johnson Society of Japan was successfully acknowledged as one of what is termed "the cooperative science and research bodies" by the Science Council of Japan. The society's emphasis had been on its autonomy and independence—indeed, it has been proud of its long tradition of academic activities maintained by the collegial group's collective commitment to move on with their studies—but becoming a member of the national organization has helped secure its place in society as well as in the academic community. Compared with powerful societies engaged in cutting-edge science and technology research, the Johnson Society of Japan is a small body with a modest voice, but its close-knit and comparatively informal milieu contributes to nurturing compelling critical views and scholarly attitudes.

Johnson in Japan

The essays in this collection, all written for the occasion, represent the richness of scholarship on Johnson in Japan, as well as Johnson's influence on Japanese education, his reception into Japanese literary culture, and how he has been translated into Japanese. The volume reflects not just the history of Johnson studies but also the broader current conditions of scholarship in Japanese academia. In addition to such works as the *Rambler* (1750–1752), *Rasselas* (1759), *Lives of the Most Eminent English Poets* (1779–1781), and *Journey to the Western Islands of Scotland* (1775), the essays in this volume engage with works by other important English writers, such as Shakespeare, Mary Shelley, Jane Austen, and Matthew Arnold, and also with later Japanese writers, including Natsume Sōseki (1867–1916). The geographical focus on Japan allows examination of a series of interlinked movements from the 1790s to the present day, a period of time during which Johnson was first introduced to Japanese writers. Contributors aim to bring to light the implications of the complex interrelations between Johnson and multiple British traditions, as well as those between Johnson and Japanese writers.

The collection begins with a historical delineation of the reception of Johnson's work in Japan. The first two chapters—by Hideichi Eto and Noriyuki Harada—look at the earliest reception of Johnson's works and biography in Japan. In "A Brief History of Johnsonian Studies in Japan" Hideichi Eto traces the shifting image of Johnson from the Meiji era onward. He argues that the dominant image of Johnson has changed from being a "moral teacher" to a "man of letters" notable for a variety of literary accomplishments. That Johnson went from being regarded as a didactic sage to a public intellectual and literary figure is demonstrated, Eto argues, by the popularity of *Rasselas* as a textbook in the 1910s and 1920s. [8] As Japan saw a significant rise in the number of university students after World War II, creating a demand for instructors trained in English literary classics, many scholars began to write essays on Johnson, while, at the same time, Johnson's works were being translated into Japanese. Eto marks these changing interests in Johnson by closely observing the nuances of successive translations of his works.

The history of Johnson's reception in Japan can be linked to a process of modernization in Britain. In "Johnson, Biography, and Modern Japan" Noriyuki Harada examines the process through which Johnson was canonized and standardized in Victorian Britain. His essay shows that the way in which Japanese people (led by Meiji intellectuals) strove to modernize society was comparable to developments in Victorian Britain, where an accumulation of information, the acquisition of encyclopedic knowledge, and the publication of literary collections and anthologies became central to its mission. In two very different cultural milieu, Johnson came to represent the very embodiment of modernity.

Chapters 3 and 4—by Kimiyo Ogawa and Yuri Yoshino—examine the significance of Johnson in terms of how Romanticism has been defined and redefined. In "Scientific Curiosity in Samuel Johnson's *Rasselas* and Mary Shelley's *Frankenstein,*" Kimiyo Ogawa focuses on some key themes of Romantic science, including knowledge, reason, and the occult. She re-examines Johnson's and Shelley's treatment of the question so deeply entrenched in Western culture, namely, happiness and human progress—whether the increase of knowledge contributes to the diminishment of one's feeling of uncertainty or unease, and therefore increases human happiness. Mary Shelley read *Rasselas* in July 1817, and looking at the theme of learning in *Rasselas* Ogawa traces Johnson's influence on *Frankenstein*, exploring how his fictional characters (such as Imlac and the scientist astronomer) provide Shelley not only with a model of a scientific overreacher, but also with a means to pose abstruse philosophical questions about life and its wonder.

Yuri Yoshino turns to Jane Austen as one of Japan's pathways to Johnson, thereby exploring the complex intermingling of realism and romance in the Romantic period novel. "Jane Austen and the Reception of Samuel Johnson in Japan" adds a new perspective to existing studies of the importance of Johnson's *Rasselas* as a popular textbook in Japanese universities. She argues that Johnson's literary views, especially his idea of fiction, were appropriated by Sōseki Natsume via his reading of Austen's novels. Relying to some extent on Sōseki's *Theory of Literature* (1907), a study of eighteenth- and nineteenth-century British literature, in which he applauds the narrative strategy of Austen, and recent scholarship that has discussed Austen's literary debt to Johnson, Yoshino argues for Johnson's influence on modern Japanese novels, particularly those by Sōseki.[9]

Chapter 5, Mika Suzuki's "Johnson the Tea Poet," also discusses Johnson's unacknowledged influence on Japanese writers. She focuses not on a literary circle but on an individual writer with a medical background, Tamotsu Morowoka, thus recognizing Johnson's active involvement in cultivating sociability, endorsing uncommon personalities, and encouraging extensive general knowledge. Among many early scholars in Japan who engaged with Johnson in their writings, Suzuki singles out Morowoka's approach as unique, and surprisingly faithful to Johnson's multifaceted personality. Morowoka's career in medicine, Suzuki suggests, may have given him particular insight into Johnson, whom he regards as a "tea poet." An interesting coincidence is that Johnson was a famous tea drinker—he once had "seventeen cups in one sitting"[10]—and that Japan's traditional tea culture is also linked to a tea master, Sen no Rikyu, who gained acceptance in the social circles of Japan's courtier and warrior elites.[11] For Suzuki, Morowoka is an interesting case of a public intellectual from a nonliterary background representing Johnson as a model scholar active in society.

Many Japanese scholars specializing in English theater have studied Johnson's approach to dramatic works. In chapter 6, "Johnson and Garrick on *Hamlet*," Miki Iwata explores the issues of Johnson's taste in what William Hazlitt and Leigh Hunt called "mental theatre." Against the background of Johnsonian critics who see him as embracing an antitheatrical tradition, this essay provides a new perspective on David Garrick and Johnson. While acknowledging the fact that Garrick is scarcely referred to in Johnson's edition of the plays of Shakespeare (1765), Iwata draws attention to the fact that he *does* mention Garrick once—in a footnote to Hamlet's line "Swear by my sword" (1.5.154). Although George Steevens, Johnson's coeditor in the 1773 revised edition of Shakespeare, remarks somewhat disparagingly that "Mr. Garrick . . . monopolizes the attention of the audience," it is highly significant that Johnson heeds Garrick's comment and not those of the two previous editors of Shakespeare, William Warburton and John Upton.

In chapter 7, "Abyssinian Johnson" Noriyuki Hattori considers the Nile as the key metaphor in *Rasselas*: as Johnson himself states, the great river with its fertility and majestic power dominates the narrative. Hattori argues that to some extent Rasselas, son of the king of Abyssinia, represents the reckless driving force of fiction, for he leaves the beautiful valley to free himself from confinement. Hattori compares moments in *A Journey to the Western Islands*, in which Johnson imagines himself to be "a writer of Romance," with the imaginative nature of the journey along the Nile in *Rasselas*.

The following two chapters—by Tadayuki Fukumoto and by Masaaki Ogura—examine Johnson's language using different approaches. In "Johnson's Prose Style and His Notion of Periodical Writer," Tadayuki Fukumoto examines the way in which Johnson sought to distinguish his prose style from those of earlier, equally commercially responsive writers. The essay, which explores Johnson's early career as a hack writer on Grub Street, compares Johnson's elaborate, sometimes convoluted, rhetoric in *The Rambler* to the hasty pressurized output of many contemporary journalists, as famously satirized in Alexander Pope's *Dunciad*.

In "An Analysis of Johnson's View of Knowledge," Masaaki Ogura applies a linguistic methodology to Johnson's style. Developing a research project based on Isamu Hayakawa's work, this essay tests his claim that Johnson's dictionary was an Enlightenment-oriented project.[12] Ogura adopts quantitative analysis in order to verify Hayakawa's working hypothesis that Johnson had a penchant for using the expression "pleasure or instruction." The advantage of using this corpus stylistics, founded on statistics-based evidence, is that it provides possible explanations for Johnson's tendency to use particular words or language clusters.

In the final essay of the volume, Hitoshi Suwabe carefully unravels the roots of the controversy over "Johnson's Final Words." His interest is not just in the possible phrases used by Johnson on his deathbed ("God bless you," as reported by John Hoole; "God bless you, my dear," as reported by James Boswell; or "Jam moriturus," as reported by Sastres) but also in what the scene implies for understanding Johnson's broader social interactions. The related questions are: "Whose words are represented or underrepresented and by whom?" and "What was the motivation to neglect such words?" Suwabe carefully reconstructs a new narrative of Johnson's last hours and the days after his death from fragmented pieces of information in the letters and diaries as well as from Boswell's, Mrs. Piozzi's, and Sastres's respective versions of Johnson's biography. He concludes that the eyewitness account of Sastres, Johnson's close and valued friend, should carry more weight in our understanding of Johnson's final words.

English studies in Japan since the nineteenth century have been subject to various influences, and research on Johnson is no exception. The modern discipline of the English language in Japan is rooted in the study of literature. Earlier scholars, therefore, paid considerable attention to the translation of the many literary works originally published in foreign languages. Most of their works are of high standard and their efforts in translation have cultivated possibilities in the Japanese literary world, the book market, and English education. However, like so many other countries, the diminishing of English literature's place in Japanese higher education and also its language teaching can be seen in terms of the broader weakening of the cultural capital of the humanities. This issue has been vocalized by many influential scholars engaged in the instruction of English language as literature specialists in Japan.[13] This may open Japanese scholars up to the global academic world, while negotiating with the current focus on teaching the language for the purposes of practical communication, which is already in danger of suffocating traditional English literary studies.

We could look back to the time when there was an unimaginable amount of pressure to modernize Japan and to develop science and technology, driving people to strive for their place in the world. We might then learn something about overcoming the present-day dilemma of promoting the humanities alongside the sciences by reading, understanding, and contemplating Johnson, for he has played a major role in the process of modernization. For the contributors gathered together for this volume, who share interests in the imminent issue of education at the university level in Japan, Johnson has been an inspiration in thinking about the significant impact that the humanities have had on the social, physical, and life sciences in Japan as well as in Britain. Of course, eighteenth-century literary studies, especially with regard to Johnson, are traditionally interdisciplinary and critics have often turned to history, continental literature, and the fine arts to develop their understanding of the field and the challenges of life. But the focus has largely been on scholarship that has been produced within Europe. The chapters in this collection, we hope, will offer some insight into Johnson and Johnsonian studies, which will take the reader beyond the boundaries that have restricted an assumed consensus about the geographical areas covered. We think that this book will open discussion of ideology and develop a revised interdisciplinary approach to literary studies in Japan, and thus encourage future scholars in the study of Johnson's works.

Notes

Part of the introduction at an early stage was written by Noriyuki Hattori.

1 James Boswell, *The Journal of a Tour to the Hebrides with Samuel Johnson; Diary of a Journey into North Wales in the Year 1774*, ed. G. B. Hill, rev. L. F. Powell, vol. 5 of *Boswell's Life of Johnson*, 6 vols. (Oxford, UK: Clarendon Press, 1934–1964), 392. Hereafter reference to and quotations from this edition of *Boswell's Life of Johnson* are indicated with the volume number and the page number(s).

2 *Boswell's Life of Johnson*, 5: 209.

3 Because Johnson did not include place names in his *Dictionary*, there is no entry in the volume for Japan as a country.

4 Mitsugi [Roan] Uchida, *Johnson* (Tokyo: Minyusha, 1894), 131; Noriyuki Harada, "Johnson in Japanese Culture," in "Johnson and the Globalization of Literature (II)," chaired by Greg Clingham at ISECS 2003 (Seminar 190), UCLA, (Wednesday 6 August 2003); Noriyuki Harada, "Johnson in Japanese Culture," *Kyorin University Review* 16 (2004): 113–136.

5 Kenji Ishida, *Johnson hakase to sono mure* (*Dr. Johnson and His Circle*) (Tokyo: Kenkyusha, 1933).

6 For updated information on the society, visit the website at http://johnson.main.jp/jsj/.

7 As for his visit to Japan and views on the society, see Greg Clingham, "A Johnsonian in Japan," *Johnsonian News Letter* 60, no. 2 (2009): 37–40.

8 Bin Ueda, preface to *The History of Rasselas,* trans. Rokusaku Shibano. (Tokyo: Dainihonntosho, 1905), 4–5.

9 As for Austen's debt to Johnson, see, for example, Gloria Sybil Gross, *In a Fast Coach with a Pretty Woman: Jane Austen and Samuel Johnson* (New York: AMS Press, 2002); Freya Johnson, "Johnson and Austen," in *Samuel Johnson After 300 Years*, ed. Greg Clingham and Philip Smallwood (Cambridge: Cambridge University Press, 2009), 225–245.

10 Peter Martin, *Samuel Johnson: A Biography*. (Cambridge, MA: Belknap Press of Harvard University Press, 2008), 354.

11 Paul Varley, *Japanese Culture* (Honolulu: University of Hawaii Press, 2000), 174.

12 Isamu Hayakawa, *Keimou shisouka no Johnson jisho: Chi no shusei wo mezashite* (*Johnson's Dictionary Under the Enlightenment: For the Purpose of Collecting Knowledge)* (Yokohama, Japan: Shunpūsha, 2013).

13 Among many contributions, Myles Chilton's *English Studies Beyond the 'Center': Teaching Literature and the Future of Global English* (New York: Routledge, 2016) and Masahiko Abe's *The Worst-Ever English Policy* (Tokyo: Hitsuji Shobo, 2017) are worth mentioning here. Professor Abe states in one of his interviews that when he was growing up as young student in a Catholic seminary in the seaside town of Shizuoka, his English-learning was nourished by his fascination with the spiritual

qualities he identified in poetry: 'poetry for me was something like an experience of trance,'" but the recent trend of language education is sadly driven by "English Industry which sells English as if it were a diet or an exercise program." (Alex Watson, "Have Something to Say: Masahiko Abe on the University of Tokyo's rejection of the Japanese Education Ministry's English Examination Reforms," *Wall Street International*, 29 September 2018).

1

A Brief History of Johnsonian Studies in Japan

HIDEICHI ETO

Introduction

In the middle of the nineteenth century, Japan opened itself to Western countries after almost 300 years of seclusion, and as a result Japanese people started learning about Western cultures and languages. In particular, the acquisition of the English language became important to the modernization of the country, and in schools and universities Japanese students were required to study the works of Western authors as a way of learning English. The works of Johnson initially formed a key aspect of the English curriculum. In this chapter, I will trace the development of Johnsonian studies in Japan following the introduction of Johnson's works to the country in the 1870s.

This chapter is divided into two parts. The first outlines the main structure of Johnsonian studies, touching on some of the estimated 1,600+ books, articles, essays, and English textbooks for Japanese students on Johnson and his works that have been published in Japan since the Meiji era (1868–1912). It also describes the transformation of the image of Johnson in Japan through the ages. The second part of the chapter addresses translations of Johnson's works and books related to him into Japanese.

In the Meiji era, the Gregorian calendar was introduced in Japan, while the traditional Japanese calendar also continued to be used. The Japanese calendar is based on the reign of particular emperors; when a new emperor succeeds to the throne, a new era name replaces the outgoing one. Since 1868, when imperial rule was formally restored, Japan has had four eras: the Meiji era (1868–1912), the Taisho era (1912–1926), the Showa era (1926–1989), and the Heisei era (1989–2019). In 2019 a new era began, the Reiwa era, with the abdication of the emperor Akihito and the advent of the emperor Naruhito. Each era is characterized by its own cultural and political trends and ethos, and the account that follows is subdivided accordingly.

The Meiji Era (1868–1912)

Rasselas was the most popular of Johnson's works in Meiji-era Japan. Roan Uchida—a leading man of letters and translator in the era—noted that *Rasselas* was used as an English textbook in so many schools during the era that it was more familiar to Japanese students than the Nine Chinese Classics.[1] Noriyuki Harada has noted that one of the reasons for the popularity of *Rasselas* during the Meiji era was that the story took a biographical form, as an account of a protagonist searching for happiness and the best choice of life. The figure of Rasselas became a model for young Japanese people attempting to widen the scope of their lives beyond the old secluded Japan.[2] Because Japanese readers valued spirituality in their daily lives, they assumed that in learning the English language they should seek moral lessons in their reading, and the rhetorical and apparently sententious nature of *Rasselas* gave them what they sought. Thus, Johnson, as the author of the fable, was regarded as a sort of mentor in life in exactly the same way Confucius was thought of as a moral teacher.

At first, students would have used copies of *Rasselas* that had been imported from overseas, but in 1884 an edition was published at the Imperial University, the oldest national university in Japan (now Tokyo University). The following year was a memorable one in Johnson studies because a Japanese translation of *Rasselas* was published for the first time by a commercial Japanese publisher. Critical essays on *Rasselas* gradually appeared, in addition to textbooks and annotated editions. This popularity continued until 1912, when the last textbook edition of *Rasselas* was published.

Other works of Johnson besides *Rasselas* were also introduced to Japan in this era. His literary criticism proved especially popular. The comments in his *Works of Shakespeare* were the first his other works introduced to Japan because Shakespeare was translated into Japanese at the beginning of the Meiji era. When Shakespeare's plays were translated into Japanese, some of Johnson's comments in his *Works of Shakespeare* were also translated and included in the plays. Tatsuo Inui and Atsuzo Nakahara included translated passages from Johnson's *Life of Milton* in an introductory essay on John Milton in 1880. In 1891 a brief summary of another biography from the *Lives of the Poets*, the *Life of Savage*, appeared in the magazine *Kokumin no tomo* (*Friends of the Nation*). Johnson's theory of translation from *Idler* no. 68 and no. 69 also appeared in the same year in *Waseda bungaku* (*Waseda Literature*).

In 1894, Uchida published the first monograph about Johnson written in Japanese. Entitled *Johnson* and composed of five chapters in 217 pages, it treats various topics such as the social background of the eighteenth century, Johnson's life and works, his literary club, and how he suffered from gout. Uchida was indeed a pioneer Johnsonian in the Meiji era because it was not long after Japan was reopened to European countries and there were very few materials available for writing essays on Johnson. Despite this, he made great efforts to obtain as many materials related to Johnson as he could, including not only Boswell's *Life*, but also Piozzi's *Anecdotes*. He also read the nineteenth-century biographies of Johnson by Francis Grant and Leslie Stephen in order to write his book, but he found that the descriptions of Johnson in both books were almost the same as in Boswell's *Life*.[3]

In 1911 the literary magazine *Eigo seinen* (*The Rising Generation*), which had been founded in 1898 and was thus one of the earliest magazines devoted to English literature in Japan, published an article concerning the purchase of 17 Gough Square—the only one of Johnson's London residences to survive into the twenty-first century—by Cecil Harmsworth, who wanted to donate it to the nation in memory of the great literary man. The property is now a museum dedicated to Johnson. The publication of an article on Harmsworth's purchase of Johnson's house demonstrates that Japanese scholars of the age were not insensitive to movements in the literary world in England, as well as to its authors and their works.

The Taisho Era (1912–1926)

Compared with the Meiji era, there were fewer publications on Johnson and his works in the Taisho era. There were only twenty-nine publications over fourteen years, mainly English textbooks of *Rasselas* for Japanese students and introductory accounts of Johnson's life, his works, and his opinions in several Japanese literary magazines and books on the history of English literature.

New developments in academic education in this era promised increased scholarly writing about Johnson. A new education law, enacted in 1918 to promote higher education in Japan, permitted the founding of private universities as well as national universities. In this age many foreign instructors were replaced by Japanese professors who had returned to Japan after studying abroad and then taught what they had learned in foreign countries. It seems, however, that they were not very interested in the Age of Johnson. These years were known as Taisho Roman in the history of Japanese literature because European Romanticism had a much greater influence on Japanese readers than English Neoclassicism. In 1916 Kenji Kaneko, one of the earliest scholars specializing in Romantic literature during this period, reaffirmed the Romantic period's response to Johnson by claiming, "Dr. Johnson was a man of erudition as well as of arrogance. He was an able and excellent writer and talker, but had an affected manner. He had a policy of hard work and he was a rough old man."[4] It seems that this was the general image of Johnson in the Taisho era.

The Showa Era: Before World War II (1926–1945)

The Showa era, which started in 1926 and ended in 1989, was the longest to date in the traditional Japanese calendar. Here the era will be divided into two parts: before and after World War II.

Before World War II, Johnson began to be the subject of renewed academic and critical attention, and the predominant image of him changed from a moral teacher to a man of literature. The first notable article in this period was an essay on the journey to Scotland by Johnson and Boswell, written by E. V. Gatenby in 1929. Gatenby was invited to Japan to teach English in 1923 and taught at Tohoku Imperial University (now Tohoku University). The essay compares Johnson's *Journey to the Western Islands of Scotland* with Boswell's *Journal of a Tour to the Hebrides*, and it appeared in *Studies in English Literature* Vol. 9, No 3, the oldest specialist journal of English literature in Japan. Before the publication of Gatenby's essay, very few Japanese scholars had paid attention to these texts in the Johnson/Boswell canon. Even after the war, it took a long time before they considered related themes such as Johnson's politics, economics, and travels.

In 1933, a memorable book in the history of the study of Johnson in Japan was published. It was Kenji Ishida's *Johnson hakase to sono mure* (*Dr. Johnson and His Circle*), a voluminous work of 600 pages based on his doctoral thesis. In describing Johnson's life, Ishida depended not only on Boswell's *Life* but also on many of the other reference materials that he could access in Japan. He notes in his preface that he had interpreted all the works he had mentioned in his book according to his own judgment, without relying on the interpretation of other scholars.[5] He placed more importance on Johnson's letters than on his conversations in Boswell's *Life*. Akio Nakahara observes that this indicates Ishida's intention to understand Johnson through his own words and not to depend wholly on Boswell's record.[6] Because of his original style of academic research, Ishida's book was a great accomplishment and made a significant contribution to the shape of Johnsonian studies in Japan.

Eighteen articles on Johnson were produced in the same year Ishida's book was published, and the following year (1934) ten more articles appeared as a result of its influence. Among them was Jiro Suzuki's *Johnson*. Suzuki was conscious of new and different viewpoints on Johnsonian studies, as is evident from the fact that he mentioned Johnson's attitude to books as well as his reading habits in his early days and advised Japanese readers, who tended to pay attention primarily to Johnson's distinctive character on the basis of Boswell's *Life*, not to ignore analysis of his major works.

Before World War II, the image of Johnson based on Boswell's *Life* was dominant, but a new and altered perspective began to emerge, as is seen in Ishida's and Suzuki's works. A key example of this new perspective on Johnson appears in a lecture by Shukotsu Togawa published in 1939, in which he said he wanted to discuss what Boswell did not mention because he doubted whether the *Life* conveyed Johnson's real character. This was a very new and progressive idea in Japanese Johnsonian studies because scholars before Togawa had depended almost entirely on Boswell's *Life* in their study of Johnson. It was only in the 1970s that this new viewpoint began to become popular among Japanese scholars of literature.

Another achievement by a Japanese scholar that deserves special attention in this era is that three of the most important works of Johnson's *Lives of the Poets*, the lives of Milton, Dryden, and Pope, were published (in English) with extensive notes in Japanese by Rintaro Fukuhara. (Translations of these works did not appear until after the war.) Publication of these *Lives* in 1943 was significant because this was the year that the war in the Pacific began to escalate. This publication was an outstanding achievement in that it showed that the study of English literature was still active, and that the level of Johnsonian studies in this country was very high, even during a critical stage of the war. Fukuhara himself gained momentum in his studies from this achievement, and he came to play a leading role in Johnsonian studies in Japan after the war.

The Showa Era: After World War II (1945–1989)

After World War II, books on Johnson were published regularly in Britain and America. Many books and magazine articles were published in Japan too, with an average of ten to thirty a year for fifty years. One innovation in Johnson studies after the war was Fukuhara's 1955 radio lecture about the life of Johnson. At that time, many ordinary Japanese people seemed to be motivated to study English literature in any way possible. There would be no audience for a radio program about the life of Johnson today.

In 1951 the Asahi Newspaper Company, one of the leading newspapers in Japan, published Fukuhara's *Asahi shin koza: eibungaku* (*Asahi New Lectures: English Literature*). In these lectures Fukuhara presented a portrait of Dr. Johnson based on Boswell's *Life*, namely, as a man who seemed to be coarse and inactive but who had a mind of acute good sense. For Fukuhara, Johnson adored

God, loved people, answered questions in epigrams, and urged the importance of order and culture. Furthermore, Johnson showed his kindness secretly, loved literature that was rich in morality, and observed the literary conventions of classicism, but was not without judicious generosity.[7] Fukuhara took an old-fashioned approach to Johnson, and he created a popular image of Dr. Johnson for Japanese readers that remained current in the country until the 1970s.

Japanese scholars began to be interested in Boswell's writings other than his *Life of Johnson* during this period after the war. In 1952, Fukuhara discussed Boswell's *London Journal* in *Eigo seinen*, a journal for scholars of English literature. Fukuhara called Boswell's *Journal* an interesting work that was reminiscent of a novel and said, in addition, that it was a very important record of Boswell's character and life and gave substantial background information regarding eighteenth-century English literature and culture. In the same year, Yoshizo Kaneo cited a book review of *Boswell in Holland 1763–1764* from the *New York Times Book Review* and *New York Herald Tribune* in *Gakuto*, Japan's longest-running magazine, published by a bookstore.

Before the 1960s, very few studies of Johnson's *Dictionary* were conducted in Japan, but in 1962 Daisuke Nagashima published an essay on the *Dictionary* in a university bulletin called *Kobe daigaku bungakukai kenkyu: bungakuhen*. He subsequently continued his studies on the *Dictionary*, writing a large number of articles in journals and university bulletins that were later collected and published in 1974 as the book *Eibei no jisho: rekishi to genjo* (*A Survey of English Dictionaries, British and American*). This book included an analysis of Johnson's *Dictionary* itself and also tackled other topics, including the English dictionaries that were published prior to Johnson's own and the academic knowledge that was required for Johnson to compile a dictionary. Nagashima also presented a brief history of the compilation of dictionaries up until the *Oxford English Dictionary* and concluded his essay with an account of American dictionaries.

Nagashima's study of Johnson as a philologist prompted other scholars to pursue the same theme, and in 1968 Tetsuro Hayashi, another leading philologist, published *Eigo hattatsu shi* (*A History of English Lexicography*); Johnson's *Dictionary* was analyzed in chapter 18. In 1967 the Nan'undo Publishing Company published *Philological Essays from Dryden to Johnson*, which included Johnson's essays on the English language, such as the "Plan of an English Dictionary," "Preface to A Dictionary of the Language," *Rambler* no.208, *Idler* no. 91, and the "Life of Roscommon," with notes and commentaries by Nagashima.

During the 1960s, books on Johnson that were first published in Britain and America were easy to obtain in Japan, so new articles based on these were written soon after their initial publication. One such article was an essay titled "Samuel Johnson the Idler," which appeared in *Aoyama gakuin bungakubu bulletin* in 1964. It dealt with Johnson's agony over his idleness and inactivity and was based mainly on the first volume (1958) of the *Yale Edition of the Works of Dr. Johnson.*

The number of universities in Japan increased from 201 in 1950 to 382 in 1970, and the number of Japanese scholars increased in proportion to the number of universities. Studies of English literature, including Johnsonian studies, also increased in number throughout the 1970s and 1980s, to the extent that after 1967 more than twenty essays and articles dealing with Johnson appeared each year. In 1972 a revised edition of Fukuhara's *Johnson dai hakase* (*The Great Dr. Johnson*), which had been one volume of his collected works, was republished as a single book. This suggests that there was still a demand for this book after its first publication in 1969.

Johnson was still popular in education in the postwar decades. Some parts of Boswell's *Life* and Johnson's essays from *The Rambler* were included in several kinds of English textbooks for university students. Hawthorne's *Biographical Stories* (1842) was also published recurrently in the form of English textbooks and two successive editions of *Biographical Stories* were published in 1965 and 1966 by two different publishers. It was assumed that students in all fields, not only English literature majors, learned about Johnson, Boswell, and their world through these textbooks. Johnson studies expanded into new areas during this period. In 1968 the economist Hiroshi Mizuta wrote an essay on the connections between Johnson and Adam Smith in a book entitled *Adam Smith kenkyu* (*A Study of Adam Smith*).

The year 1967 was memorable for Johnsonian studies because the Johnson Society of Japan was founded. The aim of the society was to promote the study of English literature from Dryden to Blake. It owed its birth to the late Professor James L. Clifford, who provided inspiration and support for the foundation of the society when he came to Japan in 1964.[8] It started to issue the *Annual Bulletin of the Johnson Society* in 1968, but it was not until the third issue in 1971 that it included an essay on Johnson himself. The society still holds an annual meeting, issues an annual bulletin, and publishes a compilation of essays on the literature of this age every four years.

In the 1970s, as more acute and meticulous research was conducted and critical reviews were issued, Johnsonians in Japan became dissatisfied with the traditional image of Johnson as a man of letters who was coarse, inactive, and arrogant, and who had an unusual (even bizarre) physical appearance. Instead they sought to develop a new interpretation of Johnson that emphasized his inner psychological world and mentality. In 1978 Genji Takahashi, a distinguished scholar of English literature, published *Samuel Johnson*, which tried to come close to its subject by explaining Johnson's works as well as his religious life. According to Takahashi, the idea of the book was to renew and refresh

Johnsonian studies for the scholars of Japan.[9] It was also the first book about Johnson written by a Japanese scholar in English.

The 1980s was considered a prelude to the golden age of Johnsonian studies in Japan. The average number of articles and books that focused on him increased to thirty or forty every year, and these covered a wider range of subjects, such as Johnson as an essayist, Johnson and Ossian, and Johnson's views on the Falkland Islands disputes. Studies of lexicography continued, and Daisuke Nagashima's book on the subject, *Johnson no "Eigo Jiten": sono rekishiteki igi* (*Johnson's Dictionary: Its Historical Significance*), was published in 1983. In the same year, Yoshiro Kojima wrote an article in *Eigo tembo* (*English Language Education Council Bulletin*), "Eigo jisho monogatari (2): Johnson no jisho to sono zengo" ("A Story of English Dictionaries (2): Before and After Johnson's Dictionary"). Further proof of this increased interest in Johnson came in the publication of a facsimile of the first edition of Johnson's *Dictionary* in the same year, and the publication of a different edition of the *Dictionary* two years later by another publisher. These publishers clearly thought, correctly, that there was a great demand for Johnson's *Dictionary* and that it was worth reprinting them in Japan.

The year 1984, the 200th anniversary of Dr. Johnson's death, saw the publication of several works on Johnson. There was a special issue of *Eigo seinen*, to which many Japanese Johnsonians contributed articles. In Oxford, a conference to commemorate the anniversary was held at Pembroke College. The conference was attended by several Japanese scholars, including Nagashima, Nakahara, and Hitoshi Suwabe. Nagashima published a book, *Doctor Johnson meigen-shu* (*Dr. Johnson through His Proverbial Sayings*), in which he introduced Johnson's famous sayings and reported the events of the conference. This report urged Japanese Johnsonians to keep in touch with their counterparts in other parts of the world. Johnsonian studies also increased in scope during this period. An essay on Johnson's Stella poems by Yutaka Izumitani appeared in the Shikoku Gakuin University bulletin in 1985, and Hideichi Eto's essay on *The Adventurer*, which appeared in the Tokoha Gakuen Tankidaigaku bulletin in the same year, was the first article on this aspect of the Johnson canon by a Japanese scholar.

Although no textbooks for Japanese students that include writings by Johnson and Boswell are currently being published, some English textbooks that were published during the 1980s included Boswell's *Dorando: A Spanish Tale*. Another textbook contained an anthology of Johnson's short stories, including *The Fountains*. Even Johnson's "Plan of an English Dictionary" was put into an English textbook (one entitled *Lessons in Language*). In 1988 two different textbooks containing some of Johnson's works were published. One was *Moral Essays: Dream, Hope and Life*, which included seven essays from *The Rambler*, two from *The Adventurer*, and three from *The Idler*. The other was *Choice Passages from English Literature,* which included several passages from the *Life of Cowley* and the famous episode from Boswell's *Life* recording Boswell's first meeting with Johnson. As if to symbolize this growth of Johnsonian studies in the 1980s, the Samuel Johnson Club of Japan was founded in 1988 with thirteen members, with Nagashima as chair. The club holds an annual meeting and publishes a newsletter in English in order to share information with other Johnsonians abroad.

In the first half of the 1990s, Johnsonian studies in Japan were approaching the period of their golden age, and thirty-five to forty-five essays, articles, and books referring to Johnson and his circle were published every year. The following gives a partial list of the major books that were published between 1991 and 1996 on topics that are relevant to Johnson studies. Akio Nakahara's 1991 *Johnson-den no keifu* (*Genealogy of the Life of Johnson*) is an extensive piece of research on major biographies of Johnson published in England, the U.S., and Japan. It traces various editions, from Johnson's earliest biographers, such as Piozzi, John Hawkins, and James Boswell, to modern ones, such as John Wain, W. J. Bate, and Thomas Kaminski, as well as to Japanese biographers, such as Ishida and Fukuhara. Yutaka Izumitani's 1992 *Kentou no bungo Johnson: Meijiki Rasselas no henei* (*The Challenge of Johnson, a Man of Literature: A Glimpse of Rasselas in the Meiji Era*) is a brilliant explication of how *Rasselas* was read in the Meiji era and how such a fantastic story was received in this era. The same author's 1993 work, *Johnson kenkyu: sono hito to sakuhin* (*Johnsonian Studies: The Man and His Works*), is composed of fourteen articles, mainly about Johnson's essays, that had previously been published in academic journals. Nagashima's 1995 *Johnson no shi to shinko* (*Johnson's Death and Beliefs*) draws on Johnson's works and several biographies to discuss Johnson's view of religion. Nagashima argued that Johnson was an Arminian—a conservative, rationalistic theist.[10] This is the only book written in Japan that is concerned with Johnson and his religious beliefs.

Johnsonian studies reached their peak in 1996, after which the number of books and articles has gradually decreased to about thirty per year. Scholars who specialize in Johnson and his circle have also decreased in number. The books published in the latter half of the 1990s are as follows. Shigeru Shibagaki's *Dr. Johnson in Boswell's Life and Journals* discusses Boswell's view of biographies and his considerations in writing the *Life of Dr. Johnson*. Nakahara's *Jisho no Johnson no seiritsu: Boswell no nikki kara denki e* (*Birth of the Dictionary Johnson: From Boswell's Diaries to His Biography*) mainly discusses Boswell's diaries and their relation to his *Life*. Nakahara also examines the quotations that are included in Johnson's *Dictionary* to consider Johnson's knowledge of other writers, including Shakespeare, Izaak Walton, and Samuel Richardson. No biographies of Johnson or guides to his literature appeared in this period.

By the end of the twentieth century, discussion in Japan of Johnson's life and works had been confined almost exclusively to Johnson specialists.

The Twenty-First Century

Although an average of thirty items per year on Johnson and Boswell were published between 2000 and 2010, there have not been new scholars based in Japan who specialize in these authors. Johnson and his position in eighteenth-century English literature are at present likely to be given less and less attention among Japanese scholars of English literature as well as Japanese intellectuals. Johnson's works are rarely read in English classes in universities, even by faculties of English literature. The fact that no English textbooks containing Johnson's essays or passages of Boswell's *Life* have been published in Japan since 2010 bears evidence to the present situation of Johnsonian studies in that country. Even Hawthorne's *Biographical Stories*, which used to be a very popular English textbook, has not appeared since the beginning of the twenty-first century.

Under such circumstances, the publication in 2006 of Tetsu Fujii's bibliography, *Nihon ni okeru Samuel Johnson to James Boswell bunken mokuroku (1871–2005)* (*A Bibliography of Samuel Johnson and James Boswell in Japan (1871–2005)*), was all the more remarkable. Fujii spent more than ten years gathering and compiling the material for this bibliography.

During the twentieth century, Japanese scholars had not adequately pursued the study of Johnson's journey to Scotland. Only nine articles were written between E. V. Gatenby's "Johnson and Boswell in Scotland" (1929) and Hideichi Eto's *Juhachiseiki no Scotland: Dr. Johnson no ryokoki o megutte* (*Scotland in the Eighteenth Century: Concerning Dr. Johnson's Journey*), published in 2008. Eto's book revealed the fictitious elements of Johnson's *Journey to the Western Islands of Scotland* by comparing it with Boswell's *Journal of a Tour to the Hebrides* and the letters from Scotland that Johnson sent to Mrs. Thrale.

Other scholars have focused on different parts of the Johnson canon. In 2009 Hitoshi Suwabe published *Johnson to Boswell: jijitsu no shuhen* (*Johnson and Boswell: Facts and Thereabout*). This book brings together into one volume several of his insightful essays, including "Boswell's Meetings with Johnson, A New Count," "A Trio in the Age of Transition: Johnson, Boswell and Hume," and "eibungaku no naka no nihonjin" ("Japanese People in English Literature"). Efforts have also been made to make information about Johnson and his world more accessible to a wider audience. For example, *Johnson hakase no kotoba* (*Dr. Johnson's Sayings*), edited by Yoshiyuki Nakano, was published in 2002. This is a collection of Johnson's sayings, referring to his view of happiness, that appear in Boswell's *Life*. The Johnson Club of Japan published *Eikoku bunka no kyojin Samuel Johnson* (*Samuel Johnson, a Giant of English Culture*) in 2009 to commemorate the twentieth anniversary of the founding of the club as well as the 300th anniversary of Johnson's birth. Edited by Hideichi Eto, Hitoshi Suwabe, and Shigeru Shibagaki, this book contains essays on a wide variety of subjects, including the historical background of Johnson's life, information about his friends and dependents, commentaries on his works, and movements of Johnsonian studies in Japan. *Samuel Johnson: sono tayonaru sekai* (*Samuel Johnson: The Diversity of His World*) was published the following year. This book, written by seven scholars belonging to a research group led by Akio Kobayashi at Sophia University, was also published to commemorate the 300th anniversary of Johnson's birth. It contains chapters on subjects as various as "Johnson as a Journalist," "A comparison of Johnson's actual travel with Rasselas's travel," "Johnson and Politics," "Johnson as a philologist," and "Johnson and Shakespeare." This is the last collection to date of articles that are solely concerned with Johnson.

Despite the relative lack of publications on Johnson and his world in recent years in Japan, Johnson's reception in this country's scholarly world continues to change rapidly. While nonspecialists still tend to depend on Boswell's *Life,* thus holding on to a more old-fashioned idea of Johnson propounded by Uchida and Fukuhara, specialist Johnsonians and eighteenth-century scholars have begun to apply more sophisticated and varied critical ideas to Johnson, and have thus begun to appreciate him as a much more dynamic and engaging writer.

A Brief History of Translations of Dr. Johnson's Works

The first translated work in Japan to refer to Johnson, an 1871 translation of Samuel Smiles's 1859 book *Self-Help*, appeared only three years after Japan had opened itself up to other countries. In 1873, J. G. Edgar's *The Boyhood of Great Men* (1853), which also refers to Johnson, was translated. This was followed in 1878 by a translation of Smiles's *Character* (1871), in which Smiles attributes Johnson's competitive spirit to the filial piety and unyielding way of life of his early years. Though almost forgotten now, these works were highly influential because it was through them that Japanese people first learned about Johnson and created their own image of him.

At the turn of the twentieth century Johnson was best known in Japan from his appearance in Nathaniel Hawthorne's *Biographical Stories* (1842). In his biography, Hawthorne mythologizes Johnson by dwelling on the iconic scene of Johnson doing penance by standing bareheaded in the rain in Uttoxeter market to atone for his prideful disinclination as a child to help his father at his bookstall.[11] The anecdote resonated with the values of Japanese people, who honored filial piety, and Hawthorne's book was, in its turn, used as a textbook for moral education as well as for learning the English language. After

Hawthorne's *Biographical Stories* was first translated into Japanese in 1895, about forty Japanese versions, including annotated editions for Japanese students to learn English, were published between 1895 and 2008.

Rasselas was the most popular of Johnson's works in Japan and the first of all his works to be translated into Japanese. Six translated versions were issued between 1886 (the year of the first translation) and 1910. After this date, however, no new editions were published until 1948, when a new version was published by Natsuo Shumuta, a distinguished Johnsonian of the time. A revised edition and pocket edition of his translation were published in 1962 and 2011, respectively.

With regard to Johnson's edition of Shakespeare, Walter Raleigh's *Johnson on Shakespeare* (1908) was translated (in 1948) by Ken-ichi Yoshida, a principal critic of the age. In 1975 Makoto Nakagawa, a scholar of eighteenth-century English literature, translated the introduction to Walter Raleigh's *Johnson on Shakespeare*, Johnson's *Proposals for Printing a New Edition of the Plays of William Shakespeare*, and Johnson's concluding critical comments on twenty-six of the plays. Yoshida's book was reissued in 1978, confirming the great interest in Japan in the1970s of both Johnson and Shakespeare. Since Nakagawa's work there have been no other translations of Johnson on Shakespeare except for a 2003 Japanese version by Tadaaki Noguchi and Hirohisa Igarashi of David Nicol Smith's 1928 study *Shakespeare in the Eighteenth Century*.

Although Johnson's essays have been the subject of substantial critical attention elsewhere in the world, they were little noticed by Japanese scholars until the mid-twentieth century. After the 1912 publication of *Sekai bungo koyukan* (*Friendships of Great Men of Letters in the World*), which contained translations by Goro Takahashi of Johnson's essays concerning friendship (*Idler* no. 23, *Rambler* no. 40 and no. 64), no other Japanese versions of Johnson's essays were published until 1944. In that year "On Wasting Time" from *Idler* no. 14 was translated by Fukuhara and published in *Eigo seinen*. Three years later, in 1947, Fukuhara also translated "Dick Minim the Critic" from *Idler* no. 60 and no. 61 for the same magazine. These essays, along with Fukuhara's translations of the *Life of Collins*, a part of the *Preface to Shakespeare*, and the section on the metaphysical poets in the *Life of Cowley*, were edited into a single book that was published in 1953 with additional commentary by Fukuhara and with the title *Eikoku kindai sambun shu* (*An Anthology of Essays in Modern England*).

In the 1970s and 1980s Izumitani made a significant contribution to the study of Johnson in Japan by translating Johnson's essays and sermons. These were anthologized in 1991 in *An Anthology of Samuel Johnson's Essays*, which contained the following essays: "Preface to *The Preceptor*," "Review of *A Free Inquiry into the Nature and Origin of Evil*," "An Essay on Epitaphs," and "On Gray's Epitaph" from *Gentleman's Magazine*, and "The Duty of a Journalist" from the *Universal Chronicle* and *Rambler* no. 145. In 1997 Izumitani published translations of Johnson's twenty-five sermons in a volume entitled *Eien no sentaku: Samuel Johnson sekkyo shu* (*Choice of Eternal Life: A Collection of Samuel Johnson's Sermons*).

Although Johnson's *Prayers and Meditations* were translated by Jiro Suzuki as early as 1933, no new Japanese translation of these works has appeared since. *The Lives of the Poets*, on the other hand, has been popular among Japanese Johnson scholars over the last century: Fukuhara published a translation of the *Life of Collins* in 1943, and Natsuo Shumuta's translation of the *Life of Milton* appeared in 1974. Two different versions of the *Life of Savage* were published the following year: one by Hitoshi Suwabe and the other by Tadashi Nakagawa, although this latter translation was only published privately. Nakagawa has subsequently published translations of the lives of Pope (1992), Swift (2005), Dryden (2006), and Addison, Gay, and Gray (all 2009). Another version of the *Lives of the Poets* was published in 2009 to commemorate the 300th anniversary of Johnson's birth. It includes the lives of Milton translated by Katsuhiro Engetsu, Dryden by Masaaki Takeda, Savage by Yutaka Semba, Pope by Akio Kobayashi, Swift by Koji Watanabe, Cowley by Noriyuki Harada, and Gray by Yuri Yoshino. Between 1982 and 1985, earlier biographies by Johnson, including those of Sir Thomas Browne, Edward Cave, and Roger Ascham, were translated by Tetsu Fujii in a university bulletin of Kassui Women's University in Nagasaki. Studies of the *Lives* tend to focus on the great poets featured in this work, while the minor poets tend to be disregarded, as are Johnson's early biographies. However, as we know, in order to understand Johnson's ideas about biography and to evaluate him fully as a critic, much more attention needs to be paid by Japanese Johnsonians to these neglected works.

The "Preface to A Dictionary of the Language" and the "Plan of an English Dictionary" were translated in 1993 and 2007 by different hands, and both versions appeared in different university bulletins. These works by Johnson—or these specific translations—would seem to have no commercial value because they have not been picked up by any publishers. However, some books that discuss Johnson's *Dictionary* have been translated into Japanese, such as Jonathan Green's *Chasing the Sun: Dictionary-Makers and the Dictionaries They Make* (1996), translated by Kiyoshi Mikawa, and Herbert C. Morton's *The Story of Webster's Third: Philip Grove's Controversial Dictionary and Its Critics* (1994), translated by Kyohei Nakamoto. Both translations were published in 1999. Melvyn Bragg's *The Adventure of English: The Biography of a Language* (2003) and Simon Winchester's *The Meaning of Everything* (2003) were translated in 2004 by Kiyoshi Mikawa and Tsunenori Karibe, respectively. A Japanese version of Henry Hitching's *Dr. Johnson's Dictionary: The Extraordinary Story of the Book that Defined the World* (2005) by Kyoko Tanaka appeared in 2007. All of these translations appeared fewer than five years after the publication of the originals, and this suggests that though the *Dictionary* itself was ignored, the romance and history of its composition, and its connections to the broader history of dictionary making, were subjects of interest and appeal to Japanese scholars.

While the poems of the Romantic period have traditionally been very popular with Japanese readers and many have been translated into Japanese, very few poems by eighteenth-century poets, including Johnson, have been accorded the same attention. One reason for this discrepancy might be the spirit of Japanese reception of European literary works in the Meiji era. Romanticism remained vibrant in English thought throughout the nineteenth century, and Japan took its cue from British cultural attitudes. Literary people of the Meiji era read the poems of the Romantic period, were deeply impressed by them, and translated them into Japanese using traditional Japanese rhythms. For most Japanese people, *poetry* meant Romantic poetry, not the heroic couplets of the Augustan age and the Age of Johnson. Only seven of Johnson's poems have been translated into Japanese. These include "An Extempore Elegy," "Burlesque of Lines by Lope de Vega," and "On Hearing Miss Thrale Deliberate about Her Hat" (1976), and "A Short Song of Congratulation" and "To Mrs. Thrale, On Her Completing Her Thirty-Fifth Year" (1977). These poems were translated by Yutaka Izumitani and appeared in *The Shimyaku* magazine. Shigeru Shibagaki's translations of Johnson's two most famous poems, "London: A Poem" and "The Vanity of Human Wishes," were published in 1985.

Although it was recognized as an important work in understanding Johnson's thought, it was not until 2006 that his *Journey to the Western Islands of Scotland* was translated into Japanese, by a research group of Chuo University whose members were Hitoshi Suwabe, Yasuo Ichikawa, Hideichi Eto, and Shigeru Shibagaki. This group invited Zenji Inamura to translate Boswell's *A Tour to the Hebrides*, Johnson's diaries of tours to Wales and France, and Thrale's diaries of the same tours. The translation of Boswell's *Tour* was published in 2010, and the translations of the Wales and France diaries in 2017. The last work is expected to be of great interest not only to Japanese Johnsonians but also to Japanese historians and scholars of French literature on account of the portraits they offer of France before the Revolution.

Biographies of Johnson have been important in Japan. One volume of an abridged version of Boswell's *Life of Dr. Samuel Johnson, LL.D.* was translated as early as 1941. Two further volumes were published in 1946 and 1948. Those three volumes were abridged by Saburo Kamiyoshi and issued in a pocket edition. Thirty-three years later, in 1981, a complete translation appeared in three volumes, translated by Yoshiyuki Nakano. Mrs. Piozzi's *Anecdotes of the Late Samuel Johnson, LL.D. during the Last Twenty Years of His Life* was translated and published privately by Choji Yokote in 1991. On the other hand, Sir John

Hawkins's *Life of Samuel Johnson* (1787), a major contemporary biography of Johhson, still awaits its translator.

Books concerning daily life and the social realities of Johnson's age have been translated sporadically since 1950. These include translations of George Trevelyan's *English Social History* (1950) by Kentaro Hayashi; Richard B. Schwartz's *Daily Life in Johnson's London* (1990) by Hideichi Eto; Bridget Irene Hill's *Eighteenth-Century Women: An Anthology* (1990) by Ryoko Fukuda; A. S. Collin's *Authorship in the Days of Johnson: Being a Study of the Relation between Author, Patron, Publisher and Public, 1726–1780* (1994) by Ken Aoki and Hiroshi Enomoto; and Roy Porter's *English Society in the Eighteenth Century* (1996) by Kimikazu Mera. In 2002, a Japanese version of Liza Picard's *Dr. Johnson's London: Life in 1740–1770* appeared in a translation by Yasuko Tashiro.

Finally, Johnson has had some popular currency in Japan. A translation of Yvonne Skargon's picture book *Lily & Hodge & Dr. Johnson* by Kaname Kitaishi was published in 1992. Translations of Lillian de la Torre's series *Dr. Sam: Johnson* began in 1958 and thirteen of these stories had been translated by 1992. In these stories Johnson represents Sherlock Holmes and Boswell represents Dr. Watson. The translators are Fukuo Hashimoto, Seiichi Yoshida, Jyunkou Nagata, Hiroshi Mitamura, Hikaru Kikuchi, Shinichi Mori, Kazuo Inoue, Mariko Fukamachi, Suzuo Sasou, Eiko Kakinuma, and Takao Miyawaki. This series introduces the names of Johnson and Boswell to general readers. Its popularity in Japan seems to lie in the traditional fondness of Japanese people for detective stories.

Conclusion

This survey of Johnson scholarship and criticism in Japan gives an idea of how deeply Johnson is rooted in Japanese academic culture. In particular, we note the popularity of *Rasselas* since the earliest stages of its reception in Japan, and the interest that Johnson's work as an etymologist and philologist holds for Japanese scholars of philology. At the same time, we note how few scholars in Japan have any interest in Johnson's thought on economics and politics, and his only drama *Irene* has never been fully studied in Japan.

Johnsonian studies in Japan in the twenty-first century are in decline: the number of young people who read and study Johnson has been decreasing, and Japanese Johnsonians are an aging society. Furthermore, Johnsonian studies have become increasingly factionalized and specialized, producing an uninviting atmosphere for younger scholars. A solution to this problem, as Fujii suggests, might be to publish high-quality articles and books, as well as engage translations of Johnson's and Boswell's works that can capture the interest of young people.[12]

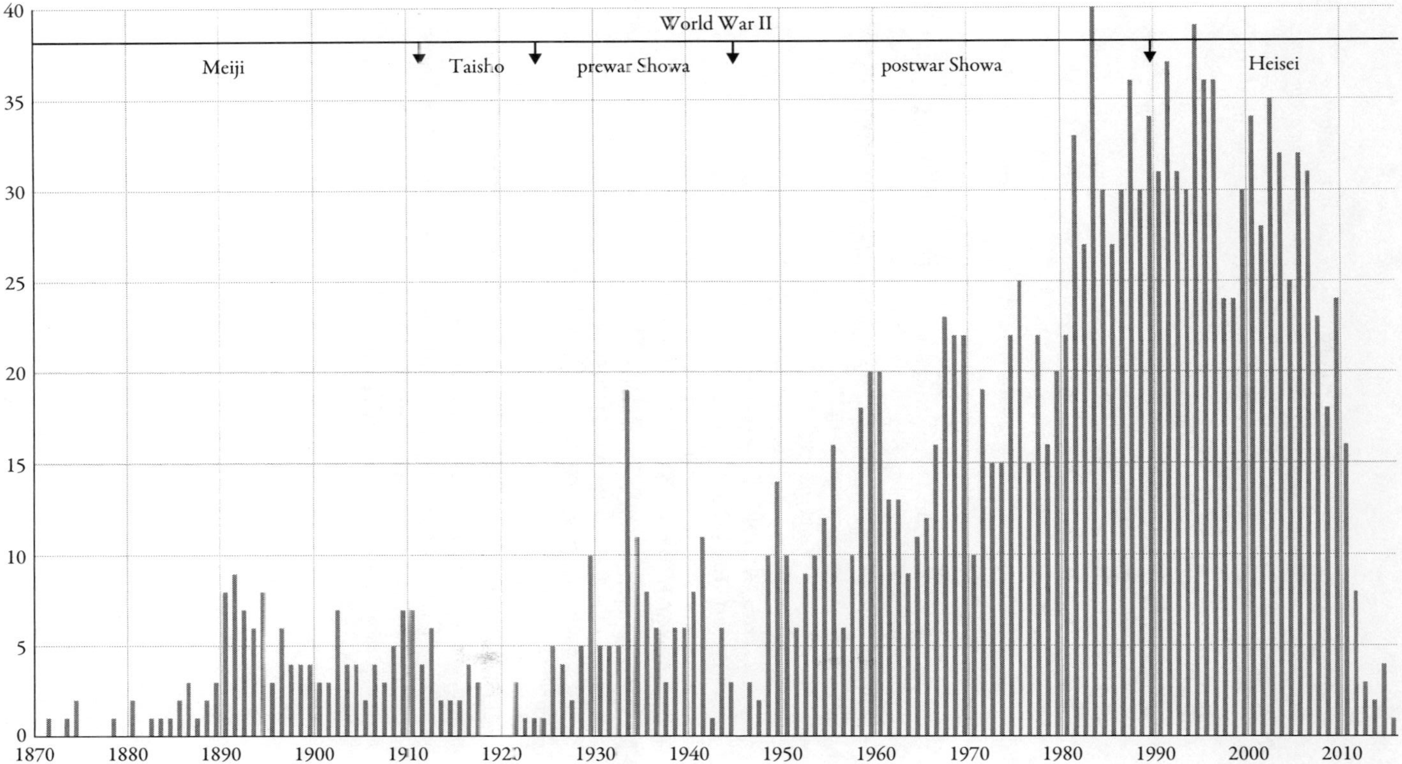

Appendix: The number of publications on Johnson and Boswell in Japan

Notes

In this chapter I have benefited greatly from the advice of Tetsu Fujii, emeritus professor at Fukuoka University, and his *Nihon ni okeru Samuel Johnson oyobi James Boswell bunken mokuroku, 1871–2005* (*A Bibliography of Johnsonian and Boswellian Studies in Japan, 1871–2005*), published by Nada Shuppan Center, Tokyo, in 2006.

1 Mitsugi [Roan] Uchida, *Junibungo: Johnson* (*Twelve Great Writers: Johnson*) (Tokyo: Minyusha, 1894), 131; also in *Uchida Roan Zenshu* (*Complete Works of Uchida Roan*) (Tokyo: Yumani Shobo, 1987), 2:369.
2 Noriyuki Harada, "Translation and Transformation: Japanese Reception and Adaptation of Eighteenth-Century English Literature," *Essays and Studies in British & American Literature* 58 (March 2012): 12.
3 Akio Nakahara, *Johnson den no keifu* (*Genealogy of the Life of Johnson*) (Tokyo: Kenkyusha Shuppan, 1991), 196.
4 Tetsu Fujii, "Johnson hen," in *Sekai bungaku sogou mokuroku* (*A Catalogue of World Literature*), ed. Michiaki Kawato and Takanori Sakakibara (Tokyo: Nada Shuppan Center, 2011), 293.
5 Kenji Ishida, *Johnson hakase to sono mure* (*Dr. Johnson and His Circle*) (Tokyo: Kenkyusha, 1933), 7.
6 Nakahara, *Johnson den no keifu*, 210.
7 Tetsu Fujii, ed., *Nihon ni okeru Samuel Johnson oyobi James Boswell bunken mokuroku, 1871–2005* (*A Bibliography of Johnsonian and Boswellian Studies in Japan, 1871–2005*) (Tokyo: Nada Shuppan Center, 2006), 57.
8 Zensuke Taira, "Nihon Johnson kyokai no sosetsu no zengo" ("Reminiscences of the Beginning of the Johnson Society in Japan"), *Annual Bulletin of the Johnson Society* no.31 (May 2007): 1–2.
9 Genji Takahashi, *Samuel Johnson* (Tokyo: Aiikusha, 1978), preface.
10 Daisuke Nagashima, *Johnson no shi to shinko* (*Johnson's Death and Beliefs*) (Tokyo: Seikokai Shuppan, 1995), 185–188.
11 Nathaniel Hawthorne, *True Stories from History and Biography*, vol. 6 of *Centenary Edition of the Works of Nathaniel Hawthorne*, ed. William Charvat (Columbus: Ohio State University Press, 1972), 245–248.
12 Tetsu Fujii, "Nihon de no Johnson jyuyo to kenkyu no rekishi" ("A History of Reception and Studies of Johnson in Japan"), in *Eikoku bunka no kyojin Samuel Johnson* (*Samuel Johnson, a Giant of English Culture*), ed. Hideichi Eto, Shigeru Shibagaki, and Hitoshi Suwabe (Kamakura, Japan: Minato No Hito, 2009), 307.

2

Johnson, Biography, and Modern Japan

NORIYUKI HARADA

Introduction

Samuel Johnson is the literary figure in the eighteenth century most frequently associated with the genre of biography, and it is in his practice of biography that he perhaps lays greatest claim to modernity. As Robert Folkenflik notes, biography was "the literary form most congenial to Johnson's assumptions about art and nature."[1] Indeed, in his early years, Johnson earned his living by contributing essays and articles to *The Gentleman's Magazine*, some of which were biographical sketches of eminent people, such as the Italian statesman Paolo Sarpi and the Dutch physiologist Herman Boerhaave. Johnson's first independent prose publication was the biography of his friend, the poet Richard Savage. Even his poetic masterpiece *The Vanity of Human Wishes* is filled with biographical sketches of kings, warriors, and writers. In his middle years, Johnson wrote important essays on biography for *The Rambler* and *The Idler*, as well as biographies such as "The Life of Dr. Francis Cheynel" and "Memoirs of the King of Prussia." In his later years, he published biographies of fifty-two English poets as *The Lives of the English Poets*. The knowledge, reading, and experience out of which the biographies of these poets were written had accumulated over decades; in a sense, *Lives* was the result of the development of his biographical thinking. In the study of the categorization of the arts in eighteenth-century England, Lawrence Lipking regards *Lives* as "literary and intellectual history," as well as "biographical encyclopedias like the *Biographia Britannica*." Alvin Kernan too argues that *Lives* combines "the hitherto scattered pieces of English literary lore," and works them "into a structure of biography, social history, and criticism sufficiently firm to constitute for the first time a history of English letters."[2] Undoubtedly, *Lives* helped to canonize certain English poets and, in general, to form the concept of English literary history through biographical description.

Johnson was, of course, also the subject of biographies written by his friends—and enemies—of which James Boswell's *Life of Johnson* was the most significant. Boswell begins his work with an intriguing remark: "Had Dr. Johnson written his own life, in conformity with the opinion which he has given, that every man's life may be best written by himself; had he employed in the preservation of his own history, that clearness of narration and elegance of language in which he has embalmed so many eminent persons, the world would probably have had the most perfect example of biography that was exhibited."[3]

But Johnson did not gather his autobiographical writings together to form a collective whole. Needless to say, it is on the basis of his own writings that Johnson had a vibrant and growing reputation after his death. At the same time, in nineteenth-century Britain, the biographies by Boswell and others helped him to become a famous literary personality, even an object of hero worship.

For Johnson, as for his society in general, Japan was a remote country. When Johnson was talking with Boswell in 1772 about buying St. Kilda, a remote island in the Scottish Hebrides, Boswell mentioned Japan as a means of illustrating St. Kilda's remoteness: "if you should advise me to go to Japan, I believe I should do it."[4] While Japan does not feature in Johnson's writings, there were memorable literary references to Japan in some eighteenth-century texts, including George Psalmanazar's *Formosa* (1704), Jonathan Swift's *Gulliver's Travels* (1726), and Tobias Smollett's *The Expedition of Humphry Clinker* (1771). Yet even Josiah Conder's thirty volumes of worldwide geographical and historical records, *The Modern Traveller* (1830), did not include Japan as an independent category. However, if we think of the intermingling of biography and prose fiction in the Japanese literary tradition, and the influence of biography in the modernization of Japan, we find some remarkable similarities between the literary scenes of Britain in the eighteenth and nineteenth centuries, and those in Japan in the nineteenth and early twentieth centuries.

Biographies were a popular feature of early eighteenth-century British literary culture. Details about the lives and deaths, not only of kings, queens, and aristocrats, but also of political leaders, priests, people of learning, merchants, famous robbers, and notable (or notorious) people from all walks of life attracted the reader's attention and biographical articles helped to increase readership figures in the publications in which these biographies appeared. The reader's curiosity about the lives of individual people was broadened by biographies. In this respect the development of biographical writing was an important factor in the development of modern society itself. Biographies that describe the lives of common people provide insights into human relationships and society. Therefore, it seems natural for Joseph Addison to begin the first issue of *The Spectator* with the narrator's own biography, saying "a Reader seldom peruses a Book with Pleasure 'till he knows whether the Writer of it to be a black or a fair Man, of a mild or cholerick Disposition, Married or a Batchelor, with other Particulars of the like nature."[5] It is interesting to note here that, though many essays of *The Spectator* recorded the authors' observations of society and were, in this sense, factual, the narrators were fictitious and the essays operated in much the way contemporary works of fiction did in representing life. In fact, many prose fictions of the late seventeenth and early eighteenth centuries took the form of a biography and the popularity of biographical writings was closely related to the birth of the novel.

The preference of Japanese readers for biographical prose fiction significantly predates the growth of the genre in Britain at the turn of the eighteenth century. It is said to date from the Heian period (794–1192); the most significant example of biographical prose fiction is *The Tales of Genji* (written in the early eleventh century), in which the life of the protagonist, Hikaru Genji, is given over several narrative romances. After the Tokugawa shogunate started a new political system in the Edo period (1603–1867), novelists such as Saikaku Ihara, Ryoi Asai, and Kiseki Ejima published prose fictions in which biographical descriptions of the characters were dominant. Ihara's *Koshoku-Ichidai-Otoko* (*The Life of an Amorous Man*) (1682) and *Koshoku-Ichidai-Onnna* (*The Life of an Amorous Woman*) (1686), both of which were fictional biographies, were well received by readers throughout the Edo period. In the early nineteenth century, we also find many popular biographical fictions, including Ikku Juppensha's *Tokaidochu-Hizakurige* (*A Journey of Tokaido on Foot*) (1802–1809), a humorous travelogue of the two protagonists, Bakin Kyokutei's *Nanso-Satomi-Hakkenden* (*The Lives of the Eight Great Dogs of Satomi Clan*) (1814–1842), the lives of eight dog warriors of a southeastern province of Japan, and Tanehiko Ryutei's *Nisemurasaki-Inaka-Genji* (*The Life of Nisemurasaki-Inaka-Genji*) (1829–1842), a popular parody of *The Tales of Genji*. In addition, in the traditional genre of theatrical performance, Kabuki, we find numerous stories in which biographies were skillfully adapted for performance.[6]

It seems natural, therefore, that when Japan sought to modernize along Western lines, books that included biographical information about eminent Westerners, such as Samuel Smiles's *Self-Help: Illustrations of Character and Conduct* (1859, 1866), were particularly well received. Masanao Nakamura's translation of Smiles's *Self-Help* (1871) appeared soon after the Meiji Restoration and was immediately used as a textbook in the earliest phase of modern primary school education. Its biographical sketches showed Japanese people the manners and achievements in modern societies; 1 million copies of the translation were sold by the end of the century.[7]

There are, of course, multiple causes of social modernization, such as the changing of old political and social systems, developments in education, technological innovation, and industrialization. In literature modernization entails changes in language, readership, and print culture. The origins of the English novel are to be found in those literary and cultural contexts. The proliferation and popularity of biographies are also important for modernization. In what follows I shall focus on Johnson's involvement with the genre of biography and the role it played in the modernization of English society. I thereby hope to shed new light on the cultural significance of Johnson's life and writing and their social influence in both Britain and Japan.

Johnson on Biography

In *The Rambler* no. 60 (1750), Johnson lays out his main ideas as to how biographies appeal to the reader's mind: "Those parallel circumstances, and kindred images, to which we readily conform our minds, are above all other writings, to be found in narratives of the lives of particular persons; and therefore no species of writing seems more worthy of cultivation than biography, since none can be more delightful or more useful, none can more certainly enchain the heart by irresistible interest, or more widely diffuse instruction to every diversity of condition."[8]

Johnson clearly places the genre of biography high among the "species of writing." In doing so, Johnson was reasserting the attitude toward biography found in one of his most significant predecessors, John Dryden. The earliest citation that the *Oxford English Dictionary* gives for the word *biography* occurs in Dryden's preface to *The Life of Plutarch* (1683). There Dryden divides "History" into three categories: "*Commentaries* or *Annals*; *History*, properly so called; and *Biographia*, or the Lives of particular men." "*Biographia*" is, according to Dryden, "the History of particular Mens Lives," in which "all things here are circumscrib'd and driven to a point, so as to terminate in one;" therefore, it must offer "less of variety" and be "inferiour to the other two" categories in terms of dignity, because "the fortunes and actions of one Man are related, not those of many." However, "in pleasure and instruction," biography "equals, or even excels both" commentaries and history. For "as the Sun Beams, uniting in a burning-glass to a point, have greater force than when they are darted from a plain superficies; so the vertues and actions of one Man, drawn together into a single story, strike upon our minds a stronger and more lively impression, than the scatter'd Relations of many Men, and many actions."[9] Dryden's preface to *The Life of Plutarch* thus not only offers a definition of biography, it also provides a substantial explanation of the characteristics and merits of the genre; more importantly, he pays attention to the effects of biography on the reader's mind.

For Dryden, and later, for Johnson, biography was a form of writing in which the author was clearly aware of the "pleasure and instruction" for the reader. According to Johnson, biography is the most delightful and useful form of writing because the "parallel circumstances" and "kindred images" that biographers describe are those to which "we readily conform our minds." Biographers need to "pass slightly over those performances and incidents, which produce vulgar greatness, to lead the thoughts into domestick privacies, and display the minute details of daily life, where exterior appendages are cast aside, and men excel each other only by prudence and by virtue."[10]

Johnson's attitude toward biography is realized in his own biographical writings. For example, he began *The Life of Mr. Richard Savage* (1744) with the following insight into the nature of human happiness: "It has been observed in all ages, that the advantages of nature or of fortune have contributed very little to the promotion of happiness; and that those whom the splendour of their rank, or the extent of their capacity, have placed upon the summits of human life, have not often given any just occasion to envy in those who look up to them from a lower station."[11]

Johnson's insight into "the promotion of happiness" drawn from Savage's life provides an effective overview of the biography and gives the reader the means of recognizing Savage's pains and pleasures as once their own.

Johnson did not forget to insert a similar biographical overview in prose fiction. His introductory remark to *Rasselas* (1759) identifies the text as a work of historical biography: "Ye who listen with credulity to the whispers of fancy, and pursue with eagerness the phantoms of hope; who expect that age will perform the promises of youth, and that the deficiencies of the present day will be supplied by the morrow; attend to the history of Rasselas prince of Abissinia."[12]

Rasselas is a story in which every member of Rasselas's party seeks happiness by traveling out of the happy valley. The conclusion of their journey only shows that every character can find no positive way for happiness and must continue the search. Nevertheless, the story is undoubtedly persuasive because the experiences of each character relating to the search for happiness is narrated biographically and so the reader can feel the experiences as their own.

We cannot overlook Johnson's views on moral behavior with regard to the writing of biography. If "exterior appendages" of the objects of biographies are cast aside, as he says, we find that "men excel each other only by prudence and by virtue." For Johnson, the truth of biography lies here. But his emphasis on prudence and virtue does not dismiss a variety of personalities. Instead, he observed various walks of life and tried to find the truth of each real life through biographical description. Narrating the truth was pivotal for Johnson and he believed that it could serve as an effective means of providing the reader with "pleasure and instruction."

Johnson as the Subject of Biographies

When we consider the reception of Johnson's achievements in nineteenth-century Britain, we need to examine carefully the relationship between his writing—his critical commentary—and his reputation as a man of letters. Boswell's biography of Johnson was so widely read in the nineteenth century that Johnson's name became identified with the idiosyncratic manners that were highlighted by Boswell, rather than with Johnson's works; in other words, Boswell's biographical vision overshadowed the reception of Johnson's writings. By as early as 1825, Walter Scott observed in his *Lives of the Novelists*:

> Of all the men distinguished in this or any other age, Dr. Johnson has left upon posterity the strongest and most vivid impression, so far as person, manners, disposition, and conversation are concerned. We do but name him, or open a book which he has written, and the sound and action recall to the imagination at once his form, his merits, his peculiarities, nay, the very uncouthness of his gestures, and the deep impressive tone of his voice. . . . All this, as the world well knows, arises from Johnson having found in James Boswell such a biographer as no man but himself ever had or ever deserved to have.[13]

Scott here still intimates that people are reading Johnson's works, but he cannot forget to suggest that the readers are predisposed to find in Johnson's own writings a version of Johnson in Boswell's *Life*. Thomas Carlyle, who regarded Johnson as one of the heroes of modern men of letters, states in his *On Heroes, Hero-Worship, and the Heroic in History* (1841), "Johnson's Writings, which once had such currency and celebrity, are now, as it were, disowned by the young generation."[14] As James T. Boulton concisely remarks, for Carlyle Johnson was "a man, not a writer; a Carlylean hero distinguished by his courage, honesty, compassion and sense of purpose to become one of 'the guides of the dull host.'"[15] Like Carlyle, Thomas B. Macaulay too was forced to refer to the unpopularity of Johnson's works in 1856: "Since his death, the popularity of his works—the Lives of the Poets, and, perhaps, the Vanity of Human Wishes excepted—has greatly diminished. His Dictionary has been altered by editors till it can scarcely be called his. An allusion to his Rambler or his Idler is not readily apprehended in literary circles. The fame even of Rasselas has grown somewhat dim."[16]

From these accounts, we easily imagine the response of nineteenth-century British readers to Johnson. Like Becky Sharp in Thackeray's *Vanity Fair* (1847–1848), who, putting "her pale face out of the window" of the carriage, "flings the book [Johnson's *Dictionary*] back into the garden" of Chiswick Mall,[17] readers might respect Johnson's name, but they shunned his works.

However, the supposed neglect of Johnson's writings in the nineteenth century needs to be carefully examined. It is certain that Boswell's description is vivid, lively, and humorous, while Johnson's writing is sometimes magisterial and has few thrilling developments of plot or fantastic flights of imagination of the kind Victorian readers sought. And yet, though Macaulay thought the fame of Johnson's writings was "grown somewhat dim," new editions of *Rasselas* were published almost every year throughout the nineteenth century, as J. D. Fleeman's bibliography indicates.[18] In *Vanity Fair* Thackeray characterizes Becky Sharp as a typical young woman of the time, but it is obvious that her copy of Johnson's *Dictionary* is not a folio or quarto edition; it must be one of the smaller, miniature editions that were so popular in the nineteenth century. It was editions of this type that Macaulay had in mind when he lamented that Johnson's *Dictionary* had "been altered by editors till it can scarcely be called his." These are clearly not authentic editions of Johnson's *Dictionary*, which is what the London Philological Society (founded in 1842) used as the basis for a new dictionary, one that would eventually become the *Oxford English Dictionary*.

The relation between Johnson's reputation and the unpopularity of his own works in the nineteenth century seems, therefore, to have at least two elements. First, the popularity of Johnson's life, based mainly on Boswell's biography, can be considered the result of the mania for biography among Victorian readers. It is not necessarily related to the readers' regard for Johnson's writings. Second, although Carlyle's and Macaulay's observations that Johnson's writings were obsolete are not untrue, we should not forget that they were primarily imagining the preferences of a newly literate mass reading public. The bibliographical record shows that the publication of Johnson's texts did not decline in the nineteenth century relative to their publication within his lifetime. The comment that Johnson's writings became obsolescent is based on a relative critical point reflecting a particular value judgment; it did not mean that readership of Johnson's writings necessarily changed drastically.[19]

Moreover, it is a mistake to think that the popularity of Johnson as the subject of biographies in the nineteenth century had nothing to do with his own writings. Indeed, we can say that Johnson's biographical reputation was based on the ideas observed in his own works. Carlyle comments on Johnson's writings when discussing the importance of Johnson's "sincerity:" "I find in Johnson's Books the indisputablest traces of a great intellect and great heart;—ever welcome, under what obstructions and perversions soever. They are *sincere* words, those of his; he means things by them.... For the phraseology, tumid or not, has always *something within* it."[20] Johnson's biographical reputation was not totally isolated from his own works in nineteenth-century Britain; biographers who contributed to his reputation were all close readers of Johnson's works.

Biographical Thinking in Modern Japan

The new government established after the last Tokugawa shogun resigned grappled with the issue of modernization but paid little regard to matters of language. There was no discussion of the possibility of making English an official language. Instead, the modernization of the Japanese language and, in particular, the harmonization of its written and spoken forms, was accomplished chiefly through the translation into Japanese of books in English and other European languages. Publishing houses adopted a system of movable-type and printed translations in forms that were highly readable, and helped to create a wide readership for translations. Undoubtedly, translations helped to innovate the Japanese language and accelerate the communication of new ideas and information.[21]

During this period of great cultural change people turned to the reading of biographies as a way of accommodating themselves to new circumstances; for, as Johnson says, biographies are filled with the "parallel circumstances, and kindred images, to which we readily conform our minds."[22] Japanese people have a long history of reading life writing and they had been familiar with biographical thinking even before the drastic change in society in the middle of the nineteenth century. It was therefore natural for Japanese people during the transitional period to be taken with biographies; now they could read about the lives of Western individuals in a form that introduced them to the cultural background in question and made it possible to feel that they were connecting with the wider world.

Indeed, as early as 1870, Robun Kanagaki, who had started his journalistic career before the Meiji Restoration, published a biographical fiction. He adapted Ikku Juppensha's *Tokaidochu-Hizakurige* to describe the two protagonists' humorous travels in the West. Although much of his description was fanciful and not based on reality, the biographical form in which the two travelers in the West were presented appealed to Japanese people and persuaded them to take the fiction for reality. Actually, most Japanese readers at the time seem to have understood many translated English novels and dramas, including *Hamlet* and *King Lear*, as works of biography. Johnson's *Rasselas* was also widely read by the younger generation as a biographical inquiry about happiness and the choice of life. It is certain that the popularity of *Rasselas* was partly due to its use as an English textbook in the newly established universities and high schools, but the travels of Rasselas's party clearly impressed Japanese readers and students as biographical descriptions of each character's search for happiness.[23]

The biographical understanding of Western culture in post-Meiji Restoration Japan overlapped with the popularity of biography and hero worship in Victorian Britain. In many ways, Victorian Britain was an important model for Japan and translations from English books gradually gained more influence than those from French or German books. It is in this period of modernization in Japan that Johnson's achievements came to be interpreted biographically in books on English literary history and, as he was canonized as a hero in Victorian Britain, so his character as "Ursa Major" attracted the attention of Japanese readers and scholars. As Boswell's image of Johnson came to prevail over Johnson's works in nineteenth-century Britain, so Johnson came to be understood in a similar way among Japanese readers and especially scholars of English literature. *Rasselas* was widely used as an English textbook with extensive circulation, which embedded Johnson biographically deep in the culture.

Teijiro Kobinata's *A History of English Literature* (1924), a very popular book on English literary history in Japanese universities in the early twentieth century, exemplified the predominant image of Johnson among Japanese scholars and students of English literature. Kobinata, a graduate of the (Imperial) University of Tokyo and professor of the National University of Hiroshima (of Humanities and Sciences), describes the history of English literature of the long eighteenth century in four chapters: "The Age of Dryden," "Classical Period," "The Age of Johnson," and "The Age of Wordsworth." This division and nomenclature are clearly based on largely biographical notions; readers are expected to understand eighteenth-century English literature as an extension of the personality of important men of letters, not through aesthetic, formal, or other literary characteristics. These chapters are, as it were, stages in the progress of a Kabuki play in which the story line follows the accumulation of personality in the presentation of representative characters and the remarkable events in their lives. In the section on "The Age of Johnson," Kobinata's biographical thinking is obvious, for Johnson's works are totally assimilated into the biographical account of his life. Kobinata begins the biographical sketch of Johnson as follows: "Almost all men of letters in the eighteenth century hoped for worldly reputation and success. Steele and Pope were far from such a tendency, but their circumstances were exceptionally wealthy. Johnson, on the other hand, was born and lived in poverty, but nevertheless, he was always independent, got a strong footing in the literary world, and was deeply venerated by people around him as a saint. By his learning, impartial judgments, and lofty character, he was highly respected as a sovereign."[24]

After this introductory remark, Kobinata continues by developing the biographical sketch of Johnson with some references to other men of letters of

Johnson's circle; the description of the chapter ends with Johnson's death in 1784 and his burial in Westminster Abbey.

Kobinata's biographical approach was not unusual for the time; his book was popular and widely used as a textbook in courses on English literature. Or rather, his biographical description of English literature was popular along with Japanese literary histories published at the time. Japanese people of the nineteenth and early twentieth centuries were naturally in haste to acquire knowledge of Western countries and an outline of their intellectual traditions; as a result, names were first introduced into the country and then the substance of their work and thought followed. However, it is noticeable that Kobinata's account of Johnson is more biographical than those of Dryden or Wordsworth, in which more attention is given to other contemporary authors and social events. Indeed, the particular circumstances of Johnson's life and works in Kobinata are presented so as to transform him "a saint" or "a sovereign." How are we to understand this transformation?

To answer this question, we need to remind ourselves that Johnson's personality as a man of letters was new to Japanese readers at the time. At the beginning of the period of modernization, Japanese people needed to harmonize the written and spoken forms of their language; translations were instrumental for the transformation of written Japanese. And in the process of transformation, the basic written form relied on by many translators was the one used by novelists of the late Edo period such as Ikku Juppennsha, Bakin Kyokutei, and Tanehiko Ryutei. In fact, Robun Kanagaki draws on this style as well as on Juppensha's *Tokaidochu-Hizakurige* for his biographical travelogue. Since the late Edo period, their works have generally been known as *gesaku* (popular, lowbrow, or dime novels). The authors of such works were not highly regarded, though they were very popular. However, circumstances drastically changed after the Meiji Restoration. The transformation of written Japanese was urgently needed to express new ideas and materials; many of the novelists of the Meiji period served as translators and they became regarded highly as important introducers of new ideas, thoughts, and literature. Indeed, Shoyo Tsubouchi, Ogai Mori, and Sōseki Natsume are all distinguished novelists of the Meiji period and they all also published many translations and taught at the newly established universities.

Therefore, bearing in mind the transformation of the cultural context of the writers under discussion, it becomes clear that an author such as Johnson, who "was always independent, got a strong footing in the literary world, and was deeply venerated by people around him as a saint," became a perfect model and example of the new social status of men of letters, scholars, and translators. Kobinata did not embroider the biography of Johnson; what he did was introduce Johnson to Japanese readers, and faithfully use the biographical descriptions of Johnson's life and works that were already widely known and accepted by contemporary British people. Although Johnson's life and works were colored by interesting anecdotes and events, his adherence to principles of "prudence" and "virtue," as essential to his idea of the great strengths of biography, made him particularly appealing and interesting to Japanese people who, as part of the process of modernization, were faced with social change, rapid scientific and technological development, and religious skepticism.

Biography and Modernization

Discussing the value of biography, Johnson states that "instruction" in biography can be diffused widely to "every diversity of condition."[25] The use of biography for "every diversity of condition" obviously suggests that biography is different from the old genres of life writing like hagiographies and the chronicles of kings or sages; the object of life writing as biography was now widened to include the life of individuals in general. The expansion of the object of life writing can be interpreted as an aspect of modernization of society; the participation of a more diverse range of people in political and social reforms, and in cultural life, needed a genre like biography that was attuned to them in detail. From its outset as a genre, biography was inseparable from modernization.

At the same time, biography is a genre in which the author needs to pay special attention to the reader; as Dryden and Johnson clearly state, biography excels other writings with respect to the "pleasure and instruction" of the reader, and it "enchain[s] the heart" of the reader "by irresistible interest."[26] The frequent references to the "reader" made by Dryden and Johnson suggest the wide readership associated with biography as well as the novel. Such a wide readership characterizes literature in a modern society. Johnson sometimes couches his critical evaluation of a work of literature by directly addressing the reader's response. For example, he says of the importance of the continuance of reputation among readers in the preface to his edition of the plays of Shakespeare: "what has been longest known has been most considered, and what is most considered is best understood. . . . He [Shakespeare] has long outlived his century, the term commonly fixed as the test of literary merit."[27] As for the novel, though it was not necessarily Johnson's favorite genre, he was well aware of the importance of the reader's response in understanding the force of novelistic fiction. In *The Rambler* no. 4 (1750), he writes that "works of fiction" are chiefly read by "the young, the ignorant, and the idle" and therefore they should operate "as lectures of conduct, and introductions into life."[28]

Johnson's reception in nineteenth-century Britain shows that the fondness for Johnson that was felt by what Johnson himself called the "common reader" came mainly through biographies.[29] It is ironic that Johnson was so well treated by the biographies of his life, for the popularity of the form in nineteenth-century Britain was a natural consequence of its development by Johnson himself in the previous century. As Johnson says, biography shows that "men excel each other only by prudence and by virtue;" and if an author wants to convey to the reader the importance of being true to life, biography is the form in which to do this. In addition, as Carlyle mentions, the biographical reception and canonization of Johnson as a literary hero in the nineteenth century were based on his works and were not merely groundless overstatements or fictionalizations. Boswell also was faithful to Johnson's words. In stating his principle of biographical writing, after quoting Johnson's critical remarks from *The Rambler* no. 60, Boswell refers to Julius Caesar's book of apothegms: "in his [Caesar's] book of Apothegms which he collected, we see that he esteemed it more honour to make himself but a pair of tables, to take the wise and pithy words of others, than to have every word of his own."[30] In short, the image of Johnson created by biographical accounts of his life in nineteenth-century Britain effectively became the model for Japanese readers in the period of modernization.

Conclusion

Biography was a new genre of writing in modern British society. When the genre emerged in the seventeenth century, it was regarded as "inferior" but the "pleasure and instruction" it brought to the common reader were appreciated widely in the eighteenth century and it became one of the most familiar genres of literature in the nineteenth century. Johnson's writings—especially his biographical writings—were instrumental in bringing about this critical transformation. However, in the nineteenth century Johnson's biographical achievements took an ironic turn; he came to be regarded as a literary hero mainly through Boswell's biography. Ironic as this may be, the reception of Johnson in Victorian Britain exhibits the significance of biographical thinking in a modern society. In Japan, too, though biographical writings had been present, they became remarkably popular in the middle of the nineteenth century and accelerated people's appreciation of the lives of individuals in modern society and culture. It was in this way that Johnson was introduced to Japan, and in which his life and achievements became exemplary.

Literary culture naturally changes as a society modernizes and one of the most typical aspects of change is the development of biography. Biographies, particularly of individuals who are not from social elites, develop in tandem with the process of modernization, widen readership, and help orientate people to the workings of modern society and culture. In the modernization of Britain and Japan, biography in general and Johnson's biography in particular played an essential role.

Notes

1 Robert Folkenflik, *Samuel Johnson, Biographer* (Ithaca, NY: Cornell University Press, 1978), 214.

2 Lawrence Lipking, *The Ordering of the Arts in Eighteenth-Century England* (Princeton, NJ: Princeton University Press, 1970), 409; Alvin Kernan, *Samuel Johnson and the Impact of Print* (Princeton, NJ: Princeton University Press, 1987), 275.

3 *Boswell's Life of Johnson*, 1:25.

4 *Boswell's Life of Johnson*, 2:149.

5 Donald F. Bond, ed., *The Spectator*, 5 vols. (Oxford, UK: Clarendon Press, 1965), 1:1.

6 For a concise explanation of Japanese literary history, see Donald Keene, ed., *Dawn to the West: Japanese Literature in the Modern Era* (New York: Holt, Rinehart and Winston, 1984) and Earl R. Miner, Odagiri Hiroko, and Robert E. Morrell, *The Princeton Companion to Classical Japanese Literature* (Princeton, NJ: Princeton University Press, 1985).

7 As for the wide readership of Nakamura's translation of Smiles's *Self-Help*, see Shoichi Watanabe's "Masanao Nakamura and Samuel Smiles," in Samuel Smiles, *Self-Help*, trans. Masanao Nakamura (Tokyo: Kodansha, 1981), 544–556.

8 Samuel Johnson, "The Rambler No. 60," in *The Rambler*, ed. W. J. Bate and Albrecht B. Strauss, vols. 3, 4, and 5 of *The Yale Edition of the Works of Samuel Johnson* (New Haven, CT: Yale University Press, 1969), 3:319.

9 John Dryden, "Contributions to *Plutarch's Lives*," in vol. 17 of *The Works of John Dryden (Prose 1668–1691)*, ed. Samuel Holt Monk, A. E. Wallace Maurer, and Vinton A. Dearing (Berkeley: University of California Press, 1971), 221–224.

10 Johnson, "The Rambler No. 60," *The Rambler*, 3:319, 321.

11 Samuel Johnson, "Savage," in *The Lives of the Poets*, ed. John H. Middendorf, vols. 21, 22, and 23 of *The Yale Edition of the Works of Samuel Johnson* (New Haven, CT: Yale University Press, 2010), 22:850.

12 Samuel Johnson, "Rasselas," in *Rasselas and Other Tales*, ed. Gwin J. Kolb, vol. 16 of *The Yale Edition of the Works of Samuel Johnson* (New Haven, CT: Yale University Press, 1990), 7.

13 James T. Boulton, ed., *Samuel Johnson: The Critical Heritage* (London: Routledge, 1971), 420.

14 Thomas Carlyle, "The Hero as Man of Letters: Johnson, Rousseau, Burns," in *On Heroes, Hero-Worship and the Heroic in History* (London: Chapman and Hall, 1897), 182.

15 James T. Boulton, ed., *Samuel Johnson*, 34.

16 Thomas Babington Macaulay, "Life of Johnson," in *The Six Chief Lives from Johnson's "Lives of the Poets" with Macaulay's "Life of Johnson,"* ed. Matthew Arnold (London: Macmillan, 1886), 41.

17 William Makepeace Thackeray, *Vanity Fair: A Novel without a Hero*, ed. Helen Small (Oxford: Oxford University Press, 1983), 10.

18 J. D. Fleeman, *A Bibliography of the Works of Samuel Johnson*, 2 vols. (Oxford, UK: Clarendon Press, 2000), 1:818–930. Roughly estimated, thirty editions of *Rasselas* were published in the eighteenth century, while in the nineteenth century 400 editions were published.

19 Even a respect for Johnson's works is observed by some Victorian authors. We can take Elizabeth Gaskell's *Cranford* (1851–1853) as an example. In the first chapter of *Cranford,* Gaskell describes two contrasting characters: Miss Jenkyns who claims

the merits of Johnson's *Rasselas* and Captain Brown who asserts the qualities of Charles Dickens's *Pickwick Papers*. Although a change of literary taste in the middle of the nineteenth century may be reflected in the scene, what we should notice is that while Captain Brown, who introduces the new topic, soon passes away in a miserable way, the memory of Miss Jenkyns survives and is decisive for the tone of the novel. See Noriyuki Harada, "Johnson to Gaskell" ("Johnson in Gaskell: Diction, Narrative, and Print Culture"), *Gaskell Studies* 20 (2016): 1–14.

20 Carlyle, "The Hero as Man of Letters," 244–245.

21 For Japanese history from the middle of the nineteenth to the early twentieth century and the language reformation, see vols. 5 and 6 of John Whitney Hall, ed., *The Cambridge History of Japan*, 6 vols. (Cambridge: Cambridge University Press, 1988–1999) and also Noriyuki Harada, "Power in Modernization of Language and Literature in Eighteenth-Century Britain and Modern Japan," *IAFOR Journal of Literature and Librarianship* 4, no. 1 (2015): 20–31.

22 Johnson, "The Rambler No. 60," *The Rambler*, 3:319.

23 As for the reception of Johnson's *Rasselas* in Japan, see Yutaka Izumitani, *Rasselas Juyoshino Kenkyu* (*A Study of the Reception of Rasselas in Japan*) (Hiroshima, Japan: Keisuisha, 2001); Noriyuki Harada, "Translation and Transformation: Japanese Reception and Adaptation of Eighteenth-Century English Literature," *Essays and Studies in British and American Literature (Tokyo Woman's Christian University)* 58 (March 2012): 1–22; and Isamu Hayakawa, "Meijini okeru seiyo bunkano jyuyo: Samuel Johnson no baai" ("The Reception of Western Culture in Meiji-era: A Case of Samuel Johnson"), *Aichi Daigaku Bungaku Ronso* (*Aichi University Departmental Bulletin for Literary Studies*) 151 (2015): 112–192.

24 Teijiro Kobinata, *Eibungakushi* (*A History of English Literature*), (Tokyo: Bunken-shoin, 1924), 307.

25 Johnson, "The Rambler No. 60," *The Rambler*, 3:319.

26 Dryden, "Contributions to *Plutarch's Lives*," 273; and Johnson, "The Rambler No. 60," *The Rambler*, 3:319.

27 Samuel Johnson, *Johnson on Shakespeare*, ed. Arthur Sherbo, vols. 7 and 8 of *The Yale Edition of the Works of Samuel Johnson* (New Haven, CT: Yale University Press, 1967), 7:60–61.

28 Samuel Johnson, "The Rambler No. 4," in *The Rambler*, ed. W. J. Bate and Albrecht B. Strauss, vols. 3, 4, and 5 of *The Yale Edition of the Works of Samuel Johnson* (New Haven, CT: Yale University Press, 1969), 3:21.

29 Johnson, "The Rambler No. 4," *The Rambler* 3:20.

30 *Boswell's Life of Johnson*, 1:34.

3

Scientific Curiosity in Samuel Johnson's *Rasselas* and Mary Shelley's *Frankenstein*

KIMIYO OGAWA

Introduction

Researchers have begun to examine how the Johnsonian and Romantic worldviews are more intimately interwoven than earlier critics had suggested. There has also been a growing interest in the theme of Romanticism's connections and continuity with its Johnsonian past, and many have attempted to revise a long-held view that Johnson lacked "imagination" or "enthusiasm."[1] James G. Basker traces the humanitarian sensibility of abolitionists (including Romantic writers) to Johnson.[2] Fred Parker has re-examined the alleged disagreements between Romantic writers and Johnson on Shakespeare's plays, noting how "the romantic insistence on the mind's creativity [has become] the direct antagonist of Johnson's feeling for general nature." While recognizing these disagreements, Parker avows that their values are not mutually exclusive, as he states, "[there] need not be . . . a simple hardening of boundaries." Parker argues that Coleridge, like Johnson, perceived nature, or the material world, and imagination as profoundly intertwined, for he was "ill at ease with his own body . . . so painfully cramped and disabled whenever it came to realizing his great powers, and great desires, in the world of fact and flesh."[3] And Philip Smallwood demonstrates that Johnson's "allusions to [music and paintings] as dimensions of experience" may be linked to his empirical approach to things.[4]

Another crucial point of connection between Johnson and Romanticism concerns materialism and scientific learning. For Helen Deutsch, Johnson's interests reflected an eighteenth-century culture in which the competing authorities of aesthetic subjectivity and scientific objectivity had not yet diverged. She gives an example, that Johnson's portrait of the mad astronomer in *Rasselas* was treated as medical evidence, and even as a medical case history, by two of the earliest psychiatric doctors, Thomas Arnold and John Haslam.[5] We also need to contextualize Johnson's *Rasselas* within the recent academic emphasis on the connections between scientific empiricism and Romanticism. In the past two decades, there has been an explosion of scholarly interest in how science and the mind is represented in Romantic literature, especially in the work of Samuel Taylor Coleridge, Percy Bysshe Shelley, and John Keats. These poets explored various natural phenomena under the rubrics of chemistry, botany, astronomy, medicine, and, in relation to this, the mysteries of the mind. The mind was beginning to be treated as part of the material universe rather than something that remains aloof from it. Studies by Nicholas Jardine, Alan Richardson, Richard Holmes, and Sharon Ruston have been particularly helpful in this area.[6] By contrast, there are only a few substantial accounts of Johnson and the scientific approach to the mind, but Richard B. Schwartz's *Samuel Johnson and the New Science* and John Wiltshire's *Samuel Johnson in the Medical World: The Doctor and the Patient* have demonstrated the importance of modern science to understanding Johnson, and Wiltshire has illustrated Johnson's awareness of the material interconnectivity of body and mind.[7]

Critical insights such as these have often stopped short of comparing Johnson's discussion of scientific knowledge and the nature of the mind with how novels from the Romantic period, such as Mary Shelley's *Frankenstein*, explore the same topics. We know from William Godwin's *Memoirs of the Author of A Vindication of the Rights of Woman* that Mary Shelley's mother, Mary Wollstonecraft, met Johnson.[8] According to Katherine Turner, Percy Bysshe Shelley's "Defence of Poetry" is influenced by Imlac's observations in *Rasselas*. Despite these personal family links with Johnson and his writings, *Frankenstein* has more frequently been seen as a progeny of Milton's *Paradise Lost*, with its theme of transgression, and has hardly ever been related to *Rasselas*.[9] Although little or no attention has been paid to *Rasselas* as a source of Mary Shelley's inspiration for her novel, my proposition is that *Frankenstein* would not have been written in the way it was without her deep interest in and connection with Johnson's text. Shelley read *Rasselas* in 1814 and (probably) again in 1817, just when she was writing *Frankenstein*,[10] and the existence of significant parallels between these texts is striking. In this chapter I discuss how these parallels are rooted in Shelley's knowledge of eighteenth-century debates on the materiality of the soul as potentially a life-enhancing, life-creating force, and in the eighteenth-century medical interest in how the mind interacts with and reacts to the bodily condition, giving rise to new and more complex notions of imagination and insanity.

Johnson and Science

Johnson's *History of Rasselas, Prince of Abissinia* (1759) outlines the choice of life by painting pictures of different life experiences: a life in a "happy valley" in which the "soft vicissitudes of pleasure and repose . . . [are] gratified with whatever the sense can enjoy,"[11] a hermit's life of "pastoral simplicity"[12] which is "disunited from society,"[13] or a life that explores the scientific interest in the natural world and aims to acquire "knowledge."[14] Imlac, the mentor of the prince and princess of Abissinia, however, does not seem to suggest that any of these choices would give ultimate or eternal happiness. It is only when Rasselas meets a poet who has traveled to various parts of the world that he begins to understand Johnson's precept that "life must be seen before it can be known."[15] Critics such as Nicholas Hudson and Robert J. Mayhew have foregrounded Johnson's religious concerns in writing this novel, pointing out his reservations as an Anglican about a visionary—or, to be more precise, irrational—goal that would be beyond human limitations. Mayhew argues that the novel repeatedly makes the point that it is wrong to believe that human beings can attain a godlike perspective that overlooks and controls nature. The precept here is that a scientist must recognize himself or herself as one with limited power and perception,[16] and this seems to underline Johnson's view that humanity has had no certain evidence of eternal happiness "till we had a positive revelation" of the divine.[17]

Other critics who see a deep tie between Johnson's novel and his lifelong embrace of Christianity argue that the shortfall between what is wished for and what is actually obtained in *Rasselas* constitutes a warning against desire that exceeds our human capacity for fulfillment. For example, in chapter 48, Imlac, Rasselas, and his sister Nekayah encounter an astronomer and debate with him about the human yearning for immortality. While this astronomer suggests that they may learn what they can "no longer procure from the living" from Egyptian mummies, Imlac argues that this ancient practice of mummifying the body actually teaches them a lesson about the futility of hoping to "elude death" (*Rasselas*, 169). From a traditional perspective of seeing Johnson as a devout Christian, these desires and intellectual aspirations might well be represented as a didactic device to teach the importance of humility. Of course, no thoughtful reader of Johnson would doubt the truth of Boswell's remark that "the history of [Johnson's] mind as to religion is an important article."[18] Therefore, this materialist—non-Christian—discourse on the soul in *Rasselas* may well have been inserted with a view to reinforcing the idea of religious humility, for Imlac says, "we must humbly learn from higher authority" (*Rasselas*, 174). Also, Hudson claims that *Rasselas* is much indebted to the *Laws of Ecclesiastical Polity* (1594), by Richard Hooker, an Anglican theologian and philosopher.[19] He suggests that Johnson approved of Hooker's argument that "our worldly desires are inexorable and have a potentially useful function in the Christian life."[20] In this sense, even sensual desires and intellectual aspirations have their roles to play in supplementing the limited religious knowledge offered by reason.

In the Enlightenment, scientific method gained superiority over other modes of knowledge, discrediting other methods such as superstition, revelation, authority, or tradition. I argue that Johnson's treatment of the soul in chapter 48 of *Rasselas* cannot be interpreted as straightforwardly as Hudson has suggested, and that Johnson was a much more scientifically and medically engaged thinker than some critics have tended to believe. Some articles on Johnson's medical condition have considered him as a "patient," and much has been made of his melancholy and depression, his gout, his "tics and gesticulations."[21] But Johnson's status as an amateur doctor or scientist has rarely been discussed. One of the primary reasons Johnson's scientific observations on physiological phenomena have been lost or at least devalued may be due to Boswell's representation of him.[22] For example, on 7 August 1779, Johnson performed an experiment to find the length of time required to grow hair after shaving "[his] right arm, next the wrist, and the skin round the right nipple."[23] Boswell saw this experiment merely as filling "moments which admit of being soothed only by trifles."[24] But closer examination reveals Johnson's enthusiasm for science and his depth of understanding of medicine.[25]

In fact, Johnson's knowledge comes from both empirical practice, as in these experiments, and from reading or translating books, for he wrote lives of famous physicians for Dr. Robert James's *Medicinal Dictionary*. One of those was Herman Boerhaave (1668–1738), professor of medicine at Leiden University.[26] According to Peter Martin, these lives illustrated Johnson's powers not only as a biographer but also as a translator. Johnson's "Life of Boerhaave," his first published work on a medical topic, is an abridged English translation of a Latin eulogy on the physician that had previously been published in Leiden.[27] Johnson understood the content of Boerhaave's thinking, which he perhaps shared, and recommended it to Boswell. Boerhaave's system was empirical, and built upon the premise that "the human body, then, is composed in such a manner that its united parts are able to produce several motions of very different kinds which derive—fully in accordance with the law of mechanics—from the mass, the shape, and the firmness of the parts and from the way in which they are linked together."[28]

This passage from Boerhaave's "Oration on the Usefulness of the Mechanical Method in Medicine" applies Newtonian mechanics to the phenomenon of the circulation of the blood.[29] Boerhaave's medical approach was based on a hydraulic system of mechanics, as he states that a physician should know "the forces exerted by fluids in mechanisms, and by mechanisms on fluids, with mathematical rigour, and he may consolidate his insights by hydraulic experiments, elucidate them by mechanical and chemical ones, observing the nature and effects of fire, water, air, salts, and other bodies of the same kind."[30]

Thus, the notion that physical abnormalities are caused by the state of the solids, or the "Blood vessels" and the humors and the blood that run through them, was important for clinical practice in the eighteenth century. The smallest blood particles became the "nervous fluid" that is transmitted to every part of the body through a nervous system, affecting the individual's mental condition.[31] Johnson recommended that Boswell read *English Malady* (1733) and *Essay of Health and Long Life* (1724), two important works by the English physician George Cheyne, which more or less upheld Boerhaave's system.[32] The degree to which Cheyne's medical language permeated Johnson's vocabulary can be observed from its playful usage in one of Johnson's letters to Hester Thrale: "Air, and Vacancy, and novelty, and the consciousness of his own value, and the pride of such distinction, and delight in Mr. Thrale's kindness would as Cheney [sic] phrases it, afford all the relief that human art can give, or human nature receive." Here he parodies Cheyne's original sentence from his medical book, "this Method . . . will afford all the Ease which human Art can give, or human Nature receive."[33] In other words, through controlling the material condition of the body, the patient's "Ease" or her psychological comfort can be attained.

Does this suggest that Johnson and his contemporaries wholeheartedly supported materialism? Christian confidence in the existence of the soul may have been somewhat eroded by Johnson's time but, nevertheless, a belief in spirituality survived to produce ambivalent linguistic expressions in medical or philosophical writings. John Locke's approach was strictly empirical, but we can say that his "association of ideas" is a strange blend of abstract and physiological concepts: "all . . . seems to me to be but trains of motion in the animal spirits, which once set a-going, continue in the same steps they have been used to, which by often treading, are worn into a smooth path, and the motion in it becomes easy, and, as it were, natural."[34] R. M. Burns claims that Locke's *Reasonableness of Christianity* (1695) shows his belief in the miraculous and thus vouches for the authenticity of divine revelation. While admitting that "nothing can be taken to be a miracle but what is judged to exceed those laws," Locke implicitly shows that a miracle could in fact exist: the perception of a "miracle" varies from one person to another because each judges those natural laws "only by his own acquaintance with Nature."[35] Burns illustrates a similar case with David Hume, who held skeptical opinions on religious matters. According to Burns, there is abundant evidence that Hume's cool attitude toward, or detachment from, issues of religion was deliberately cultivated,[36] and hence contradicts what may have been his natural inclination. Hume, for example, wrote to his friend Gilbert Elliot, "any propensity you imagine I have to the other Side, crept in upon me against my Will." Hume is here referring to the "Propensity of the mind," which tries to seek something that is beyond "our Sense & Experience"[37]—in a word, something transcendental or, as a Romantic like Wordsworth might phrase it, "something evermore about to be."[38]

This kind of wavering between experiential evidence and the existence of something beyond human senses is also observed in George Cheyne's scientific study of the human body. Materialistic though his nerve theory is, the agent of nervous communication was left ambiguous by his notion of "animal spirits" that are neither spiritual nor substantial. Cheyne maintained that what actuated and governed the operations of such a mechanism were "spiritual Substances."[39] He suggests that there are "some other more aetherial and subtil Fluid[s]" that may be "intermediates between pure, immaterial Spirit and gross Matter" forming the "Cement between the human Soul and Body."[40] Thus he tries to reconcile his paradoxical ideas of material immateriality by having the "animal spirits" as an intermediary between "aethereal" and more "gross" material.

Like Locke and Cheyne, Johnson often resorts to metaphors of force, of motion, of attraction and repulsion, or momentum and balance, exemplifying his internalization of the legacy of Newtonian mechanics,[41] while also showing keen interest in the "spirits" which act as a missing link between soul and body:

> It is natural for those who have raised a reputation by any science, to exalt themselves as endowed by heaven with peculiar powers, or marked out by an extraordinary designation for their profession; and to fright competitors away by representing the difficulties with which are supposed to be not generally conferred, and which no man can know, *but by experience*, whether he enjoys. To this discouragement it may be possibly answered, that since a genius, whatever it be, is like *fire* in the flint, only to be produced by collision with a proper subject, it is the business of every man to try whether his faculties may not happily co-operate with his desires; and since they whose proficiency he admires, knew *their own force* only by the event, he needs but engage in the same undertaking, with equal *spirit*, and may reasonably hope for equal success.[42]

Johnson, in describing a "genius," uses "scientific" or "empirical" words metaphorically, such as "experience," "fire," or "force." What is more relevant may be that these words, widespread in eighteenth-century medical and scientific texts, also suggest a palpable image of the internal "motion" of the body that was also associated with the soul's promptings. In his *Physiological Essays* (1745), Edinburgh physician Robert Whytt illustrates the basic nerve mechanism of spinal reflexes in vertebrates. He was one of the first to present a general picture of how the interior human mechanism really works, postulating that the agent which he calls "Soul," residing in the intestine as well as in other organs of the body, "perceives" or "feels" a physical stimulus.[43] A muscle reaction for Whytt, therefore, becomes a mode of "unconscious perception."[44] This view promoted the development of sciences that tried to intervene in the internal movement of the animal spirits: magnetic attraction or electricity could, for instance, be used to affect physiological conditions in the muscular, material body. Patricia Fara illustrates various ways in which the study of magnetism, electricity, and mesmerism became prominent among eighteenth-century scientists. Electrical therapy, which was initiated in Italy, also enjoyed very high prestige in England.[45] With such a growing awareness about the internal causes of motion, scientists began to perceive the "occult" as something more wholly and mysteriously "unintelligible" and inexplicable, as opposed to "insensible agencies" that could now be explained in terms of physical science and mechanics.[46]

Read from this perspective, one of the central concerns of *Rasselas* seems to be the nature of the soul and its movement within the material, or at least metaphorical, body. When Prince Rasselas meets Imlac, a man of learning, he is curious to know what the "effect" of knowledge will be on him, whether he would be "happier" if he left his "happy valley," which is characterized as a "tasteless tranquillity."[47] Imlac answers, "Knowledge is certainly one of the means of pleasure, as is confessed by the natural desire which every mind feels of increasing its ideas. Ignorance is mere privation, by which nothing can be produced: it is a vacuity in which *the soul sits motionless and torpid for want of attraction*; and, without knowing why, we always rejoice when we learn, and grieve when we forget. I am therefore inclined to conclude, that if nothing counteracts the natural consequence of learning, we grow more happy as our minds take a wider range."[48]

Imlac explains in scientific terms that ignorance is a state in which "the soul sits motionless and torpid for want of attraction." W. K. Wimsatt observes that Johnson's use of science "even when it is correct, is on the whole far from precise,"[49] but Johnson's use of the word "*attraction*" in the passage quoted is quite apt: only those with some knowledge of magnetism would be likely to resort to this image.

Imlac, as a poet and philosopher, epitomizes the drive toward learning. Through many travels, continuously moving from one region to another, from Agra to Persia, his knowledge of different cultures and languages increases. From his own experience, he reassures Rasselas that "we grow more happy as our minds take a wider range," which seems to substantiate Johnson's own claim in *The Rambler*: "He that enlarges his curiosity after the works of nature, demonstrably multiplies the inlets to happiness."[50] Imlac is also measuring one's happiness by the movement of "the soul," dismissing a lack of motion as a grievous "vacuity." The motion of the soul here refers to the internal activity that is concatenated with the process of "learning," and the soul activated by this process is positively depicted—reinforcing the idea that the acquisition of any knowledge should be encouraged.

In chapter 48, Imlac, Rasselas, and Nekayah meet and discourse with the astronomer about the nature of the soul. Imlac states, "it is commonly supposed that the Egyptians believed the soul to live as long as the body continued undissolved, and therefore tried this method [mummification] of eluding death."[51] We get a sense of Johnson's engaging in the contemporary medical discussion by following this dialogue because this idea about the soul prompts Nekayah to think about materialist philosophy, as she questions, "could the wise Egyptians . . . think so grossly of the soul?" To this, the astronomer answers, "the nature of the soul is still disputed amidst all our opportunities of clearer knowledge: some yet say, that it may be material, who, nevertheless, believe it to be immortal."[52] The ambiguous Enlightenment idea of the soul as both material and immortal is thus put in the mouth of the astronomer. Johnson is clearly aware of the arguments put forward by the contemporary medical theorists who increasingly saw matter as being endued with life force.

Greg Clingham has shown that this discussion of the embodied soul or spirit can be linked to Johnson's style and narrative. Because Johnson was fascinated by the mind's power to move out from the present moment and to embody both the past and the future, he represents this power of human fantasy as something that interrogates the notion of happiness. It is consciousness (or consciousness of thought) that separates human beings from animals or other living creatures, but this very capacity to think imaginatively enables Rasselas to feel connected to animals—or to imagine a sense of "what it feels like to be seen as animal."[53] Happiness is always contemplated in retrospect or considered teleologically, but Johnson's narratological perspective from this ambiguous, fluid standpoint, embodying both the past and the future, or beginnings and ends, complicates the very notion of happiness itself. The narrative is in continual flux and, as it were, never-ending.

Materialist Philosophy in *Frankenstein*

Throughout the eighteenth century, there was an ongoing debate as to whether matter is endued with some kind of life force—the animal spirits, magnetism or electricity. It is hard to judge whether Mary Shelley was inspired by the materialist debate in *Rasselas,* or saw its relevance to the contemporary scientific discourse in the early nineteenth century, or both, but having read Johnson's book, the image of the soul living in the undissolved or uncorrupted body of a mummy may well have lingered in her mind. She evokes the image of the mummy in the creation scene: "a mummy again endued with animation could not be so hideous as that wretch."[54] One of the most difficult tasks for Shelley's scientist is to re-create the physiological body with "all its intricacies of fibres, muscles, and veins."[55] Interestingly, the focus here is on the material body, and not the soul, and yet Frankenstein reiterates the word "causation" and "cause" of generation: "I paused, examining and analysing all the minutiae of causation," "I succeeded in discovering the cause of generation and life."[56] When Shelley writes that Frankenstein collected "materials" or corpses to prepare the "frame" for the "reception" of animation,[57] she is inheriting a typical eighteenth-century paradox that the "lifeless thing"[58] or matter contains an immaterial life force.

Mary and Percy Shelley shared an ambivalence about the materiality of the soul. Erasmus Darwin, whose work was the subject of discussion by Percy Shelley and Byron at the Villa Diodati just before Mary conceived her story, claims that "chemic changes" have the power to breach the barrier between the condition of living and that of death. Using a formula that foreshadows Frankenstein's scientific experiment, Darwin states in his poem *The Temple of Nature* that "Organic forms with chemic changes strive, / Live but to die, and die but to revive!"[59]

William Lawrence, a materialist and Percy Shelley's physician, held views similar to Whytt's regarding the presupposition of bodily organization not merely in the external arrangement of the whole, but in each part, and in all the details of each. For Lawrence, "life is the result of the mutual actions and reactions of all parts" of the material body.[60] The reason Frankenstein turns to corpses is, like the astronomer in *Rasselas*, because empirical science delved into the realm of matter in order to understand the workings of the soul: "To examine the causes of life, we must first have recourse to death."[61]

In fact, Mary and Percy Shelley both believed that the brain, a material organ of the body, responded to physical impulses of magnetic energy, and this may have had a significant impact on the way they perceived the causality of life.[62] Galvanism gave Mary Shelley a valuable insight into the workings of the organic body with its own life energy; as she states, "Perhaps a corpse would be re-animated; galvanism had given token of such things: perhaps the component parts of a creature might be manufactured, brought together, and endued with vital warmth."[63] "Galvanism's method" generally meant that "the muscles and the nerves were the source of electric action."[64] Erasmus Darwin shared this interest in electricity, and although he was skeptical of Galvanic "animal electricity"[65] he did believe that "repeated and strong shocks of electricity" could have positive therapeutic effects.[66] Although Mary Shelley also perceived the corporeal body as being "endued with vital warmth," she paradoxically saw the body as being inert. Frederick Burwick has remarked that Thomas Medwin, a friend of the Shelleys, remembered a conversation with Mary and Percy about the limitations of materialist philosophy. Medwin records their discussion about the influence of animal magnetism: "a separation from the mind and the body [takes] place—the one being most active and the other an inert mass of matter."[67] In his poems, "[Percy] Shelley was endorsing the same conception of the interchange between vital energy and inert matter that had been assumed by Victor Frankenstein in Mary Shelley's novel."[68]

If Mary Shelley was struck by Johnson's depiction of the soul in *Rasselas*, how and when did Johnson's own interest in the soul emerge? Was it his Christian faith that led him to thematize it in *Rasselas*? Could he have perceived, like Cheyne, the soul as partially chained to the animal spirits, or the body? Was he acquainted with scientific ideas about electricity or animal magnetism as a possible activating force? According to Schwartz, there is ample evidence of Johnson having "more than a passing interest in electricity." Long before Galvani's discovery of animal electricity in the 1780s, Johnson recorded a case in which an electrical spark was witnessed, which gave rise to an idea that there is an interlocking relation between electricity and life force.[69] Anna Williams, the daughter of Johnson's friend Zachariah Williams, acted as assistant to a physician, Stephen Gray, and became one of the first to observe the emission of an electrical spark from a human body. Johnson even suggested that Anne write a poem in response to the event, "On the Death of Stephen Grey, F. R. S. The Author of the Present Doctrine of Electricity."[70] This poem was published thirteen years before *Rasselas* in Williams's *Miscellanies in Prose and Verse* in 1746, which was assembled and partly written by Johnson for her benefit.[71]

Naturally, the word *electricity* cannot be found in Dr. Robert James's *Medicinal Dictionary*, published between 1743 and 1745. Although Johnson "helped [Dr. James] in writing the proposals . . . and also a little in the Dictionary itself,"[72] recent discoveries about electricity could not be included in James's *Dictionary*. It had to wait until Johnson's own *Dictionary of the English Language* (1755), where he quotes as follows in defining the term *electricity*: "A property in some bodies, whereby, when rubbed so as to grow warm, they draw little bits of paper, or such like substances, to them. *Quincy*."

Such was the account given a few years previously of electricity; but the industry of the present age, first excited by the experiments of Gray, had discovered in electricity a multitude of philosophical wonders.

The discovery of electricity had evidently revealed philosophical wonders to Johnson. His fascination with Newtonian science is expressed through his imagery, such as "the force of this [electrical] vapour," which implies that electricity has the property to promote the internal movement of a body.[73] Suffering various illnesses, Johnson was always in search of new treatments. He applied electricity to his swollen legs and thighs, and had also previously suggested this remedy to his friend and physician, Dr. Lawrence, to treat his paralyzed hands.[74] Johnson's understanding of electricity as an activating force of the body is refreshingly modern, and the controversy over the soul's materiality discussed in chapter 48 of *Rasselas* can also be understood in much the same scientific terms.

Solitude and Imagination

Curiosity, a byword of the Enlightenment, especially in the *scientific* study of humanity, was puzzling and troublesome for Johnson. He admits that there is a paradox entailed in trying to pursue a scientific inquiry—such as finding the cure for a mental malady, and by doing so, actually causing that disease. Johnson is highly aware of how interconnected life is, and that movement in one direction usually entails a countermovement in another direction. In other words, there are not only moral but also physical consequences to all actions. While encouraging us to "keep curiosity in perpetual motion," he states that "study requires solitude, and solitude is a state dangerous to those who are too much accustomed to sink into themselves." He calls this tendency a "formidable and obstinate disease of the intellect." When one is in danger of such mental disorder, one is encouraged to "adopt the joys and the pains of others, and excite in his mind the want of social pleasures and amicable communication."[75] This point is repeated by Imlac, who says that his acquirements are "useless" and make him "sorrowful." At first, Imlac boasts of his "less unhappy" state in which he can "amuse [his] solitude by the renovation of the knowledge" by varying and combining the images which he has stored up in his "mind," and we feel reassured that his exploration of the world was not in vain. Yet Imlac, like Johnson himself, perceives too much solitude as harmful.[76]

Solitude is not the only cause of mental unrest. In *The Rambler*, Johnson takes this argument further and states that the kind of "endeavour" made by "a man of mental excellence" can also damage his body—"they . . . will learn perhaps too late, how much it is endangered by diseases of the body, and find that knowledge may easily be lost in the starts of melancholy."[77] The healthy body could be damaged as a result of "incessant revels," "inactivity," and above all, "intemperate studies."[78] Physical ill health could cause serious and painful attacks, from which Johnson himself suffered.[79] In a letter to Hester Lynch Piozzi, Johnson wrote, "I pine in the solitude of sickness, not bad enough to be pitied, and not well enough to be endured."[80]

With no fewer than fifty-seven physicians treating him over the course of his life, Johnson's illness and mental disorder may be more remembered and written about than his reputation as a medical expert. But objects of his scientific inquiry ranged from the human body, which could be comprehended largely in dynamic or even hydraulic terms, to the brain, which was the cause of mental disorder.[81] In fact, Johnson's contention that "elevated minds" are more likely to suffer from melancholy may not be a contradiction after all.[82] A characteristic feature of eighteenth-century medical theory was its assumption that there was a single explanatory concept linking the body and the mind. Johnson's argument that "there are perhaps very few conditions more to be pitied than that of an active and elevated mind, laboring under the weight of a distempered body"[83] reflects a keen psychological insight.

Cheyne divides "Mankind, into Quick Thinkers, Slow Thinkers, and No Thinkers,"[84] commending in this context a quick reaction of the nerves. Contemporary medical men such as Whytt observe that the state of feelings, whether they are "quick" or "dull, slow, and difficult to be roused,"[85] depends on a person's material constitution. This was also Cheyne's argument: "there is a certain Tone, Consistence, Firmness, and a determin'd Degree of Elasticity and Tension of the Nerves or Fibres . . . necessary to the perfect Performance of the Animal Functions."[86] The whole debate about the "firmness" of the nerves seems to demonstrate that a soul or intelligence is in some way in keeping with the material body. For this reason, it seems contradictory when these physiologists characterize nerves alone as weak, for weakness in the nerves has a wider physical and pathological resonance. For Cheyne, weak nerves were a cause of intelligence *and* the effect of straining them too much. According to Cheyne, "Persons of slender and weak Nerves are generally of the first Class: the Activity, Mobility, and Delicacy or their intellectual Organs make them so, and thereby weakens and relaxes the Material Organs of the intellectual Faculties."[87]

Many eighteenth-century writers such as William Godwin and Mary Wollstonecraft held an equivocal position about the origin of self and whether "sensibility," which was the "*manie* of the day,"[88] could be the potent force of human action. Weak and delicate nerves, which connote the sophistication that is required for intellectual pursuits, also bear the potential stigma of physical degeneration.

Another feature of mental malady, which can be found in the second and third definitions of *melancholy* in Johnson's *Dictionary of the English Language*, is "a kind of madness, in which the mind is always fixed on one object," and "a gloomy, pensive, discontented temper."[89] The astronomer in *Rasselas*, who is obviously deluded, has devoted his life to controlling the climate. The astronomer talks about "the jury of my imagination" to "send rain on the southern mountains, and raise the Nile to an inundation." He "sometimes suspected [him]self of madness,"[90] but he persists in his perverse intellectual pursuits, stating "I reasoned long against my own conviction, and laboured against truth with the utmost obstinacy."[91] It has been largely agreed that Johnson's perennial concern with "mental aberration" was to warn of the danger lest it should "force [a man] to hope or fear beyond the limits of sober probability."[92]

Johnson may indeed have considered reason as the heart of things, but it is equally plausible that his protagonist, Imlac, and the astronomer embody Johnson's anxiety about his own melancholic inclination of a typical intellectual. Scholars and intellectuals are especially prone to this kind of morbid "self-indulgence."[93]

If Mary Shelley thought about the typical eighteenth-century paradox between the advantage of having delicate nerves and the disadvantage of being more exposed to mental diseases, we can also identify sources of Frankenstein's character in *Rasselas* or *The Rambler*. For example, Shelley's scientist describes his own devotion to creating his creature as his "endeavours";[94] he "was engaged, heart and soul, in the pursuit of some discoveries."[95] He confines himself in a "solitary chamber, or rather a cell" shunning any society.[96] Although he knew that his father would wish Victor to return home, he could not tear his thoughts from this "employment . . . which had taken an irresistible hold of [his] imagination."[97] Based on contemporary psychiatric treatises, this condition would be characterized as a symptom of mental disorder.[98] The disease involves that state of alienation or weakness of mind that renders people incapable of enjoying the pleasures, or performing the duties of life, and may be caused by "intense thinking, especially where the mind is long occupied about one object" or "a sedentary life; solitude."[99]

It is ironic that despite his pursuit of knowledge, or perhaps because of this obsessive, isolated state, Frankenstein comes very close to the image of the astronomer in *Rasselas*. Although Frankenstein denies that his narrative is the vision of a madman, his imagination does compel his mind to pursue a single, intensely desired objective. This powerful imaginative drive as the source of genius—and also the cause of melancholy—is mirrored by the creature's narrative too, which is also filled with the "pain of reflection."[100] I emphasize Shelley's debt to *Rasselas* because both authors are very much concerned about the spark of life and the fear that it might be eternally confined in the body. The scientific question for Shelley is, how was it possible for the creature to rise above the intellectual level of brutes from a mere spark? Of course, the creature's self-indulgence or self-pity is aggravated by his condition of being deprived of parents, food, money, or an amiable appearance that may win him the sympathy of a stranger, but we must note that his unhappy state is caused as well by an intellect that is equal to—or even goes beyond—that of a human. He accuses his creator, Frankenstein: "Why did I live? Why, in that instant, did I not extinguish the spark of existence which you had so wantonly bestowed?"[101] This passage has the same implication as Rasselas's comment: "How gloomy would be these mansions of the dead to him who did not know that he shall never die."[102]

Frankenstein also reiterates a Johnsonian theme in that it pursues the question of happiness in relation to one's "ease." When Frankenstein says that his "life might have been passed in ease and luxury; but I preferred glory to every enticement that wealth placed in my path,"[103] he is echoing, or perhaps playing on, the slightly didactic tone of Johnson. Frankenstein shuns those "social pleasures and amicable communication" Johnson had recommended and indulges in reveries that keep his imagination active. What is the fundamental difference between the brutes and the humans? What causes humans to feel the discontent or unease that animals may not feel? Rasselas compares himself with a "beast" (a goat) and says, "I am, like him, pained with want, but am not, like him, satisfied with fullness [of being fed]."[104] Despite the fact that human consciousness separates people from animals, Johnson felt that the capacity of animals to imagine meant that the boundaries between human and animal life were porous and fluid. In this context, Greg Clingham argues that Johnson's view has been influenced by Dryden's translations of Ovid's *Metamorphoses*, and had much to do with Johnson's defining *animal* in the *Dictionary of the English Language* as a "living creature corporeal, distinct, on the one side, from pure spirit, on the other side, from mere matter."[105] The lines of Dryden quoted by Clingham in support of his argument are most pertinent in linking this "distinct" yet ambiguous entity, neither material nor spiritual:

> [A]ll things are but altered, nothing dies,
> And here and there th'unbodied spirit flies,
> By time, or force, or sickness dispossessed,
> . . . All suffer change; and we that are of soul
> And body mixed, are members of the whole. (ll. 239–242)[106]

These lines from Dryden's "Of the Pythagorean Philosophy" suggest that humans "are members of the whole" of creation and not separate from or superior to the animal world.

Interestingly, the story that Frankenstein's creature tells of himself is a miniature or compressed version of natural history describing the continuity from an animal state to that of a human. At first, the creature could only perceive light, hunger, thirst and darkness, and he only wept from physical pain like an animal. The primitive sensations of Frankenstein's creature are directed toward the "clear stream that supplied me with drink, and the trees that shaded me with the foliage," and he was "delighted when [he] first discovered a pleasant sound" of the little winged animals "who had often intercepted the light from my eyes."[107] Thus, just as Rasselas contemplates the simple life of the "goats that were brousing among the rocks,"[108] Shelley's creature recollects his initial stage of being. His sense of self was not even formed until he acquired "ideas" through his senses of vision and hearing, for "no distinct ideas occupied [his] mind; all was confused."[109] This logic, that insatiable passions are born from the proliferation of ideas and the linguistic capacity to categorize them, follows that of theorists of sensation such as Locke and David Hartley. Gradually the creature understands psychological pain by observing the De Lacey family express pain, and by hearing them speak the words that produced pleasure or pain, smiles or sadness in the minds and countenances of the hearers.[110]

The agitation of the mind the creature experiences after learning that he was deserted by his creator is no less human than his creator's, whose fierce passion for intellectual pursuit is not extinguished until the toil is finally over. The creature cannot overrule his "sentiment of hatred"[111] or "burning passion."[112] Frankenstein's rage after the creature takes the lives of William, Clerval, and Elizabeth (and implicates Justine in William's murder, thereby indirectly causing her death) is described as "the devouring and only passion of [his] soul."[113] But in the end, he advises Walton, who takes him on board, to "seek happiness in tranquillity, and avoid ambition, even if it be only the apparently innocent one of distinguishing yourself in science and discoveries."[114] This state of a mind "in continual flux" is, in Johnson's work, elaborated by Imlac:

> "The state of a mind oppressed with a sudden calamity," said Imlac, "is like that of the fabulous inhabitants of the new-created earth, who, when the first night came upon them, supposed that day would never return. When the clouds of sorrow gather over us, we see nothing beyond them, nor can imagine how they will be dispelled; yet a new day succeeded to the night, and sorrow is never long without a dawn of *ease*. But they who restrain themselves from receiving comfort, do as the savages would have done, had they put out their eyes when it was dark. Our minds, like our bodies, are in continual flux; something is hourly lost, and something acquired.[115]

In Johnson's view, this cycle is repeated throughout one's life. One sees a "dawn of ease" but it is elusive because humans experience the loss and the gain of the "vital powers": "something is hourly lost, and something acquired."[116] When Johnson said, "My health has been since my twentieth year such as has seldom afforded me a single day of ease,"[117] he hints at his state of perpetual irritation and fretfulness. Johnson suggests that being released from "uneasiness" does not necessarily make for the perfect state of happiness, for even when "curiosity" is gratified and temporarily "frees us from uneasiness," it "flames and torments us."[118]

Shelley has *Frankenstein*'s narrator, Walton, explain that release from this state of unease is the sole means of delivering him from suffering: "when he [Frankenstein] composes his shattered feelings to peace and death."[119] One of the most prominent features of Shelley's novel is that not only do many characters die, they hasten to face death. Frankenstein, on his deathbed, says "this hour, when I momentarily expect my release, is the only happy one which I have enjoyed for several years,"[120] and the creature also cannot wait to "find rest" in death: "I shall die." He is glad that he "shall no longer feel the agonies which now consume [him], or be the prey of feelings unsatisfied, yet unquenched."[121]

Conclusion

Shelley's *Frankenstein* and Johnson's *Rasselas* both thematize science and Enlightenment ideas of intellectual transcendence. They are also both interested in the scientific process of sustaining or reanimating the soul within the body. Both portray scientific pursuit paradoxically: while shedding light on fascinating truths about human nature, these texts have misgivings about the dark facets of suffering. Yet Rasselas and Nekayah do learn to think about the soul and its relation to life. Shelley's challenge, too, is much like Johnson's in that her novel explores the "effect of knowledge": whether Europeans are happier because they "cure wounds and diseases with which [non-Europeans] languish and perish."[122] There is an ultimate irony in *Frankenstein*, for the protagonist is an enlightened subject whose fanatical drive to acquire knowledge breeds an incurable disease, melancholy, and a death wish. It is true, as Thomas Kass has argued, that Johnson is wary of the dangerous propensity in human nature to eschew religious responsibilities and to prefer "the gay sallies of the imagination."[123] But Johnson's curious, exploratory nature expressed through his narrative of *Rasselas* has much in common with Shelley's style. We have looked at two scientific approaches to human nature—the materialist's scientific consideration of the soul, and the possibility that too much intellectual stimulation may become a cause of madness and melancholy. Connections between materialism, ideal truth, and mental unrest preoccupied eighteenth-century scientific thinkers, and shaped some less overtly scientific preoccupations of later Romantic writers. In *Rasselas* Johnson is located strikingly between the two, alert to recent scientific discoveries and debates, and acutely aware of the peculiarly Romantic affliction of living too intensely in the imagination.

Notes

1 Katherine Turner, "Critical Reception to 1900," in *Samuel Johnson in Context*, ed. Jack Lynch (Cambridge: Cambridge University Press, 2012), 49.

2 James G. Basker, "Johnson, Boswell, and the Abolition of Slavery," *The New Rambler: Journal of the Johnson Society of London* serial no. EVI, 2002–2003 (September 2003): 36–48. Also see James G. Basker, '"The Next Insurrection': Johnson, Race and Rebellion," *The Age of Johnson: A Scholarly Annual* 11 (2000): 38–39.

3 Fred Parker, *Shakespeare's Johnson* (Oxford, UK: Clarendon Press, 1991), 65, 155, 68.

4 Philip Smallwood, "Johnson's Criticism, the Arts, and the Idea of Art," in *Johnson After 300 Years*, ed. Greg Clingham and Philip Smallwood (Cambridge: Cambridge University Press, 2009), 180.

5 Helen Deutsch, *Loving Dr. Johnson* (Chicago: University of Chicago Press, 2005), 37.

6 Nicholas Jardine, *Romanticism and the Sciences*, coedited and introduced with Andrew R. Cunningham (Cambridge: Cambridge University Press, 1990); Alan Richardson, *The Neural Sublime: Cognitive Theories and Romantic Texts* (Baltimore, MD: Johns Hopkins University Press, 2010); Richard Holmes, *The Age of Wonder: The Romantic Generation and the Discovery of the Beauty and Terror of Science* (New York: Vintage, 2010); Sharon Ruston, *Creating Romanticism: Case Studies in the Literature, Science, and Medicine of the 1790s* (New York: Palgrave, 2013).

7 John Wiltshire, *Samuel Johnson in the Medical World: The Doctor and the Patient* (Cambridge: Cambridge University Press, 1991), 64. Richard B. Schwartz, *Samuel Johnson and the New Science* (Madison: University of Wisconsin Press, 1971).

8 During her residence at Newington Green, Wollstonecraft was introduced to the acquaintance of Dr. Johnson who was at that time already considered the father of English literature. Godwin writes, "the doctor treated her with particular kindness and attention, had a long conversation with her, and desired her to repeat her visit often," although his death prevented her from doing so. William Godwin, *Memoirs of the Author of A Vindication of the Rights of Woman*, vol. 1 of *Collected Novels and Memoirs of William Godwin*, ed. Mark Philp (London: William Pickering, [1798] 1992), 99.

9 The creature's speeches, for example, are "laden with Miltonic overtones," and as John Lamb has argued, for the Romantics, it is Lucifer who best represents the drive to be "free, not over-rul'd by Fate / Inextricable, or strict necessity." Quoted in John B. Lamb, "Mary Shelley's Frankenstein and Milton's Monstrous Myth," *Nineteenth-Century Literature* 47, no. 3 (December 1992), 307. Among the many works that perceive Mary Shelley as, in some ways, inheriting Milton's legacy are Harold Bloom, "Frankenstein, or the new Prometheus," *Partisan Review* 32 (1965): 611–618; Sandra M. Gilbert and Susan Gubar, *The Madwoman in the Attic: The Woman Writer and the Nineteenth-Century Literary Imagination* (New Haven, CT: Yale University Press, 1979), 213–247; Chris Baldick, *In Frankenstein's Shadow: Myth, Monstrosity, and Nineteenth-Century Writing* (New York: Oxford University Press, 1987), 100–119.

10 See "Mary Shelley's Reading: Alphabetical List," *Romantic Circles*, accessed June 21, 2017, https://www.rc.umd.edu/editions/frankenstein/MShelley/readalph.

11 Samuel Johnson, *The History of Rasselas, Prince of Abissinia*, in vol. 16 of *The Yale Edition of the Works of Samuel Johnson*, ed. Gwin J. Kolb (New Haven, CT: Yale University Press, 1990), 16:11.

12 Johnson, *The History of Rasselas*, 16:76.

13 Johnson, *The History of Rasselas*, 16:75.

14 Johnson, *The History of Rasselas*, 16:49.

15 Samuel Johnson, "Review of Free Inquiry into the Nature and Origin of Evil," in vol. 2 of *The Works of Samuel Johnson, LL.D. with an Essay on His Life and Genius*, ed. Arthur Murphy (New York: George Dearborn, 1837), 606.

16 Robert J. Mayhew, "Nature and the Choice of Life in 'Rasselas,'" *Studies in English Literature, 1500–1900* 39, no. 3 (Summer 1999): 550.

17 Nicholas Hudson, "Three Steps to Perfection; *Rasselas* and the Philosophy of Richard Hooker," *Eighteenth-Century Life* 14, no. 3 (November 1991): 35.

18 See Charles E. Pierce, *Religious Life of Samuel Johnson* (Hamden, CT: Archon Books, 1983), 9. Maurice Quinlan also places Johnson firmly within Anglicanism,

the main tradition of English Protestantism that began with Richard Hooker. See his *Samuel Johnson: A Layman's Religion* (Madison: University of Wisconsin Press, 1964).

19 Hudson, "Three Steps to Perfection," 29.

20 Hudson, "Three Steps to Perfection," 31.

21 Wiltshire, *Samuel Johnson in the Medical World*, 1.

22 Schwartz, *Samuel Johnson and the New Science*, 31.

23 Samuel Johnson, *Diaries, Prayers, and Annals*, ed. E. L. McAdam Jr., Donald Hyde, and Mary Hyde (New Haven, CT: Yale University Press, 1958), 297–298.

24 *Boswell's Life of Johnson*, 4:110.

25 Gloria Sybil Gross argues that Johnson distrusted rationalism, which was based on knowledge gained through the isolated activity of theorizing and abstraction. See Gross's "Dr. Johnson's Practice: The Medical Context for *Rasselas*" in vol. 14 of *Studies in Eighteenth-Century Culture*, ed. O. M. Brack Jr. (Madison: University of Wisconsin Press, 1985), 277.

26 Some scholars have attempted to discern Johnson's authorship through looking at his style, and attributed to Johnson biographies of Boerhaave as well as other ancient doctors such as Aesculapius. O. M. Brack Jr. and Thomas Kaminski, "Johnson, James, and the Medicinal Dictionary," *Modern Philology* 81, no. 4 (May 1984): 380.

27 Peter Martin, *Samuel Johnson: A Biography* (Cambridge, MA: Harvard University Press, 2008), 181.

28 Hermann Boerhaave, "Oration on the Usefulness of the Mechanical Method in Medicine," in *Boerhaave's Orations*, trans. E. Kegel-Brinkgreve and A. M. Luyendijk-Elshout (Leiden, Netherlands: E. J. Brill, 1983), 96–97.

29 Johnson's first published work in the medical field was "a life of Herman Boerhaave, translated, or in parts paraphrased." See Wiltshire, *Samuel Johnson in the Medical World*, 74.

30 Boerhaave, "Oration," 116.

31 Lester S. King, *The Medical World of the Eighteenth Century* (Chicago: University of Chicago Press, 1958), 72.

32 These medical texts were not chosen as *Dictionary* sources but they had appeared as early as 1733 and 1724. See W. K. Wimsatt, *Philosophic Words: A Study of Style and Meaning in the "Rambler" and "Dictionary" of Samuel Johnson* (New Haven, CT: Yale University Press, 1948), 35.

33 George Cheyne, *The Natural Method of Curing the Diseases of the Body, and the Disorders of the Mind Depending on the Body* (1747). Quoted in letter to Hester Thrale, Saturday 29 July 1775, in *The Letters of Samuel Johnson*, 3 vols., ed. Bruce Redford (Oxford, UK: Clarendon Press, 1992), 2:258.

34 John Locke, chap. 32, sec. 6 in *An Essay Concerning Human Understanding*, ed. Roger Woolhouse (Harmondsworth, UK: Penguin, 1997), 355.

35 John Locke, *Discourse of Miracles* (London, 1706), abridged and reprinted with *The Reasonableness of Christianity* and a portion of *A Third Letter Concerning Toleration*, on the question of miracles, ed. I. T. Ramsey (London: A. & C. Black, 1958), 80.

36 R. M. Burns, *The Great Debate on Miracles: From Joseph Glanvill to David Hume* (Plainsboro, NJ: Associated University Press, 1981), 66, 135.

37 "To Gilbert Elliot [1751]," in *The Letters of David Hume*, ed. Y. T. Greig, 2 vols. (Oxford, UK: Oxford University Press, 1932), 1:153–155.

38 William Wordsworth, *The Prelude: Or, Growth of a Poet's Mind (Text of 1805)* (Oxford, UK: Oxford University Press, 1970), book 6, line 542.
39 George Cheyne, *The English Malady*, ed. Roy Porter (London: Tavistock, 1991), 94.
40 Cheyne, *The English Malady*, 81, 85, 87.
41 Wiltshire, *Samuel Johnson in the Medical World*, 161.
42 Samuel Johnson, *The Rambler*, no. 25, ed. W. J. Bate and Albrecht B. Strauss, in *The Yale Edition of the Works of Samuel Johnson* (New Haven, CT: Yale University Press, 1969), 3:139.
43 Robert Whytt, *Physiological Essays* (Edinburgh, UK: Hamilton, Balfour and Neill, 1745), 188, 144, 168.
44 R. K. French, *Robert Whytt, the Soul, and Medicine* (London: Wellcome Institute of the History of Medicine, 1969), 71.
45 Patricia Fara, *Sympathetic Attractions: Magnetic Practices, Beliefs, and Symbolism in Eighteenth-Century England* (Princeton, NJ: Princeton University Press, 1996), 19.
46 Fara, *Sympathetic Attractions*, 176.
47 Johnson, *The History of Rasselas*, 16:72.
48 Johnson, *The History of Rasselas*, 16:49, emphasis mine.
49 Wimsatt, *Philosophic Words*, 79.
50 Johnson, *The Rambler*, no. 5, 3:29.
51 Johnson, *The History of Rasselas*, 169.
52 Johnson, *The History of Rasselas*.
53 Greg Clingham, "Johnson, Ends, and the Possibility of Happiness," in *Johnson After 300 Years*, ed. Greg Clingham and Philip Smallwood (Cambridge: Cambridge University Press, 2009), 40.
54 Mary Shelley, *Frankenstein*, in *Novels and Selected Works of Mary Shelley*, ed. Nora Crook (London: Routledge, 1996) 1: 40.
55 Shelley, *Frankenstein*, 36.
56 Shelley, *Frankenstein*, 35–36.
57 Shelley, *Frankenstein*, 36–38.
58 Shelley, *Frankenstein*, 39.
59 Erasmus Darwin, *The Temple of Nature; or, The Origin of Society* (Menston, UK: Scholar Press, [1803] 1973), canto II, 46, ll. 41–42.
60 William Lawrence, *Lectures on Physiology, Zoology, and the Natural History of Man* (London: Callow, 1819), 93. Lawrence's physiological theories are mentioned in explaining Shelley's interest in materialism by Marilyn Butler. See also Introduction by Marilyn Butler, Mary Shelley's *Frankenstein or The Modern Prometheus*, The 1818 Text, ed. Marilyn Butler (Oxford and New York: Oxford University Press, 1993), xix.
61 Shelley, *Frankenstein*, 35.
62 Frederick Burwick, "'The Revolt of Islam': Vegetarian Shelley and the Narrative of Mental Pathology," *Wordsworth Circle* 40, no. 2/3 (Spring–Summer 2009): 89.
63 See author's introduction, Appendix A, in Shelley, *Frankensein*, 195–196.
64 William Sturgeon, *A Course of Twelve Elementary Lectures on Galvanism* (London: Sherwood, Gilbert, and Piper, 1843), 18.
65 Erasmus Darwin, *Zoonomia; or, The Laws of Organic Life*. Vol. I, Part I (London: J. Johnson, 1794), 66.
66 Darwin, *Zoonomia*, 39.
67 Thomas Medwin, *The Life of Percy Bysshe Shelley*, ed. H. Buxton Forman (London: Oxford University Press, 1913), 269–270.

68 Burwick, "The Revolt of Islam," 89.
69 Schwartz, *Samuel Johnson and the New Science*, 42.
70 Schwartz, *Samuel Johnson and the New Science*.
71 Anna Williams, *Miscellanies in Prose and Verse* (London: T. Davies, 1746), 42–43.
72 *Boswell's Life of Johnson*, 3:22; 1:159.
73 Samuel Johnson, *A Dictionary of the English Language* (London: Printed by W. Strahan, for J. and P. Knapton, et al., 1755–1756), 1:681.
74 Wiltshire, *Samuel Johnson in the Medical World*, 60. These curative properties had been promoted by John Wesley among others.
75 Johnson, *The Rambler*, no. 89, 3:107.
76 Johnson, *The History of Rasselas*, 16:54–55.
77 Johnson, *The Rambler*, no. 48, 3:263.
78 Johnson, *The Rambler*, no. 48, 3: 262.
79 Serge Soupel, '"The True Culprit Is the Mind Which can Never Run Away from Itself:' Samuel Johnson and Depression," *Studies in the Literary Imagination* 44, no. 1 (2011): 46.
80 "To Hester Lynch Piozzi [1773]," in *The Letters of Samuel Johnson*, 3 vols., ed. Bruce Redford (Princeton, NJ: Princeton University Press, 1992), 2:5.
81 Wiltshire, *Samuel Johnson in the Medical World*, 161.
82 Johnson states "There are perhaps very few conditions more to be pitied than that of an active and elevated mind, laboring under the weight of a distempered body." *The Rambler*, no. 48, 3:260.
83 Johnson, *The Rambler*, no. 48, 3:260.
84 Cheyne, *The English Malady*, 182.
85 Robert Whytt, *Observations on the Nature, Causes, and Cure of Those Disorders Which Have Been Commonly Called Nervous, Hypochondriac, or Hysteric*, 2nd ed. (Edinburgh, UK: Printed for T. Becket, and P. Du Hondt, London, and J. Balfour, 1765), 113.
86 Cheyne, *English Malady*, 66.
87 Cheyne, *English Malady*, 182.
88 Mary Wollstonecraft, *Vindication of the Rights of Men (1791)*, vol. 5 of *The Works of Mary Wollstonecraft* (London: William Pickering, 1989), 8.
89 Gross, "Dr. Johnson's Practice," 275. According to Wiltshire, the influence of Johnson on Haslam's book *Observations on Madness and Melancholy* (1808) is pervasive. See Wiltshire, *Samuel Johnson in the Medical World*, 179.
90 Johnson, *The History of Rasselas*, 16:147.
91 Johnson, *The History of Rasselas*, 16:147.
92 Johnson, *The History of Rasselas*, 16:150.
93 Thomas Kass, "Morbid Melancholy, the Imagination, and Samuel Johnson's Sermons," *Logos: A Journal of Catholic Thought and Culture* 8, no. 4 (Fall 2005): 56, 47–63.
94 Shelley, *Frankenstein*, 36.
95 Shelley, *Frankenstein*, 34.
96 Shelley, *Frankenstein*, 38.
97 Shelley, *Frankenstein*, 38.
98 Some of the most influential medical treatises on imagination were written by Samuel Tissot, William Falconer, Erasmus Darwin, and William Buchan. See Samuel Tissot, *Onanism; or a Treatise upon the Disorders produced by Masturbations or, the Dangerous Effects of Secret and Excessive Venery*, trans. A. Hume

(London: Thompson, 1781); Darwin, *Zoonomia*; William Falconer, *Dissertation on the Influence of the Passions upon Disorders of the Body* (London: Dilly, 1791); William Buchan, *Domestic Medicine, or a Treatise on the Prevention and Cure of Diseases by Regimen and Simple Medicines* (London: Printed by A. Strahan, T. Cadell jun. and W. Davies Strand; and J. Balfour, and W. Creech, Edinburgh, 1800).

99 Buchan, *Domestic Medicine*, 426

100 Shelley, *Frankenstein*, 106.

101 Shelley, *Frankenstein*, 101.

102 Johnson, *The History of Rasselas*, 16:174.

103 Shelley, *Frankenstein*, 11.

104 Johnson, *The History of Rasselas*, 16:13.

105 Clingham, "Johnson, Ends, and the Possibility of Happiness," 42.

106 *The Poems of John Dryden: Volume Five 1697–1700*, ed. Paul Hammond and David Hopkins (Harlow, UK: Pearson Longman, 2005), 672–673.

107 Shelley, *Frankenstein*, 77.

108 Johnson, *The History of Rasselas*, 16:13.

109 Shelley, *Frankenstein*, 80.

110 Shelley, *Frankenstein*, 83.

111 Shelley, *Frankenstein*, 104.

112 Shelley, *Frankenstein*, 107.

113 Shelley, *Frankenstein*, 153.

114 Shelley, *Frankenstein*, 166.

115 Johnson, *The History of Rasselas*, 16:127, emphasis mine.

116 Johnson, *The History of Rasselas*, 16:127.

117 "Letter to Edmund Hector [1778]," in *The Letters of Samuel Johnson*, ed. Bruce Redford (Oxford, UK: Clarendon Press, 1994), 5:7.

118 Johnson, *The Rambler*, no. 103, 4:186, emphasis mine.

119 Shelley, *Frankenstein*, 160.

120 Shelley, *Frankenstein*, 166.

121 Shelley, *Frankenstein*, 169.

122 Johnson, *The History of Rasselas*, 16:50.

123 Quoted by Kass, "Morbid Melancholy," 60.

4

Jane Austen and the Reception of Samuel Johnson in Japan

The Domestication of Realism in Sōseki Natsume's *Theory of Literature* (1907)

YURI YOSHINO

Introduction

Critics have agreed that the first phase of the reception of Johnson in Japan was during the Meiji era (1868–1912) and was characterized by the evaluation of Johnson as a moral rather than a literary authority.[1] According to these critics, *Rasselas* was a popular text for undergraduates studying English, but its moral implications were valued over its literary qualities.[2] In order to complement the existing criticism on this subject, this chapter aims to provide a more nuanced approach to understanding how Johnson's literary achievements were received in Japan by drawing attention to the reception of Jane Austen (who was herself influenced by Johnson) during the same period.[3] I will argue that Johnson's literary views, especially his view of realist fiction as outlined in *The Rambler*, were endorsed by the writer and critic Sōseki Natsume (1867–1916) via his analysis of Austen's work as examples of domestic realism. Sōseki's own fiction and his theories of literature were deeply influenced by his study of British literature, and he is arguably the most canonical novelist in Japan. My proposition is that the reception of Johnson and Austen by Sōseki enables us to appreciate how subtly and significantly Johnson's literary achievement was received in Meiji-era Japan.

Johnson in Sōseki Natsume's *Theory of Literature* (1907)

It has been noted that Sōseki undervalued Johnson's literary merits.[4] In fact, Sōseki declares in *Bungakuhyoron*, or *Literary Criticism* (1909) that he is "not necessarily fond of Johnson" and "does not admire Johnson's writings and arguments so much," except for Johnson's famous 1755 letter to Chesterfield.[5] Sōseki was "impressed with the letter since he read it for the first time" because he felt that it articulated the idea that "the age of patronage was gone for good in the Republic of letters."[6] Sōseki evaluates Johnson's declaration of independence from Chesterfield "in terms of literary history," and finds that the letter testifies to Johnson's upstanding moral character.[7] Beyond Sōseki's citation of the letter to Chesterfield, his discussion of eighteenth-century British literature occasionally refers to Johnson's critical works, such as *The Lives of the Poets*, but he does not necessarily find these to be authoritative.[8]

We can, however, find numerous references to Johnson in Sōseki's quotations from works by other British writers elsewhere in his criticism, particularly in book 5, chapter 6 of his study on eighteenth- and nineteenth-century British literature, *Bungakuron* (*Theory of Literature*) (1907).[9] In this volume, Sōseki introduces lengthy quotations from Elizabeth Gaskell's *Cranford* (1853) and William Makepeace Thackeray's *The Newcomes* (1855) as remarkable novelistic representations of "conflicts between old and new [literary] tastes."[10] To Sōseki, "the war between two representative tastes in novelistic genre at the beginning of the nineteenth century is the most interesting" case.[11] Moreover, its repercussions for novels such as *Cranford* and *The Newcomes* are "even more intriguing to him as a scholar in the field."[12] The quotations are both from dinner party scenes, where characters argue about literary works, including *Rasselas*. In these quotations Sōseki identifies Johnson as a figure of old-fashioned literary authority.[13]

In the section in chapter 1 of *Cranford*, Johnson's *Rasselas* is juxtaposed with Dickens's *Pickwick Papers*.[14] Sōseki's excerpt runs from the sentence, "When the trays re-appeared with biscuits and wine, punctually at a quarter to nine, there was conversation; comparing of cards, and talking over tricks; but, by-and-by, Captain Brown sported a bit of literature" to the end of the chapter.[15] Captain Brown, who is a newcomer to the female community with "elegant economy," holds a "literary dispute" with Miss Jenkyns, who "was daughter of a deceased rector of Cranford; and, on the strength of a number of manuscript sermons, and a pretty good library of divinity, considered herself literary, and looked upon any conversation about books as a challenge to her." Captain Brown dares to convince Miss Jenkyns of the literary merits of *The Pickwick Papers* and reads "the account of 'swarry' which Sam Weller gave at Bath."[16] In response, Miss Jenkyns

> read one of the conversations between Rasselas and Imlac, in a high-pitched majestic voice; and when she had ended, she said, "I imagine I am now justified in my preference of Dr. Johnson, as a writer of fiction." The Captain screwed his lips up, and drummed on the table, but he did not speak. She thought she would give a finishing blow or two.
>
> "I consider it vulgar, and below the dignity of literature, to publish in numbers."
>
> "How was the 'Rambler' published, Ma'am?" asked Captain Brown, in a low voice; which I think Miss Jenkyns could not have heard.
>
> "Dr. Johnson's style is a model for young beginners. My father recommended it to me when I began to write letters.—I have formed my own style upon it; I recommend it to your favourite."
>
> "I should be very sorry for him to exchange his style for any such pompous writing," said Captain Brown.
>
> Miss Jenkyns felt this as a personal affront, in a way of which the Captain had not dreamed. Epistolary writing, she and her friends considered as her *forte*. Many a copy of many a letter have I seen written and corrected on the slate, before she "seized the half-hour just previous to post-time to assure" her friends of this or of that; and Dr. Johnson was, as she said, her model in these compositions. She drew herself up with dignity, and only replied to Captain Brown's last remark by saying with marked emphasis on every syllable, "I prefer Dr. Johnson to Mr. Boz."[17]

Immediately after this quotation from *Cranford*, Sōseki comments that Captain Brown represents "the new school" and Miss Jenkyns is attached to "the old school," and, because their conversation is focused on their uncompromised partiality, it is "a war rather than a dialogue."[18] Here Sōseki avoids siding with either Captain Brown's literary taste or Miss Jenkyns's because his purpose in this chapter is to "analyze the mechanisms driving change in shared literary taste."[19] The emphasis of his argument is that "our shared literary tastes are constantly shifting"[20] and competitive, and that the dominance of a certain literary taste or movement takes time.

The quotation by Sōseki from chapter 21 in *The Newcomes* focuses on Colonel Newcome's surprise and subsequent emotional reaction to literary opinions held by his son's friends: "Doctor Johnson not write English! Lord Byron not one of the greatest poets of the world! Sir Walter a poet of the second order! Mr Pope attacked for inferiority and want of imagination; Mr Keats and this young Mr Tennyson of Cambridge, the chief of modern poetic literature! What were these new dicta, which Mr Warrington delivered with a puff of tobacco-smoke; to which Mr Honeyman blandly assented, and Clive listened with pleasure? Such opinions were not of the Colonel's time."[21]

Sōseki observes that this passage depicts a shift in literary tastes (in England) during the colonel's approximately thirty-year absence from England while he was serving in India.[22] The novel is set in the 1830s, and in the passage, Clive's friends dismiss Johnson as a writer of the bygone era along with Pope, Byron, and Scott, while they approve of Wordsworth, Keats, and Tennyson as the influential writers of the time.[23] Sōseki continues to quote the narrator's description of the colonel's subsequent emotional reactions: "A dim consciousness of danger for Clive, a terror that his son had got into the society of heretics and unbelievers, came over the Colonel; and then presently, as was the wont with his modest soul, a gentle sense of humility."[24] Rather than expressing sympathy for the colonel's attachment to Johnson and his sense of "terror" and "humility," Sōseki coolly comments that the passage simply marks "a difference in literary tastes" between the old colonel and a younger generation.[25] Sōseki adds that a shift in literary tastes takes a long time to occur precisely because members of society are of different ages with different gifts, education, and habits; and, furthermore, that such a shift would usually provoke extreme opposition.[26] It is noteworthy that the quotations from *Cranford* and *The Newcomes* deployed by Sōseki identify Johnson as an icon of the old literary taste, whereas the former episode refers to Dickens and the latter refers to Keats and Tennyson as icons of new literary tastes.

Jane Austen in *Theory of Literature*

Theory of Literature commends the narrative strategy and approach of Jane Austen, whose literary debt to Johnson has been the subject of scholarly attention since the nineteenth century.[27] One of the major references to Austen's work in the treatise is made in chapter 7, book 4, "Technique of Realism," which opens with the lavish praise that "Jane Austen is the leading authority in the world of realism."[28] It follows that "Anyone who is unable to appreciate Austen will be unable to understand the beauty of realism."[29] In order to support this enthusiastic endorsement, Sōseki quotes all of Mr. and Mrs. Bennet's conversation from chapter 1 in *Pride and Prejudice*, from Mrs. Bennet's "My dear Mr. Bennet," to Mr. Bennet's "Depend upon it, my dear, that when there are twenty, I will visit them all."[30] On "the innocuous conversation between an ordinary married couple,"[31] Sōseki argues as follows:

> While it is difficult to know whether the couple [Mr. and Mrs. Bennet] will be blessed in its hopes—no one can know what twists of fate lie in store—it is easy to see the general drift of their lives from this one passage. In other words, the deepest meaning of this passage lies in the distillation of an entire life in a single page. The deep meaning, though, is not merely in the distillation. The point is that once we have grasped their character in its normal state of affairs through this distillation, we can foresee its potential transformations as well.
>
> . . . .
>
> The description in this passage has depth not simply because it so skillfully distills their characters in a normal state but rather because it simultaneously encloses within it the capacity for change in unusual circumstances. If we accept the implications of this, it seems mistaken to argue that one cannot achieve depth—and a subtle insight into life—without deploying striking events and situating ordinary people in extreme circumstances. They say there needs to be blood on the floor to grab people's interest, that one needs to call down thunder and lightning to create the drama, that it requires one to grind the bones and gouge out the eyeballs to make people cry. That's fine to say, but to mistake this for depth is to miss the point. There is no great trick to impressing the majority of people by placing a marvel before their eyes.[32]

Sōseki recognizes "Austen's profundity" in the opening scene of *Pride and Prejudice*, as the scene succeeds in portraying "ordinary people" in "a normal state of affairs" with "the capacity for change in unusual circumstances," without depending on "striking events," "extreme circumstances," or "a marvel." This endorsement of Austen's realism seems to resonate with Johnson's view on fiction, as I will argue subsequently.

In *Rambler* no. 4 on realist fiction, Johnson criticizes the tendency of "the romances formerly written" to recycle the supernatural "wonder" of the "heroic romance."[33] According to Johnson, the "province" of "the new kind of writing" or "the romance of comedy" is "to bring about natural events by easy means, and to keep up curiosity without the help of wonder: it is therefore precluded from the machines and expedients of the heroic romance, and can neither employ giants to snatch away a lady from the nuptial rites, nor knights to bring her back from captivity; it can neither bewilder its personages in deserts nor lodge them in imaginary castles."[34]

Johnson's disapproval of the usage of "wonder" and examples of "the machines and expedients of the heroic romance" in fiction surely finds an echo in Sōseki's analysis of realism in the opening scene of *Pride and Prejudice*, quoted previously. The Japanese word translated as "marvel" in Sōseki's commentary is much like what Johnson calls "wonder." Furthermore, Johnson's view that the new fiction must "bring about natural events by easy means" seems to be further developed by Sōseki's analysis of the opening scene of *Pride and Prejudice*. Sōseki finds what Johnson calls "easy means" in Austen's craft of characterization, which convincingly suggests the potential changes to the status quo of a normal setting "in a single page." We may also note that Sōseki's examples of the "marvelous" are reminiscent of the Gothic romances that are parodied in *Northanger Abbey* (1817).[35]

Rambler no. 4 also observes that readers respond more strongly to representations of common life, and that realist representations of this kind were beyond the abilities of many writers. For Johnson, novelists should be "engaged in portraits of which every one knows the original, and can detect any deviation from exactness resemblance."[36] This idea of the modern novel emphasizes the significance and technical challenges of realism and raises the status of domestic fiction. It follows that, although he hardly quotes Johnson's work in *Theory of Literature*, Sōseki's praise of Austen's realism appropriates Johnson's view of the new fiction. According to Isobel Grundy, "*Rambler* no. 4 is still sometimes interpreted as hostile or at best grudging towards the new-style novel, yet many of Johnson's pronouncements about the business of fiction were seized on by novelists."[37] Both Austen and Sōseki may well be among these novelists.

The Reception of Austen's Domestic Realism

The anonymous review of *Emma* in the *Quarterly Review* (October 1815), generally attributed to Sir Walter Scott, contributed significantly to the successful reception of Austen's work in nineteenth-century Britain. Sōseki quotes part of this review, where Scott praises Austen's realism and makes an analogy between her art and that of "the Flemish school of painting": "The author's knowledge of the world, and the peculiar tact with which she presents characters that the reader cannot fail to recognize, reminds us something of the merits of the Flemish school of painting. The subjects are not often elegant, and certainly never grand; but they are finished up to nature, and with a precision which delights the reader."[38]

While the passage highlights Austen's original "tact" of representation, critics have been quick to identify an undermining implication in Scott's characterization of Austen's work as domestic realism.[39] The scope of Austen's domestic realism is characterized here as limited to "ordinary commonplace things and characters." It is, therefore, held by Scott and others to be an implicitly female mode of writing in contrast to the "Big-Bow wow strain" of Scott's own historical novels with "grand" subjects.[40]

In an earlier passage of his *Emma* review, Scott compares Austen and her contemporary, Maria Edgeworth: "In this class she [Austen] stands almost alone; for the scenes of Miss Edgeworth are laid in higher life, varied by more romantic incident, and by her remarkable power of embodying and illustrating national character. But the author of Emma [*sic*] confines herself chiefly to the middling classes of society."[41]

It was Edgeworth's *The Absentee*, a "national" tale published in 1812, rather than Austen's "domestic" romance confined to a small local community that inspired Scott to write *Waverley* and launch the historical novel.[42] In the chapter in *Waverley* entitled "A Postscript Which Should Have Been a Preface," Scott acknowledges that "It has been my object to describe these persons, not by a caricatured and exaggerated use of the national dialect, but by their habits, manners, and feelings, so as in some distant degree to emulate the admirable Irish portraits drawn by Miss Edgeworth."[43] Scott's review of *Emma* has thus led a recent commentator on the history of the novel in English to argue convincingly that the canonical status of Austen's domestic fiction "has been simultaneously assured and ambivalent since soon after her death in 1817."[44]

It is then noteworthy that in *Theory of Literature* Sōseki chooses *Pride and Prejudice* rather than *Emma* as an example of the masterpiece of realism. He refuses to rest entirely on Scott's view of *Emma*. He also omits commentary about "the faults" of *Emma*, "which arise from the minute detail which the author's plan comprehends," in quoting Scott's review.[45] In taking this line of exposition, Sōseki presents the excellence of Austen's domestic fiction much less ambivalently than Scott does, and, moreover, thereby associates himself more closely with Johnson's view of domestic fiction.

Rambler no. 4 posits an author from the past—a male author—"who had no further care than to retire to his closet, let loose his invention, and heat his mind with incredibilities." This author would then be able to publish a book "without fear of criticism, without the toil of study, without knowledge of nature, or acquaintance with life."[46] In the mid-eighteenth century women writers generally did not have rooms of their own in which to do their work.[47] Johnson's remarks suggest that the demand for realist novels creates opportunities for women to become writers because they are attuned to the "that experience which can never be attained by solitary diligence, but must arise from general converse, and accurate observation of the living world" rather than just to "that learning which is to be gained from books."[48] *Theory of Literature* thus resists Scott's undervaluation of domestic realism and reinstates Johnson's expectations for "our present writers."[49]

Austen's Domestication of Romance and Sōseki's Domestication of Realism

Despite Sōseki's emphasis on the realist aspects of Austen's work, her novels do not abandon the concept of fantastical romance all together. For instance, critics have pointed out that *Northanger Abbey* does not necessarily denounce the device of Gothic romance in the characterization of General Tilney; the general's cruel behavior to Catherine is, after all, comparable to that of Montoni, the Gothic patriarch in *The Mysteries of Udolpho* (1794).[50] Rather, Austen's novel domesticates the exotic motifs of Gothic romance within a familiar English context. Her writing thus shifts the arena of romance from mock medieval settings on the Continent to the modern domestic sphere in England. By doing so, Austen's novels represent the romance that underpins family life in England.

Recent scholarship on the fiction of the Romantic era has sought to situate Austen more securely among her contemporaries.[51] It has been argued that the mixture of realism and romance in the Romantic-era novel is a strength rather than a weakness.[52] This is an attempt to revise the conventional narrative regarding the "rise of the novel" as established by Ian Watt, and redress the overemphasis on realism as the key merit of the novel. Sōseki, however, plays down the romantic tendency of Austen's domestic fiction. He cites the example of Marianne's fevered "delirium" in *Sense and Sensibility* and identifies Austen as "a realist" rather than a "romantic author."[53] He gives Charlotte Brontë as an example a "romantic author" and cites the scene in *Jane Eyre* in which Jane hears Rochester calling her name from across a huge distance, as "the contrasting attitude of a romantic author in similar circumstances."[54] More recent criticism has challenged this comparison of Brontë and Austen. Comparing *Pride and Prejudice* and *Jane Eyre*, Simon Dentith argues that Brontë is "far more profoundly realist than Jane Austen, in that far more of human life is present and represented in her texts: extremes of depression, passion, and isolation, certainly, but also a much fuller feeling of human presence and intensity than in Austen."[55] It is important to notice that Sōseki's choice of Charlotte Brontë rather than male "romantic authors" effectively avoids identifying Austen's domestic realism as a distinctively female subgenre. In doing so, Sōseki questions Scott's belittlement of the domestic novel, against which Scott designates his historical novels as a male genre.

Given the ways that *Theory of Literature* introduces Austen as the master of realism, one might conclude that the treatise endorses Austen's realism as primary. At the same time, however, Sōseki is implicitly tracing Austen's practice to Johnson's views about realist fiction. His treatise attempts to probe the Western modern literary tradition and to tackle the artistic challenges that confronted men of letters in Meiji Japan. He appropriates Johnson's view of a new kind of fiction, which domesticates the Western novel, by demonstrating Jane Austen's domestic realism to be its embodiment. By such subtle means were Johnson's literary achievements appropriated by Japanese literary criticism.

Notes

1 For example, see Tetsu Fujii, "Nihondeno Johnson jyuyo to kenkyu no rekishi" ("A History of Reception and Studies of Johnson in Japan"), in *Eikoku bunkano kyojin Samuel Johnson* (*Samuel Johnson, a Giant of English culture*), ed. Hideichi Eto, Shigeru Shibagaki, and Hitoshi Suwabe (Kamakura, Japan: Minato No Hito, 2009), 289–311, and Yutaka Izumitani, *Kentou no bungo Johnson: Meijiki Rasselas no henrin* (*The Challenge of Johnson, a Man of Literature: A Glimpse of Rasselas in the Meiji Era*), (Hiroshima, Japan: Keisuisha, 1992). Isamu Hayakawa has revised this view on the reception of Johnson and pointed out that writers such as Shoyo Tsubouchi (1859–1935), Tokoku Kitamura (1868–1894), and Bin Ueda (1874–1916) recognized the literary value of *Rasselas*. Sōseki's appropriation of Johnson's literary view is, however, beyond Hayakawa's scope, because the critic considers that Sōseki's work has no affinity with Johnson's literary view. See Hayakawa, "Meijini okeru seiyo bunkano jyuyo: Samuel Johnson no baai" ("The Reception of Western Culture in Meiji era: A Case of Samuel Johnson)," *Aichi Daigaku Bungaku Ronso* (*Aichi University Departmental Bulletin for Literary Studies*) 148–151 (2013–2015), esp. 151: 103.

2 Fujii, "Nihondeno Johnson," 291–292.

3 For recent examples, see Freya Johnson, "Johnson and Austen," in *Samuel Johnson After 300 Years*, ed. Greg Clingham and Philip Smallwood (Cambridge: Cambridge University Press, 2009), 225–245, and Gloria Sybil Gross, *In a Fast Coach with a Pretty Woman: Jane Austen and Samuel Johnson* (New York: MAS Press, 2002).

4 Hayakawa has considered Sōseki's few quotations from Johnson's work in *Bungakuhyoron* (1909) as a sign of low evaluation. See Hayakawa, "Meijini okeru seiyo bunkano jyuyo," 151: 102.

5 Sōseki Natsume, *Bungakuhyoron* (*Literary Criticism*), 2 vols. (Tokyo: Iwaniami Shoten, 1985), 1:176. This book evolved from Sōseki's lectures on eighteenth-century British literature given at Tokyo Imperial University as a successor to Lafcadio Hearn (1850–1904) from 1905–1907 on his return from his studies in London, where he attended some lectures on English literature delivered by Professor William Paton Ker (1855–1923) before switching to the combination of private lessons with William James Craig (1843–1906) and self-directed studies in his own accommodation. For an English-language biography of Sōseki, see John Nathan, *Sōseki: Modern Japan's Greatest Novelist* (New York: Columbia University Press, 2018).

6 Sōseki, *Bungakuhyoron*, 1:176.

7 Kojin Karatani has pointed out that Sōseki did not endorse the concept of literary history because "he [Sōseki] was aware of the historicity of the very term 'literature.'" See Karatani, *Origins of Modern Japanese Literature*, trans. edited by Brett de Bary (Durham, NC: Duke University Press, 1993), 13. The original book in Japanese was published under the title of *Nihon Kindaibungakuno Kigen* (Tokyo: Kodansha, 1980).

8 Sakuko Matsui has observed that Sōseki's discussion of Addison "ignores" Johnson's critical assessment of the poet's major contribution. See Matsui, *Natsume Sōseki as a Critic of English Literature* (Tokyo: Centre for East Asian Cultural Studies, 1975), 173–174, 178.

9 *Bungakuron*, or *Theory of Literature* (1907), is based on Sōseki's lectures given at Tokyo Imperial University from 1903 to 1905. See Michael K. Bourdaghs, Joseph A. Murphy, and Atsuko Ueda, introduction to *Theory of Literature and*

Other Critical Writings by Sōseki Natsume (New York: Columbia University Press, 2009), 2–12. For studies of Sōseki as a scholar of English studies, see also Kasumi Miyazaki, *Hyakunengo ni Sōseki wo yomu* (*Reading Sōseki after 100 Years*) (Tokyo: Transview, 2009), and Shunsuke Kamei, *Eibungakusha: Natsume Sōseki* (*Scholar of English: Sōseki Natsume*) (Tokyo: Shohakusha, 2011).

10 Sōseki, *Bungakuron*, 2 Vols (Tokyo: Iwanami Shoten, 2007), 2:320. Chapters 4–6 of book 5 are omitted in the English translation, *Theory of Literature and Other Critical Writings*, for the reason that the chapters "explore further applications of the book's basic principles to additional authors and literary movements." See the editorial note in *Theory of Literature and Other Critical Writings* by Sōseki Natsume, edited by Michael K. Bourdaghs, Joseph A. Murphy, and Atsuko Ueda (New York: Columbia University Press, 2009), 121.

11 Sōseki, *Bungakuron*, 2:311.

12 Sōseki, *Bungakuron*, 2:311.

13 Sōseki, *Bungakuron*, 2:318–320.

14 When *Cranford* was initially published in *Household Words*, Dickens "forced Gaskell to change the reference: to take out his name and substitute Thomas Hood's," and Gaskell "furiously resented his editorial imposition." See Hilary M. Schor, *Scheherezade in the Market Place: Elizabeth Gaskell and the Victorian Novel* (Oxford, UK: Oxford University Press, 1992), 91–92.

15 Sōseki, *Bungakuron*, 2:311–315. *Cranford* is cited from the Oxford World's Classics edition, edited by Elizabeth Porges Watson (Oxford, UK: Oxford University Press, 2011).

16 Borslav Knezevic has reasonably contended that Captain Brown's choice of Sam Weller's episode represents threats caused by his arrival to the "local genteel culture" of Cranford because Weller's speech is "instantly traceable to the Cockney precincts of London" and subverts "the uniform idiom of gentility," modeled on Dr. Johnson's style. Knezevic, "An Ethnography of the Provincial: The Social Geography of Gentility in Elizabeth Gaskell's 'Cranford,'" *Victorian Studies* 41, no. 3 (1998). 421.

17 Sōseki, *Bungakuron*, 2:313–315.

18 Sōseki, *Bungakuron*, 2:318–319. As for Miss Jenkyns's attachment to Johnson's style, Jeffrey Cass has persuasively argued that it "reveals how completely she misreads *Rasselas*" in "'The Scraps, Patches, and Rags of Daily Life': Gaskell's Oriental Other and the Conservation of Cranford," *Papers on Language and Literature* 35, no. 1 (1999): 421. Schor has furthermore contended that *Cranford* "never hesitates to mock gently" Miss Jenkyns's Johnsonian style taught by her father, and that Miss Jenkyns is portrayed as a "letter-writing daughter" who is "not a wife, not a son, not even her own writer," *Scheherezade in the Market Place*, 90–91.

19 Editorial commentary in Sōseki, *Theory of Literature*, 121.

20 Bourdaghs, Ueda, and Murphy, introduction to *Theory of Literature*, 15–16.

21 Sōseki, *Bungakuron*, 2:321. The quotation from *The Newcomes* is from the Everyman's Library edition, edited by D. J. Taylor (London: Everyman, 1994).

22 According to Catherine Maxwell, *The Newcomes* was "considered by the Victorians to be one of his two most important books," in spite of Henry James's negative assessment as one of "large loose baggy monsters." Catherine Maxwell, "Swinburne and Thackeray's *The Newcomes*," *Victorian Poetry* 47 (2009): 734.

23 R. D. McMaster notes that "Thackeray is marking the transitions between artistic movements as also being markers between larger eras of manners and values, and

he is also playing upon the associations of that part of his readership old enough to remember the tastes of a quarter of a century ago. To most of them in 1854, it must have been amusing to see the Poet Laureate and author of *In Memoriam* skeptically regarded as 'young Mr. Tennyson of Cambridge'." See McMaster, *Thackeray's Cultural Frame of Reference: Allusion in The Newcomes* (Basingstoke, UK: Macmillan, 1991), 16.

24 Sōseki, *Bungakuron*, 2:323.

25 Sōseki, *Bungakuron*, 2:326.

26 Sōseki, *Bungakuron*, 2:326–327.

27 See note 3.

28 Sōseki, *Theory of Literature and Other Critical Writings*, 107.

29 Sōseki, *Theory of Literature and Other Critical Writings*, 107.

30 Sōseki, *Theory of Literature and Other Critical Writings*, 108–109. *Pride and Prejudice* is cited from the Cambridge edition edited by Pat Rogers (Cambridge: Cambridge University Press, 2006).

31 Sōseki, *Theory of Literature and Other Critical Writings*, 110.

32 Sōseki, *Theory of Literature and Other Critical Writings*, 111.

33 For Johnson's earlier addiction to the reading of chivalric romance and concern about its effect, see Eithne Henson, *The Fictions of Romantick Chivalry: Samuel Johnson and Romance* (Madison, NJ: Fairleigh Dickinson University Press, 1992), 19.

34 Samuel Johnson, *The Rambler*, ed. W. J. Bate and Albrecht B. Strauss, vol. 4 of *The Yale Edition of the Works of Samuel Johnson* (New Haven, CT: Yale University Press, 1969), 19.

35 *Northanger Abbey* refers to gothic romances such as Ann Radcliffe's *Mystery of Udolpho*, Mathew Lewis's *The Monk*, Eliza Parsons's *Castle of Wolfenbach: A German Story* (1793), and Regina Maria Roche's *Clermont, a Tale* (1798). Radcliffe's gothic romances heavily deploy the trope of the supernatural or the marvel to provoke readers' sensation, but her technique of "the explained supernatural" distinguishes her works from other gothic romances such as *The Monk* that excessively feature the supernatural without rational explanations. In other words, Radcliffe's narrative strategies seem to respond to the importance of realistic settings of domestic fiction. For the critical reception of Radcliffe's "explained supernatural," see Robert Miles, *Ann Radcliffe: The Great Enchantress* (Manchester, UK: Manchester University Press, 1995), 132.

36 Johnson, *The Rambler*, 20.

37 Isobel Grundy, "Early Women Reading Johnson," in *Samuel Johnson After 300 Years* (Cambridge: Cambridge University Press, 2009), 209.

38 Walter Scott, "An Unsigned Review of *Emma*, *Quarterly Review*, dated October 1815, issued March 1816, xiv, 188–201," in *Jane Austen: Critical Heritage*, ed. B. C. Southam (London: Routledge & Kegan Paul, 1968), 67.

39 For example, see Claudia Johnson "'Let Me Make the Novels of a Country': Barbauld's *The British Novelists* (1810/1820)," *Novel: A Forum on Fiction* 34, no. 2 (2001): 163–179, and Vivien Jones, "Jane Austen's Domestic Realism," in *English and British Fiction 1750–1820*, ed. Peter Garside and Karen O'Brien, *The Oxford History of the Novel in English* (Oxford, UK: Oxford University Press, 2015), 2:273–295.

40 Scott, "Journal Entry, 14 March 1826," in *Jane Austen: The Critical Heritage*, 106.

41 Scott, "An Unsigned Review of *Emma*," 64.

42 Ina Ferris has illuminated how the Waverley novels contributed to making the novel a literary genre. See Ferris, *The Achievement of Literary Authority: Gender, History, and the Waverley Novels* (Ithaca, NY: Cornell University Press, 1991).

43 Walter Scott, *Waverley*, ed. Claire Lamont and Katherine Sutherland, 2nd ed. (Oxford, UK: Oxford University Press, 2015), 376.

44 Jones, "Jane Austen's Domestic Realism," 273.

45 Scott, "An Unsigned Review of *Emma*," 68.

46 Johnson, *The Rambler*, 20.

47 For example, Jane Austen "had no separate study to retire to, and most of the work must have been done in the general sitting-room, subject to all kinds of casual interruptions. She was careful that her occupation should not be suspected by servants, or visitors, or any persons beyond her own family party. She wrote upon small sheets of paper which could easily be put away, or covered with a piece of blotting papers. There was, between the front door and the offices, a swing door which creaked when it was opened; but she objected to having this little inconvenience remedied, because it gave her notice when anyone was coming." See J. E. Austen-Leigh, *A Memoir of Jane Austen and Other Family Recollections* (Oxford, UK: Oxford University Press, 2002), 81–82. (Post nineteenth-century scholarship has challenged Austen-Leigh's account of Austen's writing methods and her "modest" attitude towards her novels, but Sōseki's *Theory of Literature* was published in 1907.) In the opening of *A Room of One's Own*, Virginia Woolf refers to Austen after Frances Burney in her lineage of female writers, stating "a woman must have money and a room of her own if she is to write fiction." See Woolf, *A Room of One's Own and Three Guineas* (Oxford, UK: Oxford University Press, 2015), 3.

48 Johnson, *The Rambler*, 20.

49 Johnson, *The Rambler*, 20.

50 For example, see Thomas Keymer, "*Northanger Abbey* and *Sense and Sensibility*," in *The Cambridge Companion to Jane Austen*, ed. Edward Copeland and Juliet McMaster, 2nd ed. (Cambridge: Cambridge University Press, 2011), 31.

51 For example, see Clara Tuite, *Romantic Austen: Sexual Politics and the Literary Canon* (Cambridge: Cambridge University Press, 2002).

52 For the reevaluation of the Romantic-era novel, see the special issue of *Novel*, 34, no. 2 "The Romantic-Era Novel" (Spring 2001) and Jillian Heydt-Stevenson and Charlotte Sussman, eds., *Recognizing the Romantic Novel: New Histories of British Fiction, 1780–1830* (Liverpool, UK: Liverpool University Press, 2008).

53 Sōseki, *Theory of Literature and Other Writings*, 113.

54 Sōseki, *Theory of Literature and Other Writings*, 113.

55 Simon Dentith, "Realist Synthesis in the Nineteenth-Century Novel: 'That Unity Which Lies In the Selection of Our Keenest Consciousness,'" in *A Concise Companion to Realism*, ed. Matthew Beaumont, rev. ed. (Chichester, UK: Wiley-Blackwell, 2010), 36.

5

Johnson the Tea Poet

A Scholarly Role Model and a Literary Doctor in Modernizing Japan

MIKA SUZUKI

Introduction

While various historical periods and cultures have emphasized or been drawn to different aspects of Samuel Johnson's life and work, he has generally been regarded as a model "man of letters" and scholar.[1] This chapter is inspired by Johnson's own definition of a scholar as one who seeks to disseminate knowledge to a wide readership from numerous intellectual backgrounds and considers Johnson's reception by a nonspecialist in English literature, the medical doctor-turned-scholarly writer Tamotsu Morowoka (1879–1946). I examine what Johnson offered to a Japanese medical doctor in the early twentieth century, and argue that Morowoka's own self-fashioning as a scholar was influenced by his knowledge of Johnson. Johnson provided Morowoka with an example of a sociable, if eccentric, individual who possessed a comprehensive insight into human knowledge and behavior. Morowoka also found in Johnson a precedent for an extensively erudite scholar whose main affiliation was not to the academic institution but who was autonomously active in wider society. Morowoka sought to bestow on Johnson the designation and honor he felt he deserved by granting him the unusual title of a "tea poet." In doing so, Morowoka hoped to advance his own understanding not only of Johnson himself, but also of a range of topics, including tea, the British, and the westernization of Japan.

A Literary Medical Doctor

Morowoka was born in 1879 and was educated at Steele Memorial Academy in Nagasaki (which was established in 1887 by the American Dutch Reformed Church) and at Kyushu Imperial University. He lived in London between 1919 and 1921, studying psychiatry at the London County Council's Pathological Laboratory. On his return to Japan he was appointed as an assistant professor in medicine at Kyushu Imperial University, but his ambitions were frustrated in the wake of a consultation fees scandal there. In consequence, he resigned from the post in 1927. Capitalizing on personal connections he had cultivated, he subsequently moved to Tokyo, and made a living by depending on his extensive learning as well as on his qualifications as a medical doctor. Morowoka's career was consequently not only shaped by the traditional education of Japanese intellectuals, but also by exposure to the newly imported westernized knowledge, the study of the sciences and humanities, and a familiarity with foreign languages, especially English and Chinese. His knowledge of tea, for example, combined Chinese classical learning and state-of-the-art scientific information of the time, and proved a great asset following his move to Tokyo. It was stimulated and exploited by the commercial impetus of the Japan Central Tea Association, which provided research funds to him. The attention to tea proved beneficial for him because it paved the way to promote himself in the book market. For Morowoka tea was at the focal point of the old and the new, the humanities and the sciences, scholarly expertise and everyday life experience, cultural refinement and commercial enterprise.

Morowoka published *Cha to sono bunka* (*Tea and Its Culture*) (1937). Because he regards tea to be a comprehensive field of study involving almost every branch of scholarship, he claims this "small" volume represents only a part of his knowledge. Accordingly, he refers to his ambition to pursue the subject further elsewhere on the scientific, geographical, and historical aspects of tea.[2] In this book he touches only briefly on the chemical, medical, and geographical features of tea and mainly discusses its political and moral effects. What he tries to do in this volume is primarily to examine through his connoisseurship and scholarship the customs and arts of tea that would appeal to the general public. He thinks about the importance of Japanese green tea while he explains about tea in Chinese history and the tea culture in Britain.

In the book only three people have their own sections: Lu Yu (733–804), Samuel Johnson, and Myoe (1173–1232).[3] Johnson is thus sandwiched between the Sage of Tea in China and the founder of tea cultivation in Japan, which appears to give him undue significance within the context of the history of tea.[4] Johnson gains additional prominence in the volume because he is frequently referred to and discussed in other sections as well. Morowoka even adapts a common phrase, *cha jin*—a refined tea master—to describe Johnson as "*cha shi jin*"—a compound of "tea master" and "poet."[5] By using this term, Morowoka tried to express something original: a search for *cha shi jin* in the Japan National Diet Library text database results in no other work than Morowoka's, while more than 500 books and articles have *cha jin* in their titles.

Morowoka's account of Johnson as *cha shi jin*, and the prominence he grants to Johnson in his volume on tea, presents certain issues, not least of which is his silence about Johnson's status as a poet. The quoted poems on tea are not by Johnson but by Edmund Waller, Nahum Tate, and Alexander Pope.[6] Without any further justification, Johnson's place as a tea poet is very awkward. If this is not whimsical, and I assume it is not, Morowoka's concept of a tea poet was special and it clearly extended beyond that of an individual who wrote poems about tea. Morowoka presents Johnson as a tea poet because he was a man of sober erudition surrounded by sociable intellectuals. He regards Johnson as the hub of conversation and common sense, which constitute democracy and modernity.[7] Additionally, Johnson's physical and mental sufferings made him still more interesting to the psychiatrist: he refers to Johnson as a "feeble genius" in his childhood with the "scrofula constitution" who became a young man full of "anxiety, melancholy, and neuroticism" as well as "imagination even excessive, to an almost psychopathic degree."[8] For Morowoka, the stimulating, healthy, and social effects of tea contributed to Johnson's health and sociability. There are plausible reasons, national, personal, and vocational, as to why Morowoka's writings on tea devote such attention to Johnson and why Morowoka felt Johnson to be a role model for his own life and career. Before examining these reasons, however, it is first necessary to consider where and how Morowoka acquired his knowledge of Johnson.

Johnson and Morowoka

Morowoka's books are not fully referenced and hence it is impossible to trace sources for much of the information he provides. However, he does include a few direct citations for the material about Johnson. The sources Morowoka gives in his text are by Kenji Ishida, Leslie Stephen, and Sōseki Natsume.[9] While it is possible that Morowoka learned more about Johnson when he was studying in London, his reference to Ishida's substantial work indicates the increasing attention to Johnson by Japanese literary scholars during this period.[10] He uses Stephen to introduce the literary climate in which Johnson lived and glances at Sōseki to place his current book within the context of eighteenth-century English studies in Japan.

By the time Morowoka was in his teens, Johnson was increasingly revered in Japan as an extraordinary figure. His perseverance and diligence in establishing himself especially made him a fine role model to the Japanese people as their society underwent rapid modernization. As Harada argues in chapter 2, biographies played an important role in forming modern minds. In the late nineteenth century, the Japanese avidly read biographies of prominent individuals, especially those who were held to have been diligent and innovative. Fujii's study of the reception of Johnson and his work reveals that Japanese interests in Johnson's life and personality were mainly inspired by Hawthorne's *Biographical Stories*, the first Japanese translation of which was published in 1895.[11] This didactic story for children focuses on the remorse even a great scholar like Johnson belatedly has for his youthful failure in filial duty; it recommends the readers to be always dutiful and never to be sorry too late.[12] In addition to Hawthorne's *Biographical Stories*, from the 1890s a series of books and articles on Johnson appeared.[13] One article in a magazine lauded Johnson as a great genius who had a difficult early life in poverty, in accordance with the fact that by the late nineteenth century accounts of Johnson's poverty had been already romanticized.[14] It is this aspect of Johnson's biography, rather than his status as a man of belated filial duty, that seems to have most appealed to Morowoka. Morowoka's description ignores Johnson's filial disobedience and remorse, and instead emphasizes the rise and success in London of a man endowed with literary abilities but lacking financial security or social status.

Morowoka probably saw personal parallels between himself and the Johnson familiar to Japanese readers at the turn of the century. Johnson's own account of his belief in the priority of an individual's talents regardless of the financial hardship and in defiance of power relations fits well with Morowoka's school days: "I was miserably poor and I thought to fight my way by my literature and my wit; so I disregarded all power and all authority."[15] One of Morowoka's friends, Yoichi Ueno, testifies to Morowoka's poverty. As a poor student, he was a working member of the school, and was engaged in doing the laundry of other pupils.[16] Such straitened circumstances may have made the adult Morowoka feel closer to Johnson.

Morowoka found parallels between his and Johnson's temperament and values, as well as their respective childhoods. He emphasizes Johnson's tenacity of mind and rebelliousness against the establishment; like Johnson, he had a staunch sense of justice.[17] During their school days Morowoka and Ueno were both keen learners and they were usually on good terms with the teachers, but when they resorted to writing, they styled themselves as rebellious students. They wrote scathing attacks of the school in the school's own magazine, which resulted in their expulsion. It was not until a year later that they were repentant; they apologized and were admitted again.[18] One of Morowoka's friends, who was an MP, describes Morowoka as a person whose admirable qualities included "pure and sound high-mindedness" and "his lofty ideals."[19] Once he took up a good cause, he remained committed to it; he was, for example, enthusiastic about the promotion of temperance.[20] Johnson too described alcohol as a threat to proper use of reason.[21] For Morowoka, alcoholism was one of the most dangerous aspects of modern life, and he equated it to lead poisoning and syphilis.[22]

Like Johnson, Morowoka took pride in his eloquence. Ueno describes how "He himself regarded speeches as his forte. He was very good at delivering speeches. He was an unpretentious simple man in his daily life while on the rostrum he found himself in his element, impressing the audience with his witty remarks that invited wonders and laughs."[23] He made his way in establishing himself as a lecturer not only within the university but also in ad hoc meetings for the general public. His eloquence was such that he was invited to discussion tables featured in periodicals, including attention-grabbing forums like "a meeting of the experts to discuss how to be a beauty" for *Fujin Club* (*Women's Club*) (1931).

From the 1930s, that is, shortly after he settled in Tokyo, he became a darling of the publishers. He became a writer in commercial periodicals that presupposed a wide readership. Here too, we can see points of comparison between Morowoka and Johnson; Johnson was widely regarded, in Japan and elsewhere in this period, for resisting the older system of aristocratic patronage of the arts in favor of a more recognizably modern professional relationship with the newly commercialized literary market.[24] Morowoka wrote for, among other publications, journals specializing in medicine, business, and tea growing, each of which had a specific though considerable group of readers. He also wrote for more general audiences, including in a women's magazine.[25] In addition, he sought an English-speaking audience, presumably American traders and consumers, by writing a thirty-two-page English booklet concerning the health benefits of tea to help Shizuoka Tea Association to promote tea in the global market.[26]

His basic stance throughout his writing is that of a qualified specialist, but he was also a generalist, adapting his literary persona depending on which publication he was writing for. His forte lay in psychiatry as well as tea and he was very good at making use of his scientific and literary knowledge; sometimes styling himself as a well-educated commentator, at other times specifically mentioning his qualification as a medical doctor as well as a specialist in psychiatry. His professorship at a Buddhist university in Tokyo allowed him to feel entitled to talk about Zen and tea, including philosophical, religious, economic, and political issues.[27] He also tailored his subject matter to specific audiences: in his addresses to women he drew on his knowledge of biology and medicine to write on how to be expressive and attractive, and how to achieve mental well-being; when his target readers were businessmen, his topics included "the methods of brain training" and also advice on love and reproduction.[28] In these articles he behaves as a star critic in the mass media, speaking at ease supported by his extensive knowledge. His book, *Kai shoku, kai min, kai ben* (*Good Appetite, Sound Sleep and Regular Motions*) (1939), appealed to a still larger public by encouraging ordinary people to recognize how they could help themselves keep fit in everyday life. It was so popular that the publisher reprinted it again and again; in fact, they had the eighteenth reprint within the first six months of its publication. Across these various publications, he dedicated his erudition and scientific knowledge to educate ordinary people in culture, health, and fitness, paying particular attention to the benefits of tea drinking in these areas. His strategy worked well, and made Morowoka a popular and respected health advisor and author.

Morowoka's Ambivalence toward Britain

Morowoka's interest in tea contributed to his ambivalent feelings toward the British. In his view of the progress of civilization the British had only comparatively recently improved from a state of barbarism by the help of tea consumption. He regarded the British as the usurpers of the global tea trade, which, he felt, should have belonged to the Chinese. He felt that the British had achieved their competitive advantage and their control of the tea trade (and other industries) through their use of modern science, modern technology, and brave entrepreneurship.[29] Morowoka's admiration of the British implies both genuine respect of the success they achieved and an ambivalence regarding their manipulation and control of the world's economy and markets.

His perseverance in learning English and reading English literature was a driving force in his life but it is not certain what Morowoka thought or felt about Britain during his early adult life. What is certain is that as he matured in his career as a writer in the 1930s and 1940s, he expressed vehemently hostile feelings toward Britain. The retrospective account of his early life written as part of the afterword to the *Chakyo hyoshaku gaihen* (*Supplementary Volume to Commentaries on the Classic of Tea*) (1943) emphasizes the wartime aversion against the United States and Britain.[30] His aversion is most apparent in the preface he contributed to a book of relentless indictment against Britain, *Eikoku no spy! Kyuseigun wo utsu* (*Destroy the Salvation Army, the British Spy Organization*) (1940).[31] In the 1943 publication in which he recounts his formative years, he claims that he went to Steele Memorial Academy only to refute the Americans and the British, for which knowledge of the English language was necessary. His reason for learning English was, he maintained, out of repugnance for the wanton cruelties of the Americans and the British. Further, he claims that, even as a child, the resentment he felt for the Americans and British was so fierce that he wanted to castigate them.[32]

Because his papers at home near Shibuya were all destroyed in the Great Tokyo Air Raid on May 25, 1945, there is little hope of finding his letters, diaries, or other personal records to support or modify his own claims in print; the printed retrospective construction of his life and some comments given by his friends are the only material now available. As far as they go, the object of his indignation was sometimes the general circumstances of conventional Japanese society, sometimes the context of international affairs, and sometimes the enemy nations at war. The earlier anger led him to learn English, and later he turned, also in anger, to Chinese culture. Whatever motivated him, the shifts in the contemporary social and political climate always gave impetus to his pursuits in learning. He was such a bibliophile that he desperately wanted to protect his books during the war. Unfortunately, he lost them all. Devastated, his wife records, he wished his books, not his own life, had been saved in 1945 and he died in a state of regret and grief the following year.[33]

Morowoka was able to combine this professed hostility toward the British with his admiration for Johnson because he regarded Johnson as a model of learning and scholarship, rather than as a typical example of Englishness or Britishness. In this, he differed from other Japanese scholars who had an interest in Johnson. For example, Ishida, whom Morowoka refers to as a leading Johnsonian, tries to understand Johnson's multidimensional personality and complex views by attributing his various characteristics to his Britishness. He emphasizes Johnson's reason and good sense on top of the idiosyncratic "Romantic qualities," and resolves his multifaceted features into a "true-born Englishman," a "national institution."[34] Morowoka needed another perspective different from this approach of Johnson as a typical Englishman to accommodate his respect of Johnson. This need may have influenced Morowoka's idea of Johnson as *cha shi jin*. In the final section of this chapter, I discuss how, by putting Johnson in the context of tea, already a familiar produce for export and increasingly an important element in everyday Japanese life, Morowoka familiarizes Johnson to the Japanese reading public.

Genius and Peculiarity

Historians of the eighteenth century have regarded politeness as "one of the myths of the age," and, as Paul Langford maintains, politeness became the basic social standard in eighteenth-century Britain.[35] The examination of the behavior of, among others, scholars and authors brings to the fore conflicting expectations associated with standardized values on the one hand and individuals' intellectual originality on the other.[36] In contrast with the polite ideal, an image of Samuel Johnson as an uncouth scholar has become familiar to readers. His flair in conversation and expertise in writing go together with unsightly, inelegant, and bearish behavior.[37] One of David Garrick's friends, Lady Spencer, described her ambiguous feelings for Johnson: "Doct^r Johnson's judgement as a critic is often prejudiced, and his manners are unpolished and even brutal, but upon the whole he is one of the first geniuses we have, is possessed of great taste and extensive learning, has the strongest principles of religion, founded on the firmest conviction of the truths of Christianity."[38]

Lady Spencer's point is that Johnson's intellectual and moral virtues make up for his behavioral faults, notably arrogance and "brutality." In doing so, Lady Spencer, like many of Johnson's other contemporaries, resorts to a kind of special pleading as a way of understanding and accepting behavior that was deemed to be socially aberrant. His "otherness" stands out in the increasingly standardized society that produced numerous conduct books and manuals on regular social and personal behavior.[39] In an eighteenth-century aristocratic woman's view, the privilege of genius is to be allowed to maintain its own way, the privilege of eccentricity being generously awarded to an individual by a society that made much of politeness.[40]

Morowoka, a prewar Japanese scholar, applied his own framework in understanding Johnson. The term *Cha jin* usually means a tea master, one who is purported to have tastefully mastered the procedures of the ceremonial tea. They exemplify good taste and connoisseurship in arranging or appreciating the significance of the tea ceremony—a tea set, a seasonal flower in a nonchalantly refined vase, and a hanging scroll with calligraphy or picture. The host is to provide good tea and intelligent company to their guests with the help of literary knowledge and dilettantish accomplishments in ephemeral encounters. For the simple pleasure of enjoying tea, the host and their guests are to engage themselves in creating the locus of interaction whether in conversation or in silence. This is one of the reasons the cultured take pleasure in tea gatherings.[41] There, neatness, orderliness, and simplicity count. However, in these highly formalized procedures, deviation is paradoxically highly appreciated. Indeed, *cha jin* can also mean a person with unusual taste in the pursuit of curiosity. As a result, they can be deemed eccentric.[42] The notion of *cha jin* works as a contrivance to appreciate an invention, a deviation from the norm. By combining this *cha jin* with a romanticized notion of the poet, *cha shi jin* goes further to include the possession of unusual, iconoclastic opinions, making for a state of affairs that suggests clear parallels with Johnson's reception by his contemporaries. The acceptance and accommodation of such eccentric, antisocial individuals by society as a whole nurtures tolerance, and partly explains Morowoka's interest in Johnson, in whom he saw a great deal of himself.[43]

The topic of tea allows writers to bring together opposing states or contexts and to examine them in light of each other: the elegant and the bizarre, the luxurious and the everyday, the personal and the national, the literary and the scientific, the textual and the practical, and the great and the trivial. The disputes over tea, "the elegant and popular beverage," between the philanthropist Jonas Hanway and Johnson gave Boswell the opportunity to see "how very well a man of genius can write upon the slightest subject."[44] Hanway saw the increasing consumption of tea by the British as creating political, economic, and moral problems; he claimed that it was, as a whole, a serious national concern.[45] On the other hand, Johnson famously began his argument against Hanway and in favor of tea by confessing his personal feelings in the matter: he is a "hardened and shameless tea-drinker."[46] Boswell regarded Johnson's writing twice against the single-minded zeal of Hanway as a "condescension" motivated "chiefly to make sport" and as a means by which Johnson could ridicule the grand rigidity of Hanway.[47] Johnson's critique of Hanway, however, is not just the playful attack and self-mockery of a tea lover. One of Johnson's strengths lies in his versatility in holding various viewpoints. His aspiration to greatness is reconciled with his vindication of quotidian littleness. Isobel Grundy, for example, draws attention to Johnson's habitual structure of thought, and the comparison and simultaneous use of alternative scales that enable a juxtaposition of the great and the small. This stylistic characteristic enables Johnson to "compare one scale of measurement with another, keeping both in play,"[48] and it enables Johnson to critique Hanway's argument about tea on multiple levels. While Morowoka adamantly refuted Johnson's Christianity, he evidently much appreciated Johnson's account of tea.[49]

Conclusion

In Morowoka's argument, a conversation over tea encourages political and literary discussion where wits reign.[50] Here the idea of *wit* represents personal inventiveness as well as collective sociability. Introducing the term *wit* as borrowed from English, he explains that a wit is a genius among poets and novelists, and that wit is the capacity to create pleasure and wonder through innovation and literary skill. Morowoka argues that tea is closely connected to driving literary innovation because of its capacity to awaken and clear the mind, and, in so doing, to nurture a more refined sensibility and connoisseurship.[51] According to Morowoka, the introduction of tea to Britain in the seventeenth century invited the flowering of literature in the eighteenth century, because "Such poets as Addison and Johnson set the trend to enjoy tea and literature in the clubs."[52] In its development, wit was important both in literature and society because wit consists of cultivating pleasure and innovation in society as a whole, not just within the academy. Its emphasis is on the pleasure offered to the audience appreciating creativity; his particular wit places more clarifying emphasis on interaction and communication than the showy output by the self-contented wits. *Cha shi jin* is similar to the wit Morowoka idealizes. Both are literary and social. In other words, by reinforcing the social and conversational functions of a literary person, Morowoka presented Johnson as *cha shi jin*, an innovative and extraordinary man of letters active in society. To such a person as Morowoka, who was on the fringes of the academic community for much of his later life, this was an ideal he could pursue.

From the end of the nineteenth century, studies of Johnson in Japan emphasized his filial devotion, morality, perseverance, and the usefulness of his learning. These emphases reflected the concerns of Japan as it sought to modernize. Soon after Morowoka began to publish widely, the publication business began to have economic and political difficulties. These vicissitudes also hit the scholars who had learned Western languages and culture. Largely because of the political and cultural alterations, scholars found themselves in the situation of trying to justify what they had acquired. Accordingly, they were searching for ways to use their learning safely and effectively in their changing society. It was also an examination and vindication of their own intellectual pursuits. Morowoka adopted the aversion theory as a tool of belligerent excuse to defend his personal history: among other things, his youthful decision to opt for learning English. While this apparently nationalistic garbling justification would potentially deny part of his learning experience, namely, Western medicine, and eventually disunite his learning, he saw in Johnson an opportunity to integrate his various interests and life experiences. He saw Johnson as an eccentric, independent thinker and scholar who sought his way with his literary expertise. In addition, Johnson's collaboration with booksellers, appealing to the general reading public, presented a ready role model for a writer reliant on commercial success for his place in society.

Notes

1 For differences in Boswell's depiction of Johnson between his *Life of Johnson* and his other works, see Greg Clingham, *James Boswell, the Life of Johnson* (Cambridge: Cambridge University Press, 1992), 33–37, 79–85; W. K. Wimsatt discusses different emphases in the portrayals of Johnson by the contemporaries in "Images of Samuel Johnson," *ELH* 41, no. 3 (1974): 359–374; John Wiltshire examines various biographies, anecdotes, and visual representations of Johnson to show how the images of Dr. Johnson have been constructed in his *The Making of Dr Johnson: Icon of Modern Culture*, Icons of Modern Culture Series (Westfield, Hastings, UK: Helm Information, 2009).

2 Tamotsu Morowoka, preface to *Cha to sono bunka* (*Tea and Its Culture*) (Tokyo: Daito Press, 1937).

3 Lu Yu's *The Classic of Tea* (c. 760) was the first definitive work on tea. Morowoka published its annotated edition, *Chakyo hyoshaku* (*Commentaries on the Classic of Tea*) in 1941. Myōe was a Buddhist monk who promoted tea at its introduction in Japan.

4 For comparison, in Victor H. Mair and Erling Hoh, *The True History of Tea* (London: Thames & Hudson, 2009), Johnson makes only a very brief appearance (179–180).

5 Another poet he refers to as *cha shi jin* is Tu Tong (盧仝; 790–835), who lived as a recluse, composing innovative poems on tea (Morowoka, "Nihonbunka to cha" ("Japanese Culture and Tea"), in *Nihonbunka no seikaku* (*Japanese Culture*), edited by Shihoho hoken kyokai Shotoku (Tokyo: Bunrokusha, 1941), 305. The term *cha shi jin* was not common, while *cha shi*, tea poetry, has a long and rich tradition in China. See Tadahisa Ishikawa, *Cha wo utau shi* (*Tea Poetry in China*) (Tokyo: Kenbun, 2011).

6 Morowoka, *Cha to sono bunka,* 110, 115, 129–130.

7 Tamotsu Morowoka, "Zen to Shin-Kokka" ("Zen and a New Polity"), in *Man-Mou Koza* (*Lectures on Manchuria and Mongolia*) (Tokyo: Ritsumeikan Press, 1937), 456–457.

8 Morowoka, *Cha to sono bunka*, 134.

9 He refers to Leslie Stephen's *English Literature and Society in the Eighteenth Century* (1904), Sōseki Natsume's lectures (no title given), and Kenji Ishida, *Johnson hakase to sono mure* (*Dr. Johnson and His Circle*) (Tokyo: Kenkyusha, 1933).

10 Morowoka, *Cha to sono bunka,* 128–129, 133.

11 Tetsu Fujii, "Nihon deno Johnson juyo to kenkyu no rekishi" ("A History of Reception and Studies of Johnson in Japan") in *Eikoku bunkano kyojin Johnson* (*Samuel Johnson, a Giant of English Culture*), ed. Hideichi Eto, Shigeru Shibagaki, and Hitoshi Suwabe (Kamakura, Japan: Minato No Hito, 2009), 289–311.

12 Nathaniel Hawthorne, *Denki monogatari* (*Biographical Stories*), ed. Kiyosi Yoshida (Tokyo: Kanesashi Horyudo, [1842] 1906), 45–64.

13 For example, Monmosei, "Genkon no bungakusha" ("Recent Literary Scholars"), *Jogaku zasshi* (*Feminist Journal*) 272 (1891): 15–17; Mamashi [a playful pseudonym that could also be read as Mamako or Magamagashi], "Bungei sa dan 2: kodai no shisei to kinsei no shisen (Johnson)" ("On Literature 2: Bards Classical and Recent—Johnson," *Doshisha bungakukai zasshi* (*Doshisha University Journal of Literature*) 46 (1891): 26–27; "Hakase Samuel Johnson ryakuden" ("A Brief Biography of Dr. Samuel Johnson"), *Shonen en* (*Boys' Land)* 7, no. 73 (1891): 23–25; Teishichi Nakahara, ed. "Dokutoru Samuel Johnson shi no den" ("A Life of Dr. Samuel Johnson"), *Goyu shonen* (*Brave Boys*) (1891): 314–328; Mitsugi Uchida, "Rasselas den no sakusha" ("The Author of *Rasselas*"), *Kokumin no tomo* (*The Nation's Friend*) 222 (1894): 34–36, 223 (1894): 21–25, 224 (1894): 23–26; Mitsugi Uchida, *Johnson* [in Japanese] (Tokyo: Minyusha, 1894). For discussion of diligence and idleness, see Sarah Jordan, "Samuel Johnson and Idelness," in *The Age of Johnson: A Scholarly Annual 11*, ed. Paul J. Korshin and Jack Lynch (New York: AMS, 2000).

14 Paul J. Korshin, "Samuel Johnson's Life Experience with Poverty," in *The Age of Johnson: A Scholarly Annual 11*, 3–17.

15 *Boswell's Life of Johnson*, 1:74.

16 An afterword by Yoichi Ueno to Morowoka's *Cha* (*Tea*) (Tokyo: Taikodo, 1949), 187; Sangyo Noritsu Daigaku, ed., *Ueno Yoichi den* (*A Biography of Yoichi Ueno*) (Tokyo: Sangyo Noritsu Daigaku Press, 1967), 25. The first half of this biography is an autobiography by Ueno himself; the second half is a biography by the editorial team and Ueno's son. The parts about Morowoka are all from Ueno's own writings.

17 Morowoka, *Cha to sono bunka*, 134, 141.

18 Sangyo Noritsu Daigaku, ed., *Ueno Yoichi den,* 23, 25.

19 Masakuma Takahashi and Tamotsu Morowoka, *Shakaiteki kyoiku saku* (*On Society and Education*) (Tokyo: Kaihatsusha, 1902), 1.

20 He was a committed member of the Japan Temperance Union.

21 See Samuel Johnson, "The Vision of Theodore," in *Rasselas and Other Tales*, ed. Gwin J. Kolb, vol. 16 of *The Yale Edition of the Works of Samuel Johnson* (New Haven, CT: Yale University Press, 1990), 195–212.

22 *Jitsugyo no Nihon (Business Magazine of Japan)*, 34, no. 1 (1931): 160.

23 Ueno's afterword, *Cha*, 188.

24 As for Johnson as a champion of the modern author in the development of the book market and the traditional patronage system, see, for example, Dustin H. Griffin, *Literary Patronage in England, 1650–1800* (Cambridge: Cambridge University Press, 1996), 220–245. As for Johnson's prose style in writing in periodicals, see chapter 8 by Tadayuki Fukumoto.

25 *Fujin Club* was one of the four major periodicals for women, published between 1920 and 1988.

26 *Jitsugyo no Nihon,* popular for its articles featuring business success stories, continued its publication from 1897 until 2002, when it was suspended. The Japan Central Tea Association was established in 1884 as a parent body of local associations of tea growers and merchants to promote tea and its culture at home and abroad. Morowoka's "Tea Drinking Habit Proved Effective in Health Improvement: Medicinal Properties of Tea Scientifically Ascertained" [in English] (n.d.) was to promote tea in the U.S. market. He also emphasized women's roles in everyday tea consumption in *Gendai josei to nihon cha* (*Modern Women and Japanese Tea*) (Shizuoka, Japan: Tea Commerce & Industry's Association of Shizuoka-shi, 1938). These were part of efforts to restore the local tea industry; Shizuoka benefited from the roaring trade in tea exports in the early 1900s but suffered a decline after World War I.

27 The list of the courses in 1931 at Komazawa University includes one subject, "abnormal psychology" by Morowoka (*Komazawa daigaku bukkyo gakkai nenpo* (*Komazawa University Buddhist Studies Bulletin*) 1 (1930): 204). The president of the university, his personal acquaintance, probably invited him to teach there. Even after that, he mainly introduced himself as a medical doctor, presenting himself with the title of MD and occasionally styled himself as a professor at the Buddhist university.

28 *Fujin Club*, 11, no. 6 (1930): 358; 12, no. 4 (1931): 214–219; *Jitsugyo no Nihon* 33, no. 6 (1930): 62–65; 33, no. 7 (1930): 98–101; 33, no. 8 (1930): 61–64; 33, no. 10 (1930): 62–64.

29 Morowoka, *Cha to sono bunka*, 46.

30 Tamotsu Morowoka, *Chakyo hyoshaku gaihen* (*Supplementary Volume to Commentaries on the Classic of Tea*), (Tokyo: Shuppann kagaku sogo kenkyujo, [1943] 1978), 1.

31 Morowoka, the sixth president of the Japan Temperance Society, shared interests with Matsumoto, who published *Toyo Kinshu Taikan* (*A Survey of Temperance in the Orient*) (Osaka, Japan: Kinki Kinshu Association, 1935).

32 Morowoka, afterword to *Chakyo hyoshaku gaihen*, 1.

33 Takako Morowoka, "Chosha shouden (A short biography of the author" in *Cha*, 186.

34 Ishida, *Johnson hakase to sono mure*, 25, 45–62, 75–101.

35 Lawrence E. Klein, "Politeness and the Interpretation of the British Eighteenth Century," *Historical Journal* 45, no. 4 (2002): 870; Paul Langford, "The Uses of Eighteenth-Century Politeness," *Transactions of the Royal Historical Society* 12 (2002): 311–331; see also Paul Langford, *A Polite and Commercial People: England 1727–1783* (Oxford, UK: Oxford University Press, 1992), esp. 59–121.

36 On the relationship between talk and writing, see, for example, Catherine N. Parke, "Johnson and the Arts of Conversation," in *The Cambridge Companion to Samuel Johnson*, ed. Greg Clingham (Cambridge: Cambridge University Press, 1997), 18–33; Philip Carter discusses the scholars' difficulty in the combination of merits and deportment referring to *The Rambler* no. 14 in "Polite 'Persons': Character, Biography and the Gentlemen," *Transactions of the Royal Historical Society* 12 (2002): 341–342; see also Lawrence E. Klein, *Shaftesbury and the Culture of Politeness: Moral Discourse and Cultural Politics in Early Eighteenth-Century England* (Cambridge: Cambridge University Press, 1994), 93–96; for a discussion of the framing of the standards in personal comportment and scholarly conduct of the earlier scholars, see Anne Goldgar, *Impolite Learning: Conduct and Community in the Republic of Letters, 1680–1750* (New Haven, CT: Yale University Press, 1995).

37 Bergen Evans, introduction to James Boswell, *The Life of Samuel Johnson*, ed. Bergen Evans (New York: Modern Library, 1952), x; see also Thomas Babington Macaulay, *Life of Johnson,* ed. William Schuyler (New York and London: Macmillan, 1924), 2, 6, 13–14; Wiltshire, *The Making of Dr Johnson,* esp. 30, 34, 35.

38 Vere Brabazon Ponsonby, ed., *Georgiana: Extracts from the Correspondence of Georgiana, Duchess of Devonshire* (London: John Murray, 1955), 93.

39 Jacques Carré, ed., *The Crisis of Courtesy: Studies in the Conduct-Book in Britain, 1600–1900* (Leiden, Netherlands: E. J. Brill, 1994), 41–49; Nancy Armstrong, *Desire and Domestic Fiction: A Political History of the Novel* (New York: Oxford University Press, 1987), 59–69; Goldgar, *Impolite Learning.*

40 Helen Berry examines the eighteenth century's fascination with impolite conduct even as they took pleasure in transgressing the dominant polite code; "Rethinking Politeness in Eighteenth-Century England: Moll King's Coffee House and the Significance of 'Flash Talk': The Alexander Prize Lecture," *Transactions of the Royal Historical Society* 11 (2001): 65–81.

41 Chisako Hirose, "Cha no yu to Yedo bungaku" ("Tea and Literature in the Tokugawa Period"), in *Cha to bungei* (*Tea and Arts*) (Kyoto, Japan: Tanko, 2001), 197.

42 Shinji Nobuhiro, "Zekko bungei to cha no yu" ("Oral Arts and Tea"), in *Cha to bungee* (*Tea and Arts*) (Kyoto, Japan: Tanko, 2001), 168.

43 Morowoka was an eccentric according to Ueno (Sangyo Noritsu Daigaku, ed., *Ueno Yoichi den*, 81).

44 *Boswell's Life of Johnson*, 1:313.

45 Jonas Hanway, *A Journal of Eight Days Journey from Portsmouth to Kingston Upon Thames . . . In a Series of Sixty-Four Letters: Addressed to Two Ladies of the Partie. To Which Is Added, an Essay on Tea: Considered as Pernicious to Health: Obstructing Industry and Impoverishing the Nation . . . With Several Political Reflections on Thoughts on Public Love in Twenty-Five Letters to the Same Ladies* (London: H. Woodfall, 1756).

46 Samuel Johnson, *Literary Magazine; or, Universal Review*, no. 13 (1757), in *Johnson on Demand: Reviews, Prefaces, and Ghost-Writings*, ed. O. M. Brack Jr. and Robert

Demaria Jr., vol. 20 of *The Yale Edition of the Works of Samuel Johnson* (New Haven, CT: Yale University Press, 2018), 360.

47 *Boswell's Life of Johnson*, 1:313–314.

48 Isobel Grundy, *Samuel Johnson and the Scale of Greatness* (Athens: University of Georgia Press, 1986), 6, 235.

49 Sangyo Noritsu Daigaku, ed., *Ueno Yoichi den*, 19.

50 Markman Ellis discusses literary inspiration at coffee house in *The Coffee-House: A Cultural History* (London: Weidenfeld & Nicolson, 2004), 150–165, 185–206. See also Brian Cowan, "Mr. Spectator and the Coffeehouse Public Sphere," *Eighteenth-Century Studies* 37, no. 3 (2004): 345–366; Brian Cowan, "Café or Coffeehouse? Transnational Histories of Coffee and Sociability," in *Drink in the Eighteenth and Nineteenth Centuries*, ed Susanne Schmid and Barbara Schmidt-Haberkamp, Perspectives in Economic and Social History No. 29 (London: Pickering & Chatto, 2014), 35–46.

51 Morowoka, *Cha to sono bunka,* 69–73.

52 Morowoka, *Cha to sono bunka*, 70.

6

Johnson and Garrick on *Hamlet*

MIKI IWATA

Introduction

In *The Antitheatrical Prejudice* (1985), Jonas Barish's influential monograph on the antitheatrical tradition that lies at the very heart of Western theatrical history, Barish refers to the "Platonic overtones" of "Johnson's notorious scorn for the stage" as an English equivalent for the eighteenth-century French antitheatrical sentiment expressed by Diderot.[1] When critics discuss an eighteenth-century rupture between "stage and page," Samuel Johnson is always regarded as a central figure on the side of drama on the page. On the other hand, David Garrick (1717–1779), Johnson's former pupil in Lichfield and later a leading actor and manager at Drury Lane, unequivocally sees drama performed on the stage as superior. Michael Caines in his *Shakespeare and the Eighteenth Century* (2013), for example, names one of its chapters, "Johnson's *Plays*, Garrick's Jubilee," and contrasts the first edition of *The Plays of William Shakespeare* (1765) by Johnson with the Shakespeare Jubilee in Stratford-upon-Avon in September 1769 presided over by Garrick: "the late 1760s were remarkable, then, for producing, in the Jubilee, an event that brashly deified Shakespeare the author at the same time as his texts were coming under intense scrutiny from Johnson, the most influential critic of the age."[2] According to Caines, Garrick's Jubilee, which consisted mainly of costumed processions without a single performance of Shakespeare's plays,[3] symbolizes the emergent bardolatry. Johnson's variorum

Plays embodies a growing interest in Shakespeare from a different viewpoint: one of serious textual criticism, as opposed to simply producing new editions of the plays.

As long as we look at the jubilee and Johnson's *Plays*, this contrast is undeniably true, but it does not follow that a binary opposition can be enlarged to encompass Garrick and Johnson themselves. As Dale Townshend points out, Garrick was (especially in his earlier career) also thought of as a redeemer of true, authentic Shakespeare "through passionate and inspired performance of his dramatic roles," and the idea is well illustrated in the anonymously authored poem "Shakespeare's Ghost" (1750).[4] In the poem, Shakespeare's ghost pleads with Garrick, the Bard's Hamlet-like son,

> to vindicate my injur'd song,
> To place each character in proper light,
> To speak my words and do my meaning right,
> To save me from a dire impending fate,
> Nor yield me up to Cibber and to Tate. (ll. 84–88)

The two playwrights mentioned here—Colley Cibber (1671–1757) and Nahum Tate (1612–1715)—are the authors of notable adaptations of Shakespeare's plays. While Cibber's *Richard III* (1700) is more sensational and less rhetorical than the original—by the addition of a scene where King Edward's two young sons are murdered and by the cutting of the character of Queen Margaret—Tate's *King Lear* (1681) famously (later notoriously) transforms Shakespeare's devastating tragedy into a tragicomedy that ends happily with the victory of Lear and the marriage of Edgar and Cordelia.

When these reworkings of Shakespeare for the stage began to be questioned in the early eighteenth century in such works as John Dennis's *An Essay on the Genius and Writings of Shakespeare* (1712) and Alexander Pope's edition of Shakespeare (1725), actors could be seen either as destroyers or protectors of the poet's original text. Fortunately for Garrick, people generally thought that he belonged to the latter group, and he became interested in the burgeoning tradition of Shakespearean textual criticism. He was known for his extensive collection of old plays and quarto editions of Shakespeare. He corresponded with his French friends Jean Monnet (1703–1785), the director of the Opéra Comique in Paris, and Pierre-Antoine de Laplace (1707–1793), the first translator of Shakespeare into French after Voltaire, energetically advocating Shakespeare's true worth against the French literati's distaste for him.[5] Even though Garrick's jubilee might have promoted Shakespeare's deified status as, in Michael Dobson's words, "a ubiquitous presence in British culture," whose "reputation no longer seems to depend on his specific achievement as a dramatist," David Garrick the adaptor does not always conform to this line of interpretation.[6]

And yet, the differentiation between Garrick and Johnson in terms of stage and page was propagated by Johnson himself. Johnson ignores Garrick in his famous preface when he summarizes the history of Shakespeare criticism and the editions that were then available, from Nicholas Rowe (1709), Alexander Pope (1725), Lewis Theobald (1734), and John Upton (1746) to William Warburton (1747). To be precise, Johnson only once implies the name of Garrick in the preface, but this is to complain that he declined to let the critic read his collection of texts: "I collated such copies as I could procure, and wished for more, but have not found the collectors of these rarities very communicative."[7] Related to their disagreement, the following comment by James Boswell (1740–1795) is frequently quoted by critics: "considering the slovenly and careless manner in which books were treated by Johnson, it could not be expected that scarce and valuable editions should have been lent to him."[8]

However, Boswell's words, severed from their broader context, are a little misleading. According to Garrick, he did allow Johnson to read his rare books and lent him the key to his library. "Johnson's pride," Johnson's recent biographer Peter Martin argues, "would not let him acknowledge the favour, especially since he regarded Shakespeare's text as his own province, not Garrick's, and resented his crossing the line from stage to page through the power of his collection."[9] Because Samuel Johnson himself was eager to draw a clear line between stage and page, it was natural for later critics to follow this binary distinction. In this chapter, I would like to recalibrate the idea that the division between stage and page became clear in the era of Garrick and Johnson, and to resuscitate their ambivalent relationship by looking at their criticism of Shakespeare. This essay will thus focus on *Hamlet* (c. 1600), the only play by Shakespeare in whose notes Johnson refers to Garrick. This was also the actor's final adaptation of the Bard in his long career.

Behind the "Anti-Garrick" Shakespeare Criticism

As already mentioned, Johnson never directly mentions Garrick in his preface. Boswell records that on 19 October 1769 he "complained that he had not mentioned Garrick in his Preface to Shakespeare; and asked him if he did not admire him." Johnson's answer is as follows:

JOHNSON "Yes, as 'a poor player, who frets and struts his hour upon the stage;'—as a shadow."

BOSWELL "But has he not brought Shakspeare [*sic*] into notice?"

JOHNSON "Sir, to allow that, would be to lampoon the age. Many of Shakspeare's plays are the worse for being acted: Macbeth, for instance."

BOSWELL "What, Sir, is nothing gained by decoration and action? Indeed, I do wish that you had mentioned Garrick."[10]

In this exchange, Johnson's words appear to imply a criticism of Garrick's first attempt to adapt Shakespeare's plays: his version of *Macbeth,* which was first performed on 7 January 1744 (but not published until 1773). Compared with the preceding version by William Davenant (performed in 1664 and printed in 1674), which was still preferred as an acting text in the 1740s, Garrick's *Macbeth* could duly be described as a "restoration" of Shakespeare. Nevertheless, for Johnson, it seemed far from satisfactory. For while Garrick's version restored many of the archaic words and phrases in the original that were deleted by Davenant, he followed Davenant's stagecraft, designed to attract his audience, such as eliminating the comic porter in act 2, scene 3, and adding a dying speech for Macbeth.

Until the 1970s Johnsonian critics, such as R. W. Desai in his *Johnson on Shakespeare* (1979), could give full support to the antitheatrical tradition and assert that "when we remember that Garrick wrote a dying speech for Macbeth . . . and that he had the audacity to produce his own version of *Hamlet* . . . we can well sympathize with Johnson's disgust for the acting profession, of which Garrick was the age's greatest exponent."[11] Desai is especially acrimonious toward Garrick's *Hamlet,* as an example of "the extent to which Garrick could go in deforming Shakespeare," and in which he "omitted the grave-diggers and Ophelia's funeral, did not show the queen being poisoned on stage but let her off, only to later inform the audience that her sense of guilt had driven her insane, and showed the king defending himself vigorously against an incensed Hamlet, and finally being killed by Hamlet."[12] For Desai, Garrick's *Hamlet* represents some of the worst examples of stage adaptation of the Bard.

Notwithstanding his detailed enumeration of Garrick's deformations, however, Desai very probably did not actually read Garrick's full text. Garrick's *Hamlet* (1772) had long been thought to be lost until, in 1933, it was rediscovered by G. W. Stone, a librarian at the Folger Shakespeare Library (founded a year before). Naturally for an actor-manager, Garrick used as his source text the 1748 reprint of the acting version of *Hamlet,* first published by Robert Wilks and John Hughes in 1718, to which Garrick and others added new lines or deleted unnecessary ones for their own performance. Reconstructing Garrick's *Hamlet* from this emended Wilks–Hughes copy, Stone published the fifth act, but it had only a limited circulation. It was as late as 1982 that its full text appeared in print from Southern Illinois University Press as the fifth volume of *The Plays of David Garrick* (1980–1982).

Until then, critics of Garrick's *Hamlet* had to rely on fragmentary remarks by Garrick's contemporaries. Unfortunately, however, the most influential of these comments is neither reliable nor favorable. When *Biographia Dramatica, or a Companion to the Playhouse* was published in 1782, three years after Garrick's death, George Steevens—Johnson's coeditor in *The Works of*

Shakespeare with the Corrections and Illustrations of Various Commentators (1773)—was responsible for an article on the late actor's version of *Hamlet*. But Steevens is not complimentary:

> 10. HAMLET. Altered by Mr. Garrick. Acted at Drury Lane, 1771. This alteration was made in the true spirit of *Bottom the Weaver*, who wishes to play not only the part assigned him, but all the rest in the piece. Mr. Garrick, in short, had reduced the consequence of every character but that represented by himself; and thus, excluding Osric, the Gravediggers, &c. contrived to monopolize the attention of the audience. Our poet had furnished Laertes with a dying address, which afforded him a local advantage over the Prince of Denmark. This circumstance was no sooner observed, than the speech was taken away from the former, and adopted by the latter.[13]

Steevens's cruel sneer at every change Garrick made in *Hamlet* illustrates what Gefen Bar-On Santor calls the "quasi-religious" respect for Shakespeare's texts, with which "eighteenth-century Shakespeareans came to regard the performance of Shakespeare much as Protestants viewed the reading of the Bible . . . as a primary experience that had the potential, if done correctly, to bring the individual into contact with timeless truths."[14] To achieve this lofty goal, editors "emended his surviving texts . . . wrote exhaustive commentary on obscure words and other aspects of the text, and standardized the presentation of the plays."[15] In this context, any deviation from this process of standardization could be regarded as sacrilege.

Nevertheless, what emerges from Garrick's adaptation *per se*, which will be discussed in my final section, is somewhat different from Steevens's sarcasm. It is true that Garrick omitted many of the eye-catching scenes in act 5, but the text of *Hamlet* was (and is) obviously too long for a regular performance and most performances of the play in the late eighteenth century used abbreviated versions of the text. Compared with other versions—the 1763 text published from Hawes & Co., for example—Garrick's version has more in common with Johnson's antitheatrical taste. While the Hawes text unsparingly prunes reflective, meditational, and philosophic speeches in the play, preferring spectacular scenes to entertain the audience, Garrick did the reverse. His *Hamlet* is more a neoclassical tragedy than an eye-catching spectacle. He was conservative and radical as a man of the theater at the same time.

Furthermore, Vanessa Cunningham in *Shakespeare and Garrick* (2008) contends that Steevens was almost certainly involved in the massive reduction of the play's final act. Though Stone apparently did not notice it, she argues, there are multiple hands in the margins of the Folger Library copy of *Hamlet*, including that of Steevens. The possibility that Garrick consulted him about his version of *Hamlet* before its first performance (18 December 1772) is enhanced by an existing letter by Steevens:

> In a letter dated simply "Saturday Evening, 1771", which responds to one from Garrick, now lost, Steevens writes that he expects "great pleasure" from perusal of the alteration. . . . Steevens responds with enthusiasm: "It is a circumstance in favour of the poet which I have long been wished for". He continues: "In spite of all he [Dr. Johnson] has said on the subject, I shall never be thoroughly reconciled to tragi-comedy; . . . I am sure when you personate the Danish Prince, you wish your task concluded with the third act, after which the genius of Shakespeare retires, or only plays bo-peep through the rest of the piece."[16]

In this letter Steevens flatteringly praises Garrick's idea of producing a new *Hamlet*, and emphatically insinuates the importance of reducing the latter half of the play in order to save "the genius of Shakespeare" by removing comical and digressive scenes, thus giving the work the generic regularity of tragedy. One may then deduce that Garrick's dramaturgy in revising *Hamlet* was (at least partly) based on Steevens's advice. It is therefore odd that Steevens turned on Garrick after his death. As the *Oxford Dictionary of National Biography* entry for Steevens indicates, "it is unfortunate that Steevens should be remembered for his hoaxes and for his attacks on various of his contemporaries rather than for his valuable additions to Shakespeare scholarship."[17]

What eclipsed Garrick's reputation as the best mediator of Shakespeare of the mid-eighteenth century was a shift in editorial focus away from the theater after his death, already discernable in the Johnson–Steevens edition of 1773 in comparison with the 1765 Johnson edition. This shift made Steevens suppress his former involvement in Garrick's *Hamlet* in *Biographia Dramatica*. However, as will be discussed, Johnson's attitude toward Garrick seems not only more consistent than Steevens's but also more profoundly ambivalent than later critics have noticed.

Johnson and Garrick as Textual Critics of Shakespeare

Johnson's *Plays* refers to Garrick just once. The reference occurs not in the preface, but in a footnote to Hamlet's line, "Swear by my sword" (1.5.154 in Johnson's edition), when the prince asks Horatio and Marcellus never to reveal that they have seen the ghost. Johnson first introduces William Warburton's comment on the line, "Here the poet has preserved the manners of the ancient Danes, with whom it was 'religion' to swear upon their swords. WARBURTON," but immediately proposes a different interpretation: "I was once inclinable to this opinion, which is likewise well defended by Mr. Upton, but Mr. Garrick produced me a passage, I think in Brantôme, from which it appeared, that it was common to swear upon the sword, that is, upon the cross which the old swords always had upon the hilt."[18]

While Johnson generally respected Warburton's edition in 1747—partly because its preface set a high value on Johnson's *Miscellaneous Observations on the Tragedy of Macbeth* (1745), at the time when he was still unknown and struggling in poverty—he here gives precedence to Garrick, rejecting Warburton and Upton. Nevertheless, as is pointed out by James Gray in *Shakespeare Quarterly* 27, no. 2 (1976), the passage at issue has not been identified. There seem to be no suitable descriptions from the oeuvre of Brantôme. After his comprehensive search of the *Oeuvres Complètes de Pierre de Bourdeille, Seigneur de Brantôme*, Gray wonders, "perhaps Johnson's remarkable memory was for once at fault. It would have been reasonable for him to think of Brantôme in the context, however, both as a contemporary of Shakespeare's (ca. 1539–1614) and as an authority on war."[19]

It would not be very fruitful, after Gray, to discover the source Garrick showed Johnson. What is more noteworthy here is Johnson's critical judgment, which took the phrase "to swear by the sword" as coming from Christianity rather than from ancient Danish religion, and that the judgment was associated with his conversations with Garrick. For one thing, this shows the sagacity of his judgment; because the ghost telling his son of the murder and urging revenge is an invention Shakespeare added to his source text, a story of Amleth in Saxo Grammaticus's *Historiae Danicae* (first published in 1514), the playwright had no suitable lines from the twelfth-century Danish historian to reuse for the scene. It seems reasonable to assume, therefore, that the basic cultural context behind the lines is early modern English rather than early medieval Danish. In fact, many modern editions of *Hamlet* approve of Johnson's interpretation: the line "Upon my sword" is glossed in Philip Edwards's edition of the play for the New Cambridge Shakespeare series (1985) as "The hilt forms a cross," and in the Arden Third Series *Hamlet* (2006), edited by Ann Thompson and Neil Taylor, with the comment, "The hilt of a sword could be used to stand in for a crucifix, as at *R2*, 1.3.179."[20]

Another important aspect of Johnson's footnote is that, as mentioned, he associates Hamlet's expression with his conversation with Garrick. Whatever book (if any) the actor showed him, Johnson's (perhaps deliberately) periphrastic descriptions suggest that Garrick proposed the reading of the sword as a substitute cross, with which Johnson agreed, possibly somewhat reluctantly. Though Johnson would not admit it publicly, Garrick was far from ignorant of the contemporary debate over Shakespeare's text, as can be seen in his letter to Charles Yorke (1722–1770) written on "Xmas Day" 1768. In the letter, Garrick, hating to "appear ignorant" at Yorke's table and showing off his knowledge, reports the vigorous discussion he had with his friend Daniel Wray on the previous night about the word "mobled," which occurs in the player's account of Hecuba:

> This was my case—when we talk'd about Hamlet, & the Mobled Queen—he [Wray] ask'd me what was Mobled? I answer'd *Clouted*—but something running in my head, & the Demon of Criticism, (slipping down with ye Burgundy) possessing me at ye Instant; I said, is it not Mob-led?—When I return'd home, & was looking into a Memorandum book, where I had collected Every Scrap about Shakepear [*sic*], I found that I had met with this interpretation of Mobled, in some pamphlet, or Other, and that I had written under it—absurd and ridiculous—and most certainly it is so—Dr Warburton says—Mobled, or Mabled signifies, veiled—Johnson—huddled or grosly cover'd—Capel has it—Ennobl'd Queen—wch I don't understand—Shakespeare certainly means, wretchedly clad.[21]

While Garrick laughs at the overreaching enthusiasm for Shakespearean textual criticism, introducing a far-fetched interpretation of "mobled" as "mob-led," he is, at the same time, so intrigued by the subject that he makes demonstrations of his expertise and opinions of his own. In the latter half of the quotation, he lists the previous editors' interpretations—Warburton's "veiled", Johnson's "grossly cover'd," and Edward Capel's "Ennobl'd"—but, once again, his own view ("wretchedly clad") most resembles that of Johnson.

Johnson's contempt for Garrick's intellectual ability with regard to Shakespeare criticism is widely known. Boswell in his *Journal of a Tour to the Hebrides* (1785) laments that "Dr. Johnson is often too hard on our friend Mr. Garrick," and introduces a witty but cruel example in a footnote: when Garrick after his retirement said that he would from now on "sit down and read Shakespeare," according to information Boswell heard from Edmund Malone, Johnson exclaimed "''Tis time you should . . . for I much doubt if you ever examined one of his plays from first scene to the last.'"[22] Nevertheless, behind this kind of haughty attitude, Johnson and Garrick had much in common in terms of *reading* Shakespeare. The two small examples from *Hamlet* discussed previously—"to swear by my sword" and "the mobled queen"—suggest that not only Johnson but also Garrick had good judgment about how to interpret obsolete words and phrases in Shakespeare and that they occasionally influenced each other. Johnson, of course, still had far greater influence on scholarship. However, their mutual influence is not confined to textual criticism. Johnson and Garrick could also have affected each other in the domain of performance.

The Hidden Emotional Aspect of Johnson's Drama Criticism

It may sound unlikely that Garrick's acting style affected Johnson's reading or vice versa. While Garrick was renowned for his emotionally charged acting style, and was felt to be especially good at representing a mind divided between two extreme sentiments, like fear and anger, the keynote to Johnson's approach to Shakespeare is often considered to be "rational," which should be applied both to the playwright and to the reader.

Francis Gentleman (1728–1784), comparing Garrick's performance in the role of Jaffier in Thomas Otway's *Venice Preserv'd* (1682) with that of Spranger Barry (1719–1777), gives a decision in favor of the former. He warns himself that a judge should be cautious because "Jaffier is weak, irresolute, rash, affectionate, cruel, friendly, treacherous; an unnatural compound of such as never were jumbled in the heart of man"—in short, a character on whose behalf it is difficult to engage the audience's sympathy—and because "Messrs. GARRICK and BARRY has such an equality of merit in the representation of Jaffier."[23] And yet, as Gentleman's report progresses, he become more and more partial to Garrick: "Where Belvidera is delivered to the conspirators, we must give Mr. GARRICK considerable preference, for looks most powerfully expressive, and piercing notes of expression. In the first scene of the third act equality [between Garrick and Barry] again took place; the short subsequent interviews with Pierre and Renault were manifestly on Mr. GARRICK's side, whose merit has caused us to lament, that what the author has written so censurably, should be rendered so agreeable in action."[24]

For Gentleman, Garrick's powerful facial as well as vocal expressions move the audience so much as to arouse sympathy in them, even against the author's intention, a sign of the power and ability of the actor. For Johnson, however, it would have been a lamentable deficiency in the performance that deforms the original's didactic purpose. As Walter Jackson Bate deftly summarizes, Johnson's *Plays* is based on a quite different discipline: "the *Preface* is drenched and permeated—creatively, magnificently—by this one supreme value, 'the stability of truth.'"[25] "Stability" here implies two different, but interrelated meanings. Any work of art, according to Johnson's belief, should convey an immutable truth or a moral to enlighten the mind of the reader or audience; at the same time, these unchangeable qualities should be taught not through superficial and ephemeral sensations, but through deep and unfaltering reason.

Thus, Johnson famously grieves in his preface that Shakespeare "sacrifices virtue to convenience, and is so much more careful to please than to instruct, that he seems to write without any moral purpose."[26] Additionally, he does not forget to give players a warning: "a play read, affects the mind like a play acted. It is therefore evident, that the action is not supposed to be real."[27] The latter quotation has been often regarded as an example of Johnson's multifaceted antiperformance prejudice, especially against Garrick's acting style. James Harriman-Smith, for instance, argues that, while Johnson's view is antitheatrical in a traditional sense "in that it at best equates and at worst subordinates the stage to the page," Johnson also prefigures the Romantic version of it—"the version of the play that exists in the mind."[28]

It is true that throughout his life Johnson did not hide his distaste for "those enthusiasts who believe yourself transformed into the very character you represent," but it does not necessarily follow that he was not moved by a sensational performance.[29] Reading Johnson's commentary on Shakespeare's plays, one may notice that he often reacts quite emotionally to them. One of the most famous is his approbation of the ending in Nahum Tate's version of *King Lear*, because "Shakespeare has suffered the virtue of Cordelia to perish in a just cause contrary to the natural ideas of justice," something neither Johnson himself nor the wider public was able to endure.[30] While Johnson is equipped with a rational justification of his preference for Tate—"since all reasonable beings naturally love justice, I cannot easily be persuaded, that the observation of justice makes a play worse"—he also betrays an emotional motive in the next paragraph: "I was many years ago so shocked by Cordelia's death, that I know not whether I ever endured to read again the last scenes of the play till I undertook to revise them as an editor."[31] Consequently, his claim that "a play read, affects the mind like a play acted," could represent his hypersensitive immersion (even like that of a naïve spectator) in plays rather than his disdain for theatrical performance.

Johnson found editing *King Lear* particularly mentally exhausting; he also writes of "the extrusion of Gloucester's eyes," that it "seems an act too horrid to be endured in dramatick exhibition, and such as must always compel the mind to relieve its distress by incredulity."[32] In the eighteenth century, the lack of probability of Shakespeare's plots was often lamented by neoclassical critics, including Johnson himself. Interestingly, however, Johnson here focuses more on the reader's psychological defense mechanism than on the author's unskillfulness as the reason the scene looks implausible. As Leopold Damrosch has pointed out, "while he often quoted Shakespeare in contexts of personal suffering, this tells us more about Johnson than about Shakespeare."[33]

There are many other examples of Johnson's overidentification with Shakespeare's characters. On Desdemona's death, Johnson writes, "I am glad that I have ended my revisal of this dreadful scene. It is not to be endured."[34] He is also very sympathetic to Richard II in his decline, paying little attention to his showy self-pity: "it seems to be the design of the poet to raise Richard to esteem in his fall, and consequently to interest the reader in his favour."[35] For the generally well-balanced critic, this sounds strikingly indulgent, and has even led certain critics like Matthew M. Davis to discuss this attitude in the context of Johnson's hidden sympathy for the Stuart cause.[36] However, this can also be interpreted as Johnson's genuine human sympathy for a man who, deprived of all the power to which he was accustomed, has to face destruction.

Johnson's supposedly "rational" approach to Shakespeare can be construed as a defensive reaction to his own sentimental inclination. He could have disliked "those enthusiasts," players who identify themselves with characters they assume, all the more because he was irresistibly affected by them. Damrosch explains this mechanism as follows: "even though Johnson was fond of applying Shakespearean passages to his own emotional needs, his considered view of the plays can almost be said to repudiate that emotional experience," hence in "assessing his conception of Shakespeare's tragedies, one should probably take the word *rational* as the keynote."[37] And this self-denying academic stoicism can be seen in his comments on *Hamlet*, to which I now return.

Garrick's *Hamlet* as a Bridge between Stage and Page

Judging from his comments on *Hamlet*, Johnson seemed to find reading that play as shocking an experience as reading *King Lear*. At the close of act 3, scene 3, Hamlet, finding Claudius kneeling by himself, thinks it a good opportunity for revenge. However, he then gives up the idea because killing Claudius when he is at prayer will cleanse his sins and send him up to heaven. Thus, Hamlet concludes,

> Then trip him, that his heels may kick at heav'n;
> And that his soul may be as damn'd and black
> As hell, whereto it goes. (3.3.93–95 in Johnson's edition)

Johnson comments on this passage: "this speech, in which Hamlet, represented as a virtuous character, is not content with taking blood for blood, but contrives damnation for the man that he would punish, is too horrible to be read or to be uttered."[38] As for the poetically just death of King Claudius in the final scene of *Hamlet*, Johnson laments, in a way not much different from his grievance about Cordelia's death, that "the gratification which would arise from the destruction of an usurper and a murderer, is abated by the untimely death of Ophelia, the young, the beautiful, the harmless, and the pious."[39] Because Johnson's moral principle is interconnected with his sense of probability, his concluding remarks, not unexpectedly, include the following reservation: "the poet is accused of having shewn little regard to poetical justice, and may be charged with equal neglect of poetical probability."[40]

This double fault of *Hamlet* is, in Johnson's view, most conspicuously displayed in the protagonist. First, Hamlet does not appear to have a strong, consistent character, and therefore "Hamlet is, through the whole play, rather an instrument than an agent."[41] Even after he is convinced that Claudius murdered King Hamlet, "he makes no attempt to punish him, and his death is at last effected by an incident which Hamlet has no part in producing."[42] Moreover, because "the exchange of weapons [in the bout with Laertes] is rather an expedient of necessity, than a stroke of art," Johnson even wonders that "a scheme might easily have been formed, to kill Hamlet with the dagger, and Laertes with the bowl."[43] Johnson's sense of poetic justice would not allow a protagonist in a tragedy to die accidentally, without some clear and great cause for which he could take responsibility. While Johnson's sensibility begrudgingly accepts young Ophelia's madness and death by drowning, his reason demands that Hamlet should die more nobly, fulfilling his duty of revenge as a son and taking responsibility for what he has done as a prince.

In contrast with Johnson's serious, moral reading of the tragedy, David Garrick's alteration of *Hamlet* (first performed on 18 December 1772) has often been regarded as a histrionic deformation of Shakespeare. Nevertheless, on closer inspection, Garrick's version approximates itself to Johnson's views of the play. Though Garrick keeps Hamlet passing Claudius at prayer in act 3, scene 3 (act 4, scene 1, in the Garrick version)—possibly in order to cater to the theatergoers' taste—there is a curious textual manipulation in the scene. Because the play's text is too long to be acted on stage, Garrick marks the lines to be left out in performance with apostrophes, and the scene at issue reads as follows:

> Then trip him, that his heels may kick at heaven,
> ' And that his soul may be as damned and black
> ' As hell whereto it goes.' My mother stays.
> This physic but prolongs thy sickly days. (4.1.595–598)[44]

Here, Garrick as Hamlet, avoiding the two sensationalistic lines that made Johnson shudder, is to speak simply, "Then trip him, that his heels may kick at heaven, / This physic but prolongs thy sickly days," which would make the prince sound less cruel and despicable. When it comes to the final act, with which both Steevens and Johnson are so discontented, Garrick's response is more interventionist. He reduces the fourth and fifth acts of the original so drastically that, immediately after mad Ophelia exits, singing, "And will he not come again?" (which happens in act 4, scene 5 in Shakespeare, but in act 5, scene 2 in Garrick), the scene suddenly jumps to the graveyard (but without any graveyard, much less gravediggers). Laertes's lamentation over his deranged sister is replaced by his rage at her funeral and is then interrupted by the similarly enraged Hamlet. By radically curtailing the last quarter of the play, the altered version succeeds in both removing the comic relief of the gravediggers and Osric (widely held to be an abomination in neoclassicist readings of the play) and in making the fate of Ophelia quite ambiguous.

Furthermore, Garrick's version endeavors to make it crystal clear that *Hamlet* is a revenge tragedy of Hamlet on Claudius for his father's death. Listening to the heated argument between Hamlet and Laertes, Claudius orders the guards to take the prince into custody (following the editors of *The Plays of David Garrick* [1980–1982], lines which Garrick composed and added are italicized):

> KING. . . . *Affection hitherto has curbed my power,*
> *But you have trampled on allegiance,*
> *And now shall feel my wrath.—Guards!*
> HAMLET. *First feel mine!—(Stabs him.)*
> Here, thou incestuous, murd'rous, damned Dane.
> *There's for thy treachery, lust, and usurpation!*
> KING. O yet defend me, friends; I am but hurt—(*Falls and dies.*)
> QUEEN. *O mercy, heaven!—Save me from my son*—(*Runs out*).
> LAERTES. *What treason, ho! Thus then do I revenge*
> *My father, sister, and my King—*
> Hamlet *runs upon* Laertes's *sword and falls.*
> HORATIO. *And I, my prince and friend*—(*Draws.*)
> HAMLET. *Hold, good Horatio! 'Tis the hand of heav'n*
> *Administers by him this precious balm*
> *For all my wounds.* (5.2.294–307)[45]

In this version, Hamlet does not need the accidental motive of his mother's death by poison to revenge his father. Compared with Shakespeare's lines immediately followed by "Here, thou incestuous, murd'rous, damned Dane"—"Drink off this potion. Is thy union here? / Follow my mother" (5.2.311)[46]—Garrick's lines remain focused more on the father–son relationship. His death is also quite different from the original. Imitating the ancient Roman custom, Hamlet commits suicide by intentionally pushing himself onto the point of Laertes's sword. That Hamlet is deliberately killing himself to bring the cycle of revenge to an end is confirmed by his stopping Horatio from fighting with Laertes. Also noteworthy is Gertrude's disappearance from the stage because the contrivance, as in the case of Ophelia, relieves the play's finale from another accidental death of a female character (though it is suggested that she has swooned with agony and horror and will be insane before long). In general, however absurd this acting version may appear now, Garrick in fact adapts *Hamlet* with studious care to comply with the demands of neoclassicist critics, especially those of Johnson.

Though this influence is now quite obscure to us, it might have been less so for Garrick's contemporaries. Garrick wrote to his friend Pierre-Antoine de

Laplace on 3 January 1773, about two weeks after the first performance of this version of *Hamlet.* The now fifty-five-year-old actor is still highly excited at his experiment and takes pride in his success like a child:

> I am still upon ye Stage, & am so flatter'd by my Country's partiality to Me, that I have not yet been able to retire—just before Christmas I appear'd in the Character of the *Young* Hamlet, and receiv'd more applause than when I acted it at five & twenty. . . . I must tell You that I have ventur'd to alter Hamlet, & have greatly Succeeded; I have destroy'd ye Grave diggers, (those favourites of the people) & almost all of ye 5th Act—it was a bold Deed, but ye Event has answer'd my most sanguine expectation: if you correspond with any of the Journalists, this circumstance will be worth telling, as it is a great Anecdote in our theatrical history—[47]

The euphoric tone of the letter clearly shows that the performance was a commercial success, notwithstanding his "destroying" (as he admits) almost the entire final act, including the audience's favorite comic scenes. Garrick thinks this is a feat bold enough for French journalism to treat as a historical event—as an example of "enlightened Shakespeare" worthy of the French literati's notice. Of course, this does not mean that everybody was happy with Garrick's adaptation at the time. Arthur Murphy wrote a satiric farce, *Hamlet, with Alterations* (circulated privately before being published in 1811), which is set on "December 15, 1772"—three days before the première of the Garrick version. Closely following the structure of the first act of *Hamlet*, the farce makes parallels between the rotten Elsinore and Drury Lane under Garrick's management, and between the avenging ghost and the abused Shakespeare. However, Murphy's work is not so much a satire on Garrick's adaptation as a general personal attack. At the time, Murphy and Garrick repeatedly fell out and reconciled over Garrick's choices of plays for the stage; in 1772, Murphy was angry about the actor-manager's greedy attitude toward the success of his tragedy, *The Grecian Daughter*. In short, when Garrick performed his *Hamlet*, it was not degrading to his reputation. As Cunningham duly indicates, it is "after Garrick's death in 1779" that "the split between stage and page widened," and Steevens's harsh, cruel attack on Garrick's *Hamlet* in *Biographia Dramatica* (1782) should be read in this context.[48]

Similarly, being written in the post-Garrick cultural ambience, *The Life of Garrick* (1801) by a becalmed Murphy is more sympathetic to the actor and tactfully evasive about the merit of Garrick's alterations at the same time: "the rage for re-touching, and, as it was said, correcting and improving our best authors, was the very error of the times. Colman, with an unhallowed hand, had defaced the tragedy of King Lear. Bickerstaff was another precedent, and, unhappily, Garrick was infected with the contagion."[49] Laying the blame not on the person but on the times was a tactful way of handling an adaptation which by then was quite out of date and had lost almost all the meaning it once had.

Unfortunately, Boswell's *Life of Johnson* reports nothing about Johnson's immediate (as well as later) reactions to Garrick's *Hamlet*, partly because he was visiting Scotland during the autumn and winter months of the relevant year, whereas Johnson, refusing Boswell's invitation, stayed in London. Johnson's total silence on this theme might mean that he simply thought it was not worthy of mention. And yet, it is equally possible that he was inwardly appreciative to some degree of his ex-pupil's effort to answer his comments on the play. Perhaps the lines he composed for Garrick a quarter of a century previously, his prologue for the opening of Drury Lane in 1747—the first season under Garrick's management—may best represent Johnson's general idea of Garrick's adaptation: "Hard is his lot that here by fortune placed / Must watch the wild vicissitudes of taste" (ll. 47–48).[50] Johnson must have been able to imagine this kind of difficulty, because he himself was divided between a text-based devotion to reason and histrionic sensibility.

Notes

1 Jonas Barish, *The Antitheatrical Prejudice* (Berkeley: University of California Press, 1985), 280.

2 Michael Caines, *Shakespeare and the Eighteenth Century* (Oxford, UK: Oxford University Press, 2013), 112. Hereafter, Johnson's *The Plays of William Shakespeare* will be abbreviated as *Plays*.

3 The only use of Shakespeare's words at all was an adaptation of a single line from *Hamlet*—"I shall not look upon his like again" (1.2.187)—in Garrick's *Ode upon Dedicating a Building and Erecting a Statue to Shakespeare* (1769). For further details, see Kate Rumbold, "Shakespeare and the Stratford Jubilee," In *Shakespeare in the Eighteenth Century*, ed. Fiona Ritchie and Peter Sabor (Cambridge: Cambridge University Press, 2014), 254–276.

4 Dale Townshend, "Gothic and the Ghost of *Hamlet*," in *Gothic Shakespeares*, ed. John Drakakis and Dale Townshend (London: Routledge, 2008), 61. The poem is also quoted from Townshend's essay.

5 For Shakespeare's obscurity in France until the mid-eighteenth century and Garrick's journeys to Paris in 1751 and 1763 promoting Shakespeare's reputation among the French literati, see Frank A. Hedgecock, *David Garrick and His French Friends* (London: Stanley Paul, 1911), 191–237.

6 Michael Dobson, *The Making of the National Poet: Shakespeare, Adaptation and Authorship 1660–1769* (Oxford, UK: Clarendon Press, 1992), 214.

7 Samuel Johnson, *Johnson on Shakespeare*, 2 vols., ed. Arthur Sherbo (New Haven, CT: Yale University Press, 1968), 1:105.

8 *Boswell's Life of Johnson*, 2:192.

9 Peter Martin, *Samuel Johnson: A Biography* (Cambridge, MA: Belknap Press of Harvard University, 2008), 331.

10 *Boswell's Life of Johnson*, 2:92.

11 R. W. Desai, *Johnson on Shakespeare* (New Delhi, India: Orient Longman, 1979), 47.
12 Desai, *Johnson on Shakespeare*, 47.
13 David Erskine Baker and Isaac Reed, eds., *Biographia Dramatica, or a Companion to the Playhouse* (London: Longman et al., [1782] 1812), 2:278–289.
14 Gefen Bar-On Santor, "Shakespeare in the Georgian Theatre," in *The Oxford Handbook of the Georgian Theatre, 1737–1832*, ed. Julia Swindells and David Francis Taylor (Oxford, UK: Oxford University Press, 2014), 213.
15 Santor, "Shakespeare in the Georgian Theatre," 215.
16 Vanessa Cunningham, *Shakespeare and Garrick* (Cambridge: Cambridge University Press, 2008), 147.
17 *Oxford Dictionary of National Biography*, s.v. "Steevens, George." doi.org/10.1093/ref:odnb/26355.
18 Johnson, *Johnson on Shakespeare*, 2:971. Johnson's citation from Warburton is from the same page.
19 James Gray, "'Swear by My Sword': A Note in Johnson's Shakespeare," *Shakespeare Quarterly* 27, no. 2 (1976): 206. (Gray used the Paris 1873 edition of Brantôme.)
20 William Shakespeare, *Hamlet*, ed. Philip Edwards (Cambridge: Cambridge University Press, 1985), 112; and William Shakespeare, *Hamlet*, ed. Ann Thompson and Neil Taylor (London: Bloomsbury, 2006), 223. For Joseph Pearce, the expression reveals not only Shakespeare's Christianity in general, but his secret sympathy toward Catholicism: "In insisting that 'faith alone' is not sufficient, Hamlet and the Ghost are taking the Catholic side in the dispute between the Protestant belief in *sola fide* (by faith alone) and the Catholic doctrine of *fide et operibus* (by faith and works)" (Pearce, *Through Shakespeare's Eyes: Seeing the Catholic Presence in the Plays* (San Francisco: Ignatius Press, 2010), 162).
21 David Garrick, *The Letters of David Garrick*, ed. David M. Little and George M. Kharl, 3 vols. (Oxford, UK: Oxford University Press, 1963), 2:632, letter no. 525. The phrase placed in the paragraph just before the independent quotation—"appear ignorant"—is also cited from the same letter.
22 James Boswell, *The Journal of a Tour to the Hebrides, with Samuel Johnson, 1773*, ed. F. A. Pottle and C. H. Bennet (London: William Heinemann, 1963), 207.
23 Michael Caines, Paul Goring, Nicola Shaughnessy, Robert Shaughnessy, Gail Marshall, and Tetsuo Kishi, eds., *Lives of Shakespearian Actors I: David Garrick, Charles Macklin and Margaret Woffington by Their Contemporaries*, 3 vols. (London: Pickering & Chatto, 2008), 1:146–147.
24 Caines et al., *Lives of Shakespearian Actors I*, 1:147.
25 Walter Jackson Bate, *Samuel Johnson* (New York: Harcourt Brace, 1977), 402.
26 Johnson, *Johnson on Shakespeare*, 1:71.
27 Johnson, *Johnson on Shakespeare*, 1:79.
28 James Harriman-Smith, "The Anti-Performance Prejudice of Shakespeare's Eighteenth-Century Editors," *Restoration and Eighteenth-Century Theatre Research* 29, no. 2 (2014): 59.
29 *Boswell's Life of Johnson*, 4, 243. The quotation is from Johnson's question to the actor Phillip Kemble (1757–1823): "Are you, Sir, one of those enthusiasts . . . ?"
30 Johnson, *Johnson on Shakespeare*, 2:704.
31 Johnson, *Johnson on Shakespeare*, 2:704.
32 Johnson, *Johnson on Shakespeare*, 2:703.
33 Leopold Damrosch, *Samuel Johnson and the Tragic Sense* (Princeton, NJ: Princeton University Press, 1972), 200.

34 Johnson, *Johnson on Shakespeare*, 2:1041.
35 Johnson, *Johnson on Shakespeare*, 1:440.
36 Some recent criticism has doubted Johnson's loyalty to the Hanoverians. However, Davis's conclusion is wisely moderate: "Johnson's notes on Richard II [sic] do not prove that Johnson was a Jacobite and a Nonjuror, but they do suggest that the Tory Johnson had at least 'a kind of liking' for both causes." See Matthew M. Davis, "'Elevated Notions of the Right of Kings': Stuart Sympathies in Johnson's Notes to *Richard II*," in *Samuel Johnson in Historical Context*, ed. Jonathan Clark and Howard Erskine-Hill (Houndmills, UK: Palgrave, 2002), 259.
37 Damrosch, *Samuel Johnson*, 201.
38 Johnson, *Johnson on Shakespeare*, 2:990.
39 Johnson, *Johnson on Shakespeare*, 2:1011.
40 Johnson, *Johnson on Shakespeare*, 2:1011.
41 Johnson, *Johnson on Shakespeare*, 2:1011.
42 Johnson, *Johnson on Shakespeare*, 2:1011. (Hamlet's certainty of Claudius's guilt is clear from the play-within-the-play scene in act 3, scene 2.)
43 Johnson, *Johnson on Shakespeare*, 2:1011.
44 David Garrick, *The Plays of David Garrick*, ed. H. W. Pedicord and F. L. Bergmann, 7 vols. (Carbondale: Southern Illinois University Press, 1980–1982), 5:302.
45 Garrick, *Plays*, 5:322–23.
46 Shakespeare, *Hamlet*, ed. Philip Edwards, 238.
47 Garrick, *Letters*, 2:840.
48 Cunningham, *Shakespeare and Garrick*, 164.
49 Arthur Murphy, *The Life of David Garrick*, 2 vols. (London: J. Wright, 1801), 2:82.
50 Samuel Johnson, *The Major Works*, ed. Donald Greene (Oxford, UK: Oxford University Press, 2000), 10.

7

Abyssinian Johnson

NORIYUKI HATTORI

Introduction

Rasselas (1759) has long been considered an oriental tale, but of a very particular kind. While the tale has clearly been influenced by the popular eighteenth-century form of the oriental or Eastern tale, such as Johnson's own "The Story of Seged, King of Ethiopia,"[1] which appeared in numbers 204 and 205 of *The Rambler,* it is unusual in being set in Abyssinia, modern-day Ethiopia. While other "oriental" tales that appear in *The Rambler* are set in East Asia, India, Hindostan, and Timur, Johnson had a long-standing interest in Abyssinia—he had translated Jeronimo Lobos's *Travels to Abyssinia* when he was twenty-nine years old—and he importantly chooses the same geographical and cultural setting for *Rasselas.*[2] In this chapter I seek to explore some of the imaginative and paradoxical implications of Johnson's choice of Abyssinia for the setting of his tale. In the eighteenth-century European imagination, Abyssinia occupied two powerful and seemingly contradictory positions. As part of the Ottoman Empire, it loomed large as a locus of oriental history, power, and exoticism, while at the same time it was known to be the origin of Coptic Christianity.[3] How do these associations play out in Johnson's handling of a form that had become popular since the publication of Antoine Galland's French translation of *One Thousand and One Nights* (1704–1717)?[4]

By way of exploring Johnson's use of the oriental trope in his handling of Abyssinia, I shall place *Rasselas* in the context of several other late seventeenth- and eighteenth-century works that also locate themselves in Africa, if not Abyssinia itself. By making certain contrasts and comparisons with moments in Aphra Behn's *Oroonoko* (1688), Lady Mary Wortley Montagu's *Turkish Embassy Letters* (composed 1717–1718, published 1763), Daniel Defoe's *Captain Singleton* (1720), and Johnson's own *Journey to the Western Isles of Scotland* (1775), I aim to suggest Johnson's distinctive use of Abyssinia as a setting in *Rasselas*.

The Oriental Seraglios of *Oroonoko* and *The Turkish Embassy Letters*

The hero of *Oroonoko* is the prince of Coramantien (a region situated on the west coast of Africa, roughly corresponding to the modern nation of Ghana) who is abducted and sold into slavery in Surinam. Aphra Behn had personal knowledge of Surinam, which she describes realistically. When writing about West Africa, however, where she could not draw on personal experience, Behn's account of the country is less reliable. In her account of the West African country Behn uses tropes that are usually associated with "oriental" fiction in the seventeenth and eighteenth centuries: an autocratic ruler and transgressive sexual behavior, as well as the conventional settings of bath house and seraglio. For example, Oroonoko's grandfather, the king, has a seraglio with many wives and mistresses, but he develops an unnatural passion for Oroonoko's fiancé Imoinda. He forces her to come to his seraglio: "They brought her thus to court, and the king, who had caused a very rich bath to be prepared, was led into it where he sat under a canopy in state to receive this longed-for virgin, whom he having commanded should be brought to him, they (after derobing her) led her to the bath and, making fast the doors, left her to descend. The king, without more courtship, bade her throw off her mantle and come to his arms."[5]

Ignoring Imoinda's ardent solicitation for mercy, the old man forces her to receive his caresses, and holds her in miserable captivity in the Otan (seraglio). The narrator reveals, however, that, "alas . . . [the old king] could but innocently play" "with this gay thing [Imoinda]," suggesting his sexual impotence, in contrast to Oroonoko, who "ravished in a moment what his old grand-father had been endeavoring for so many months."[6]

In contrast to Behn's depiction of the salacious and male-centered nature of the Eastern bath house, associated with captivity and rape, Lady Mary Wortley Montagu's *Turkish Embassy Letters* (1763) offers us a vision, apparently based on empirical observation and personal experience, of the Eastern bath as highlighting the autonomy and the beauty of female sexuality.

The question of how much Montagu witnessed and how much she imagined in her evocative account of the Turkish bath houses is difficult to determine. Certainly, she accompanied her husband, the British ambassador to the

Ottoman Empire (1716–1718), and she writes how "I ramble every day, wrap'd up in my ferigé and asmak, about Constantinople and amuse my selfe with seeing all that is curious in it."[7] The bath houses of Constantinople were a cultural mixture of West and East, combining the advanced plumbing technology of Rome with exquisite massage techniques of the East Indies. Resisting the prevalent association of Turkish bath houses with sexual licentiousness,[8] Montagu describes a very different reality, in which women of different ages and different social classes accept and embrace their sexuality while mingling in a kind of social ease and harmony, beyond the gaze of men, as we see in Montagu's account in Letter 26:

> I know no European Court where the Ladys would have behav'd them selves in so polite a manner to a stranger.
>
> I believe, upon the whole, there were 200 Women and yet none of those disdainful smiles or satyric whispers that never fail in our assemblys when any body appears that is not dress'd exactly in fashion. . . . The first sofas were cover'd with Cushions and rich Carpets, on which sat the Ladys; and on the 2nd their slaves behind 'em, but without any distinction of rank by their dress, all being in the state of nature, that is, in plain English, stark naked, without any Beauty or deffect conceal'd, yet there was not the least wanton smile or immodest Gesture amongst 'em. They Walk'd and mov'd with the same majestic Grace, which Milton describes our General Mother. There were many amongst them, as exactly proportion'd as ever any Goddess was drawn by the pencil of a Guido or Titian, and most of their skins shineingly white, only adorn'd by their Beautiful Hair divided into many tresses hanging on their shoulders, braided either with pearl or riband, perfectly representing the figures of the Graces. I was here convinc'd of the Truth of a Refflexion that I have often made, that if twas the fashion to go naked, the face would be hardly observ'd. I perceiv'd, that the Ladys with the finest skins and finest shapes had the greatest share of my admiration, thÔ their faces were sometimes less beautiful than those of their companions. . . . so many fine Women naked in different postures, some in conversation, some working, others drinking Coffee or sherbet, and many negligently lying on their Cushions, while their slaves (generally pritty girls of 17 or 18) were employ'd in braiding their hair in several pritty manners. In short, tis the Women's cofffée-house, where all the news of the Town is told, Scandal invented, etc. They generally take this diversion once a-week, and stay there at least 4 or 5 hours without getting cold by immediate coming out of the hot bath into the cool room, which was very surprizing to me.[9]

As Isobel Grundy discusses at length, "Lady Mary was delighted by the beauty and courtesy of the scene,"[10] not least because this was where women in eighteenth-century Constantinople had a chance of meeting freely and socially.

While Behn and Montagu are both interested in female sexuality, the seraglio, and the baths, their works suggest two very different ways in which these tropes intersect and appeal to the Western imagination.

Captain Singleton: Anti-Oriental Africa

In 1720, when *Captain Singleton* was published, central Africa had hardly been explored by Europeans so they knew almost nothing about it. Taking advantage of this situation, Defoe presents the fictional character Captain Singleton crossing the African continent from Madagascar, where he is abandoned as a young man, to west Guinea. Singleton is at a loss whether to take the route northward to the Red Sea, west across the continent, or south to the Cape of Good Hope. He dismisses the third because the seas around the cape are notoriously dangerous. He is afraid of the first because of the danger of abduction and enslavement by Arab pirates in Ethiopia and Egypt, then part of the Ottoman Empire. He chooses the western route.

Despite this choice, Singleton and his crew remain interested in the passage north on account of the then-prevalent obsession with the pursuit of the source of the Nile. Since ancient times, the source of the Nile was believed to be in the legendary Mountains of the Moon, as we see on the world map of Ptolemy (c. 100–c. 170 A.D.), where two rivers flow out of the Mountains of the Moon to be combined as the Nile, which corresponds to the White Nile of today.[11] However, part of their interest is also practical: if they happen to find the source of the river and follow it northward by boat, they might thus escape from the depths of Africa. Having advanced 1,800 kilometers inland, they do, in fact, find a river. The gunner enthusiastically insists that this river must be close to the source of the Nile.

> We found [the river] run Northward, which was the first Stream we had met with that did so; it run [*sic*] with a very rapid current, and our Gunner pulling out his Map, assured me that this was either the River Nile, or run [*sic*] into the great Lake; out of which the River Nile was said to take its Beginning; and he brought out his Carts and Maps, which by his Instruction, I began to understand very well; and told me, he would convince me of it, and indeed he seemed to make it so plain to me, that I was of the same Opinion.[12]

Singleton's crossing of the African continent as a means of escape from a hostile environment is thus also complicated by his economic interests. The river they encounter is abundant in gold dust, so much so that the crew name the river "The Golden River." They are assisted in gathering gold from this river by a white man they encounter, who had been researching the region for trade purposes when indigenous people abducted him and took him inland. He is revealed to a be a member of the Royal African Company, a company established by the Stuart family in 1660 to trade along the west coast of Africa, and which from 1663 explicitly included slavery in its operations. Immersed as the company was in the slave trade, it also conducted scientific research, such as exploring the source of the Nile.

Defoe's fiction is responsive to these contradictory impulses and attractions associated with the Nile, financial gain, and scientific exploration. While the Nile is associated with fertility and riches, symbolizing life and prosperity, it is also a destructive force, for the river regularly floods and inundates its river basin. Singleton and the party have to wait for the flood to subside in order to acquire more gold dust. For him and his party, sailing upstream on the Nile offers an escape from death in the desert, but also raises the risk of another elemental kind of death by inundation. Seriously considering these alternatives and making the kind of economical calculation characteristic of Defoe, they abandon their desire for wealth and discovery and choose the safer option by proceeding west.

Johnson's Pursuit of the Source of the Nile

Where Behn's *Oroonoko* provides an example of an "orientalized" Africa, the "Golden River" episode of *Captain Singleton* parallels the significant presence of the Nile in *Rasselas*. As Thomas Keymer suggests, the Nile "dominates the narrative as much as any human character" in *Rasselas*, where fertility and inundation are striking themes.[13] The Nile in *Rasselas*, however, corresponds not to the White Nile, but to the Blue Nile, which originates in Lake Tana in Ethiopia. Though Johnson's narrator does not identify the location of the happy valley in *Rasselas*, he does note, "the Father of waters [the Nile] begins his course" in the emperor's dominions, "whose bounty pours down the streams of plenty, and scatters over half the world the harvests of Egypt."[14] The Nile brings fertility to Abyssinia and the country downstream, Egypt. The reader assumes that the happy valley, surrounded by high mountains with rivulets, must be close to the source of the Nile. The Nile was a real river, and so must have a source, even if the location of that source was unknown to Johnson when he was writing *Rasselas*. To locate the happy valley at the source of the Nile was therefore to attempt to locate it in reality as well as an imaginary landscape.

When Johnson met James Bruce in 1775, he was eager to hear about Bruce's travels in Africa, for Bruce had discovered the source of the Blue Nile in 1770.[15] Johnson tells Boswell that he had been "in the company of a gentleman [James Bruce] whose extraordinary travels had been much the subject of conversation."[16] Boswell "was curious to hear what opinion so able a judge as Johnson had formed of his [Bruce's] abilities," and asked, "if he [Bruce] was not a man of sense." Like many others, however, Bruce's conversational and expository powers did not impress Johnson: "Why, Sir, he is not a distinct relater; and I should say, he is neither abounding nor deficient in sense. I did not perceive any superiority of understanding." Boswell, however, retorts, "But will you not allow [Bruce] a nobleness of resolution, in penetrating into distant nations?" To which Johnson answered, "That, Sir, is not to the present purpose. We are talking of his sense. A fighting cock has a nobleness of resolution."[17]

Johnson obviously was keenly interested in the source of the Blue Nile but is disappointed that Bruce is unable to relate his discoveries in a clear and compelling way.

Travel as a Fiction

In 1775—the year in which Johnson met James Bruce—he published *A Journey to the Western Islands of Scotland*, a work that affirms the usefulness of travel: "All travel has its advantages. If the passenger visits better countries, he may learn to improve his own, and if fortune carries him to worse, he may learn to enjoy it."[18] The experience of the protagonists in *Rasselas* describes a similar arc: they leave home in order to discover and experience the world, and they return home with new knowledge and changed perspectives.

Although Johnson was committed to providing a factual and historical account of the real Scotland he visited, as in *Rasselas,* he blurs the boundaries between real and fictional landscapes in *A Journey to the Western Islands of Scotland.* For example, of Talisker in the Isle of Skye he recounts "A great part of our journey was performed in the gloom of the evening. In travelling even thus almost without light thro' naked solitude, when there is a guide whose conduct may be trusted, a mind not naturally too much disposed to fear may preserve some degree of cheerfulness; but what must be the solitude of him who should be wandering, among the crags and hollows, benighted, ignorant, and alone?"[19]

In writing thus about the experience of traveling in the gloom of the Scottish evening, Johnson realizes that "the fictions of the Gothick romances were not so remote from credibility as they are now thought."[20] In looking at the real Skye, Johnson fictionalizes it, seeing it through the lens of romance, suggesting how easily he blends empirical thinking and fictive description. Indeed, in surveying ancient Scottish castles he concludes that they "afford another evidence that the fictions of romantick chivalry had for their basis the real manners of the feudal times, when every lord of a seignory lived in his hold lawless and unaccountable, with all the licentiousness and insolence of uncontested superiority and unprincipled power."[21] The imaginative combination of fact and fiction that characterizes Johnson's account of the Scottish landscape is also a central feature of his style in *Rasselas.*[22]

In chapter 4 of *Rasselas*, Rasselas imagines himself to be "an orphan virgin robbed of her little portion by a treacherous lover;" this impression was so strong that he actually ran forward "to seize the plunderer."[23] Rasselas imagines himself to be a character in a romance, and, for a moment, cannot separate the reality of the imagined scene from its fictitiousness. This is different from the perception on display in *A Journey to the Western Islands of Scotland*. There Johnson sees fiction behind the real landscape; in *Rasselas*, Rasselas tries to see reality beyond the happy valley, and it is to that reality that he seeks to escape, with Imlac's help, to make the "choice of life."[24] However, as Robert DeMaria notes, "the prince's temporary complacency followed by disappointment sets the pattern for all of Rasselas's endeavours to find happiness."[25] In searching for solid and enduring happiness in real life, beyond the happy valley, Rasselas yearns for an unfulfillable dream associated with romance. Ironically, he leaves one utopia (the happy valley) in search of another ("the choice of life"), and this irony, like the Nile, is central to the structure of the tale. The Nile, as I have suggested, is both real and fictional in the eighteenth-century imagination. Imlac, we are told, was born in the fictitious "kingdom of Goiama, at no great distance from the fountain of the Nile."[26] In like fashion, Rasselas and his party leave their fictitious country (the happy valley) and proceed downstream to Cairo, where, in the company of Imlac, they seek a different kind of romance among ordinary people.

Reason and Imagination in *Rasselas*

The narrator of *Rasselas* indulges the dream of writing a romance that features a hero dreaming of the pursuit of the choice of life. But just as Rasselas awakens from a dream of contentment in the happy valley, so the narrator awakens from the romance constated by the tale that is *Rasselas*. In chapter 44 Imlac reflects on the power of the imagination: "to indulge the power of fiction, and send imagination out upon the wing, is often the sport of those who delight too much in silent speculation."[27] Although this might suggest Johnson's deep skepticism of the effects of imaginative activity, we have to remember that it is uttered within the context of the astronomer's peculiar solipsistic indulgence, a kind of madness; for he produces a highly meaningful fiction in the form of the tale itself. As DeMaria insightfully points out, "Johnson's hostility to the form [of the tale] was not disingenuous, for its ironic persistence in *Rasselas* explains some of the most puzzling features of the work."[28]

Indeed, the tale is full of examples in which Johnson deploys fictional means to present the dangers and articulate the meaningfulness of fiction. We see this, for example, in Imlac's words about the nature of the poet: "whatever is beautiful, and whatever is dreadful, must be familiar to his imagination."[29] Yet, this total comprehensiveness, in which the poet has a responsibility to absorb everything on earth into his imagination, quickly becomes untenable. However, what is only nonsense in Imlac becomes more deplorable and dangerous in the behavior of others with less self-knowledge.

In the case of the sage in chapter 18, who discourses with great energy on the government of the passions, we are given a speech about "the conquest of passion." He "displayed the happiness of those who had obtained the important victory, after which man is no longer the slave of fear, nor the fool of hope; is no more emaciated by envy, inflamed by anger, emasculated by tenderness, or depressed by grief."[30] However, notwithstanding the sage's declamatory style and passionate dismissal of passion, he sinks into bottomless agony when he loses his only daughter, "from whose tenderness [he] expected all the comforts of [his] age."[31] His grief and distress, which are completely natural and human, stand in ironic contrast to the madness of his aloofness and imagined self-sufficiency. In his lecture, he is beyond human "tenderness,"[32] but in his innermost feelings, he is actually soaked in the personal tenderness which looked to his future security.

The pity that we feel for this sage, however, takes on a different complexion when we encounter the case of the astronomer in chapters 40–44. Here we see that to give free and unrestrained rein to the imagination is to court not only enthusiasm but madness itself. Unlike other characters encountered in the tale—those who have become weary of life—this scientist "has spent forty years in unwearied attention to the motions and appearances of the celestial bodies, and has drawn out his soul in endless calculations."[33] Unwearied attention, of course, is beyond human capability, and in this case the astronomer's unrestrained devotion to the maintenance of a wholly imagined obligation—to secure and guide the weather by unwearied attention—has produced a kind of madness. When "the princess smiled, and Pekuah convulsed herself with laughter" at the astronomer's fantastic beliefs, Imlac admonishes them not "to mock the heaviest of human afflictions;" because "of the uncertainties of our present state, the most dreadful and alarming is the uncertain continuance of reason."[34] As Johnson knew personally, "such maladies of the mind are frequent."[35]

Awakening

If the story of the mad astronomer and the dreaming Rasselas, at the end and the beginning of the tale, are connected by the maladies of the mind, then that theme, like the Nile, runs through the episode concerned with Pekuah's abduction and rescue in Egypt (chapters 39–49). After exploring the pyramids (chapter 39), Nekayah is preparing a long narrative for Pekuah, when they learn that she and her two maids have been seized by marauding Arabs. Nekayah is distraught at the loss of Pekuah, and she ceases to communicate with others and becomes withdrawn. It is as if Nekayah's aborted narrative has itself been abducted.

Nekayah blames herself for Pekuah's tragedy, and Imlac gives comfort by saying that her tenderness toward Pekuah was the accidental cause of the evil that has befallen them.[36] Furthermore, Rasselas observes—an undercurrent of the tale—that "man cannot so far know the connexion of causes and events."[37] Indeed, Nekayah herself remarks in chapter 29, "no man can, at the same time, fill his cup from the source and from the mouth of the Nile,"[38] suggesting that she knows deep down that human beings cannot always foresee the consequences of a choice or action, just as it is not possible to be in two places at the same time (the source and the mouth of the Nile).

The kidnapped Pekuah is imprisoned on an island in the Nile, and her story is symbolically stranded between the source and the mouth of the ubiquitous river. We learn from Pekuah after her release that she had been held in a seraglio, where, unlike the world portrayed by Lady Mary Wortley Montagu, women's conversations are insipid and tedious because they know nothing about the outer world. Pekuah, however, was someone whose conversation delighted the chief, given her broad experience of life, and she was civilly treated during her captivity because the chief "delighted to hear my observations."[39] The chief's "studied procrastination"[40] of her release was designed to prolong the pleasure of her conversation, alluding to the storytelling powers and narrative function of Scheherazade in *One Thousand and One Nights*. Like Scheherazade, Pekuah worried that "I must end my days in an island of the Nile."[41] However, she realizes that though the power of conversation is very great, the Arab's avariciousness is even stronger, so she bribes him with money to secure her release. Cynical as this might appear—it confounds Rasselas's idealism: "How could a mind, hungry for knowledge, be willing, in an intellectual famine, to lose such a banquet as Pekuah's conversation"[42]—it turns out to be Pekuah's great learning experience. Her experience with the Arab teaches the travelers how to approach the mad astronomer, whose introduction follows the story of Pekuah's recovery.

The princess and Pekuah visit the astronomer, who is not only deluded in his belief that he controls the movements of the Nile (he could "raise the Nile to an inundation"),[43] but is also deprived of human company, especially the company of women. But Pekuah, who has acquired a new perspective on the banks of the Nile, has acquired a knowledge of astronomy during her imprisonment that enables her to engage the astronomer in conversation. Under the pretext of acquiring further knowledge, she gains entrance into the astronomer's house and at last access to his mind. The story of Pekuah's captivity and release, and ignorance and enlightenment, deeply moves the astronomer, who feels his conviction of omnipotence to weaken under the influence of her presence. He felt "the conviction of his authority over the skies fade gradually from his mind and [he] began to trust less to an opinion which he never could prove to others, and which he now found subject to variation from causes in which reason had no part."[44] Not only does the astronomer's sense of absolute control diminish as a result of Pekuah's visits, "the happy commerce of domestick tenderness,"[45] but so does his melancholy, which was formerly sustained by isolation.

The narrative movement of the tale thus leads us to the realization that what saves people from the dangers of imaginative overindulgence is the power of human contact and communication. But this awakening to the reality of the world has been occasioned within the fictitious form of the "oriental" tale. In Johnson's handling of the tropes of the "oriental" tale, Abyssinia appears to be both a fictional space and a real African country, part of the Ottoman Empire. Situated between Europe and the East Abyssinia is a place that evokes a paradisiacal happy imagination, yet also brings forth the unpredictable powers of the Nile, which look, on the one hand, to the oriental seraglio, and on the other, to the experience of Pekuah, and the proper blending of imagination and reality that she occasions.

Notes

1 See Samuel Johnson, *The History of Rasselas, Prince of Abissina,* ed. Thomas Keymer (Oxford, UK: Oxford University Press, 2009), xxi.

2 Beyond the texts discussed in this chapter, the Abyssinian tale is rare in the prose of the seventeenth and eighteenth centuries and does not feature as the locus of any of the numerous plays with an "oriental" setting in the period. For Johnson's extensive knowledge of Abyssinia, see Wendy Laura Belcher, *Abyssinia's Samuel Johnson: Ethiopian Thought in the Making of an English Author* (Oxford, UK: Oxford University Press, 2012).

3 See Clement Hawes, "Johnson and Imperialism," in *The Cambridge Companion to Samuel Johnson*, ed. Greg Clingham (Cambridge: Cambridge University Press, 1997), 116.

4 See Greg Clingham, "Johnson and China: Culture, Commerce, and the Dream of the Orient in Mid-Eighteenth-Century England," *1650–1850: Ideas, Aesthetics, and Inquiries in the Early Modern Era* 24 (2019): 203.

5 Aphra Behn, *Oroonoko,* ed. Janet Todd (London: Penguin, 2003), 15–16.

6 Behn, *Oroonoko*, 15.

7 Mary Wortley Montagu, *The Complete Letters of Lady Mary Wortley*, ed. Robert Halsband (Oxford, UK: Oxford, Clarendon Press, 1966–1967), 1:405.

8 Elizabeth Bohls, *Women Travel Writers and the Language of Aesthetics, 1716–1818* (Cambridge: Cambridge University Press, 1996), 29.

9 Montagu, *Complete Letters*, 1:313–314.

10 Isobel Grundy, *Lady Mary Wortley Montagu: Comet of the Enlightenment* (Oxford, UK: Oxford University Press, 1999), 164.

11 The White Nile in fact originates in Lake Victoria and the source of its waters, which flow into Lake Victoria, is the Rwenzori Mountains.

12 Daniel Defoe, *The Life, Adventures, and Pyracies, of the Famous Captain Singleton,* ed. P. N. Furbank (London: Pickering & Chatto, 2008), 87.

13 Johnson, *History of Rasselas,* xxii.
14 Johnson, *History of Rasselas,* 7.
15 Bruce did not publish an account of his travels until after Johnson's death: see James Bruce, *Travels to Discover the Source of the Nile, In the Years 1768, 1769, 1770, 1771, 1772, and 1773* (London:G. G. J. and J. Robinson, 1790).
16 *Boswell's Life of Johnson*, 2:333.
17 *Boswell's Life of Johnson*, 2:334.
18 Samuel Johnson and James Boswell, *A Journey to the Western Islands of Scotland and The Journal of a Tour to the Hebrides,* ed. Peter Levi (London: Penguin, 1984), 133.
19 Johnson and Boswell, *Journey to the Western Islands*, 87–88.
20 Johnson and Boswell, *Journey to the Western Islands*, 88.
21 Johnson and Boswell, *Journey to the Western Islands*, 146.
22 For the relation between fact and fiction in Johnson's style see, for example, Ralph W. Rader, "Literary Form in Factual Narrative: The Example of Boswell's *Johnson*," in *Boswell's Life of Johnson: New Questions, New Answers*, ed. John A. Vance (Athens: University of Georgia Press, 1985), 25–52; and Greg Clingham, *Johnson, Writing, and Memory* (Cambridge: Cambridge University Press, 2002), 70–77.
23 Johnson, *History of Rasselas*, 14.
24 Johnson, *History of Rasselas*, 32.
25 Robert DeMaria Jr., *The Life of Samuel Johnson: a critical biography* (Oxford, UK: Blackwell, 1993), 207.
26 Johnson, *History of Rasselas*, 22.
27 Johnson, *History of Rasselas*, 93.
28 DeMaria, *The Life of Samuel Johnson*, 205.
29 Johnson, *History of Rasselas*, 28.
30 Johnson, *History of Rasselas*, 45.
31 Johnson, *History of Rasselas*, 45.
32 Johnson, *History of Rasselas*, 45.
33 Johnson, *History of Rasselas*, 88.
34 Johnson, *History of Rasselas*, 93.
35 Johnson, *History of Rasselas*, 93.
36 For a deeply thoughtful discussion of Nekayah's grief, see Fred Parker, "The Skepticism of *Rasselas*," in *Cambridge Companion to Johnson*, 127–142 (esp. 139–140).
37 Johnson, *History of Rasselas*, 74.
38 Johnson, *History of Rasselas*, 66.
39 Johnson, *History of Rasselas*, 87.
40 Johnson, *History of Rasselas*, 87.
41 Johnson, *History of Rasselas*, 87.
42 Johnson, *History of Rasselas*, 87.
43 Johnson, *History of Rasselas*, 91.
44 Johnson, *History of Rasselas*, 101.
45 Johnson, *History of Rasselas*, 100.

8

Johnson's Prose Style and His Notion of the Periodical Writer

TADAYUKI FUKUMOTO

Introduction

In *Adventurer* no. 115, Samuel Johnson describes the literary culture of his age as one in which "every man is qualified to instruct every other man."[1] According to him, never before had the country seen "the province of writing" flooded by so many self-styled authors who had "not yet attained the power of executing their intentions."[2] It is particularly notable that he counted among them "the innumerable correspondents of public papers."[3] Johnson clearly regarded periodicals as outlets for amateur writers lacking literary skills.[4]

The cultural status of writing prose was not particularly high in the first half of the eighteenth century. It was widely held to be a genre that was dull, humble, or divested of artistic skill. Indeed, definitions of *prose* reflected this view. According to the *Oxford English Dictionary*, 2nd ed. (OED), the first recorded use of *prose* in 1688 understood the term to mean "A dull, commonplace, or wearisome discourse or piece of writing." The use of *prosaic* to denote "lacking poetic beauty, feeling, or imagination" has been traced to 1746, and *prosaical*, with the same meaning, to 1699. Johnson himself defined *prose* in his *Dictionary* as "Language not restrained to harmonick sounds or set number of syllables; discourse not metrical." Johnson's views on the contemporary literary situation are similar to those expressed in Alexander Pope's *Dunciad* (1728, 1729, 1743). He considered, as Johnson did a decade later, that the low status of prose and the flourishing state of hack writers were due to the appearance and popularity of periodicals. It was "Journals, Medleys, Merc'ries, Magazines" and "all the Grub-street race" that sprung from "The Cave of Poverty and Poetry" (Book I, ll. 34–44).[5] Pope characterized hack writers as people from a low social class who were hired (cheaply) to produce "low-grade" and ephemeral work. Johnson, a regular contributor to periodicals himself, shared some of these characteristics, but he differed from the early periodical writers in attitude and style.

This chapter is a stylistic investigation of the nature of early periodical writers, the cultural conditions that informed what Johnson thought his own approach to periodicals should be, and the differences between the early editors and Johnson as to their notion of the proper duties of a periodical writer. Johnson's stance on periodicals will be clarified as compared with the one Pope expressed most typically in *The Dunciad*.

The Early Periodicals and Hack Writers

There is a cause-and-effect relationship between the appearance of periodicals and of the first "hack" writers. It is well known that the lapse of the Licensing Act in 1695 led to the flourishing of periodicals.[6] As Roy Porter points out, the concept of the "hack writer" emerged in the literary world at almost the same time ("from around 1700"),[7] although he uses the less derogatory phrase "author by profession." It is more than coincidence that, according to the OED, the first recorded use of *hack* as "a literary drudge, who hires himself out to do any and every kind of literary work" (4a) dates to 1700.

The concurrence of the emergence of periodicals and hack writers is not surprising because contributors to periodicals were not required to write in an elevated literary style. Indeed, the title Richard Steele gave to his first periodical, *The Tatler*, one of the most highly regarded eighteenth-century publications, indicates the preferred mode of expression. That the style of *The Tatler* is modeled after heated arguments in coffeehouses is evident in specifying a coffeehouse as a source for each article. Indeed, in the persona of Isaac Bickerstaff, Steele says, regarding his principle in defining news, "I am still within Rules, and trespass not as a Tatler any further than in an Incorrectness of Style, and writing in an Air of Common Speech" (*Tatler* no. 5).[8] He deliberately adopted a conversational style, and *The Tatler* enjoyed phenomenal popularity: John Gay asserted that "[*The Tatler*] had brought [the coffeehouses] more Customers than all their other News Papers put together."[9] Steele's strategy was followed by many editors of subsequent periodicals, who gave their papers such names as *The Northern Tatler*, *The Grouler*, *The Grumbler*, or *The Prater*.[10]

It was therefore understandable that periodical editors introduced fictitious personae, such as Isaac Bickerstaff in *The Tatler*, Mr. Spectator in *The Spectator*, and Nestor Ironside in *The Guardian*, through which to speak. "Equality is the Life of Conversation" was one of Bickerstaff's/Steele's favorite sayings in *The Tatler*.[11] The masked narrators are presented as the readers' social and intellectual equals, which contributed to the creation of a widely accessible public arena where important issues of the day were discussed. The editors adopted the personae of ordinary people in order to converse directly and intimately with their readers.

Why did the early periodicals go for easy accessibility by adopting a conversational style in the first place? This was in part because they could not assume a high rate of literacy among their intended audience. John Brewer estimates that the literacy rate was 45% for men and 25% for women in 1714.[12] At the time, periodicals were read out loud for the illiterate,[13] which explains and substantiates Joseph Addison's apparent overestimation of the readership of *The Spectator* at twenty per copy.[14] In the early years of the century, many people were still dependent for information on illustrations in chapbooks or shop signs in London streets. As such, the primary duty of early periodicals was to disseminate practical news and information among the readership rather than impress them with elaborate ideas or style. Readers shared this expectation, and Steele was convinced that the early issues of *The Tatler* owed their popularity to factual war news rather than to the essays on other subjects that he included. In *Tatler* no. 18 he jocularly described the distress the coming peace would cause to news writers, and the contrivances they would have to resort to in order to keep their readers' interest after the end of the War of the Spanish Succession. Indeed, the circulations of two periodicals, *The Post Man* and *The Post-Boy*, suffered a dramatic drop in 1713 due to the ratification of the Peace of Utrecht.[15]

Satire on the Culture of Conversation in *The Dunciad*

I highlighted in the previous section the plainness of style used in the early periodicals due to their primary function as disseminators of knowledge. The success of *The Tatler* and *The Spectator* prompted the publication of numerous other periodicals with similar ambitions. These later periodicals were not always held in the same high regard as Steele's and Addison's publications. Because their authors were not required to write in an elaborate style, these periodicals were regarded as mass producers of hack work. In 1717 the editor of the book version of the triweekly periodical, *The Censor*, lamented how this period "may be well called the Age of Counsellors, when every Blockhead who could write his own Name attempted to inform and amuse the Publick."[16]

It is noteworthy in this context that Pope's *Dunciad*, a pioneering satire of hack writers, abounds in jibes at periodicals and the culture of conversation on which their popularity was based. The mock annotator to the aforementioned line that describes the fertility of the Cave of Poverty and Poetry explains that periodicals "were thrown out weekly and monthly by every miserable scribler."[17] As such, Pope's slighting references in *The Dunciad* to periodicals and to writers associated with them are surprisingly abundant, partly stimulated by the attacks on him and his Homer translations by periodicals.[18]

However, Pope's attitude toward periodicals was more ambivalent than his hostile comments in *The Dunciad* suggest. In fact, he himself had contributed several articles to periodicals.[19] Furthermore, some of his early works were advertised, praised, or even published in the pages of periodicals.[20] Indeed, he owed his emergence as a much-lauded poet to the universal accessibility of periodicals. Moreover, the writing styles used in periodicals were not as worthless as Pope treated them in *The Dunciad.* This is, of course, especially apparent in periodicals like *The Tatler* and *The Spectator*, written by such masters of prose as Steele and Addison. In *The Dunciad*, therefore, Pope aims not to ridicule the style used in periodicals, but to warn against the latent dangers of publishing something with a press that set itself up as a forum for public discussion.

Pope's satire of periodicals is deeply connected with his covert mockery of the culture of conversation. The implication is already noticeable at the outset of *The Dunciad*: "In eldest time, e'er mortals writ or read, / . . . / Dulness o'er all possess'd her ancient right" (Book I, ll. 9–11) and "Still her old Empire to restore she tries" (Book I, l.17). Thus, the imaginative scene of *The Dunciad* depicts the contemporary literary situation in which dunce writers *can only talk*.

Pope's mockery of the culture of conversation helps us understand the significance of the cumbersome mock-scholarly annotations to the text of *The Dunciad* that he added in the 1729 edition of the poem "The Dunciad Variorum." These annotations are present from the outset of the poem, as can be seen in the comments regarding the correct spelling of the poem's title:

> *The DUNCIAD,* sic MS. It may well be disputed whether this be a right reading: Ought it not rather to be spelled *Dunceiad,* as the Etymology evidently demands? *Dunce* with an *e*, therefore *Dunceiad* with an *e*. . . . THEOBALD.
>
> This is surely a slip in the learned author of the foregoing note; there having been since produced by an accurate Antiquary, an *Autograph of Shakspeare* himself, whereby it appears that he spelled his own name without the first *e*. . . . BENTL.
>
> It is to be noted, that this great Critic also has omitted one circumstance; which is, that the Inscription with the Name of Shakspeare was intended to be placed on the Marble Scroll . . . ANON.
>
> Though I have as just a value for the letter *E*, . . . and the same affection for the Name of this Poem, as any Critic for that of his Author; . . . SCRIBLERUS.[21]

What is immediately noticeable about these annotations is the overwhelming number of utterances by different alleged dunces. There is fairly general agreement that Pope's intention in including these lengthy, trivial annotations was to satirize the excessive pedantries of the assumed contributors.[22] However, I do not entirely share this view because the annotations also mock the contemporary public sphere in which "every Blockhead who could write his own Name attempted to inform and amuse the Publick." The hypercriticism and garrulity developed on the margins of the pages of *The Dunciad* mimics an animated coffeehouse conversation in contemporary London.

In this context, we should pay more attention to one of the prefatory sections of the poem "Testimonies of Authors" because literary critics have so far not fully appreciated its significance. In this parody of the critical apparatus in a typical learned edition of a literary text, Pope, in the guise of Martinus Scriblerus, introduces various utterances of different critics. Many of these were actually taken from contemporary periodicals about Pope himself and his works.

> . . . beginning with his ESSAY on CRITICISM, of which hear first the most ancient of Critics,
>
> Mr. JOHN DENNIS.
>
> "His percepts are false or trivial, or both; his thoughts are crude and abortive, his expressions absurd, his numbers harsh and unmusical, his rhymes trivial and common;— . . ." No less peremptory is the censure of our hypercritical Historian
>
> Mr. OLDMIXON.
>
> "I dare not say any thing of the Essay on Criticism in verse; but if any more curious reader has discovered in it something *new* . . . , I should be very glad to have the benefit of the discovery." . . .
>
> To all which great authorities, we can only oppose that of
>
> Mr. ADDISON.
>
> "The Art of Criticism (saith he) which was published some months since, is a master-piece in its kind. . . ."[23]

Once again, Pope reproduces a widely accessible public forum, and thereby represents on the printed page a heated oral struggle between dunces that he expected to find in a coffeehouse or other aspect of the public sphere.

Johnson's Approach to Periodicals

Let us now turn to Johnson's attitudes toward conversation and periodical writing. Johnson was an adept conversationalist himself and was aware of the inherent potential of a conversational style. Catherine N. Parke has discussed how "[Johnson] was also actively curious about how the mind works and believed that much can be learned with pleasure, often with little conscious effort, by conversing with well-informed people, not necessarily scholars or intellectuals in the narrow sense."[24] Indeed, in *Rambler* no. 177, Johnson has his fictional contributor, Vivaculus, represent his view by saying, "I therefore resolved for a time to shut my books, and learn again the art of conversation; to defecate and clear my mind by brisker motions and stronger impulses; and to unite myself once more to the living generation."[25] Being an incredibly avid reader, Johnson put great value not only on how much knowledge one acquired but how that knowledge was conveyed to others. He says in *Idler* no. 85, "He that conveys knowledge by more pleasing ways, may very properly be loved as a benefactor."[26]

Johnson was also convinced of the important role periodicals played in public education and enlightenment. Boswell records Johnson saying, "The mass of every people must be barbarous where there is no printing, and consequently knowledge is not generally diffused. Knowledge is diffused among our people by the news-papers."[27] Johnson may have been ironic, but he admits the contribution of periodicals to promoting literacy. Like the editor of *The Censor*, he links thriving periodicals with a greater accessibility to discussion: "[The universal diffusion of instruction] certainly fills the nation with superficial disputants; enables those to talk who were born to work."[28] He is even concerned about the possibility that his own periodical may cause readers to neglect their normal duties. In an early edition of *The Idler*, he warns his would-be correspondents against forgetting their place: "I should be indeed unwilling to find that, for the sake of corresponding with the Idler, the smith's iron had cooled on the anvil, or the spinster's distaff stood unemployed."[29] Clearly, Johnson was well aware that the availability of periodicals promoted the practice of reading among ordinary people.

Despite Johnson's appreciation of the potential of a conversational style in periodicals, he did not follow suit in his own periodicals, *The Rambler, The Adventurer*, and *The Idler*. Johnson regarded his articles as works possessed of an artistic value exceeding their status as vehicles of information. The contemporary social structure was parallel to this specialization within print culture. Porter remarks, "Indeed, the key polarity in Georgian England, . . . was . . . that between those swimming in the metropolitan culture pool created by print and those excluded, those whose culture was still essentially oral."[30]

Johnson's periodical essays were apparently designed for the former, while *The Tatler* and *The Spectator*, published mostly before the Georgian era and often read aloud in coffeehouses, were originally intended for the latter. This historical context informs Robert DeMaria Jr.'s contention: "*The Rambler* is not the most perfect periodical essay because it has less of the flavour of daily life than *The Tatler* or *The Spectator* or many other periodicals. *The Rambler* was not written for the coffee house."[31]

Johnson's own words confirm his belief in targeting his audience. He says in *Idler* no. 70, "Every author does not write for every reader; many questions are such as the illiterate part of mankind can have neither interest nor pleasure in discussing . . . and many subjects of general use may be treated in a different manner, as the book is intended for the learned or the ignorant."[32]

Johnson's point here can be applied to his periodical essays. He acknowledges the desirability of writing in the style appropriate to the intellectual level of the targeted readers. Accordingly, he appreciates Addison's endeavors to enhance the accessibility of his writings: "An instructor like Addison was now wanting, whose remarks being superficial, might be easily understood, and being just, might prepare the mind for more attainments."[33] However, Johnson's periodicals were not aimed at achieving universal accessibility. Addison paid more attention to the enlightening function of his essays among ordinary people, whereas Johnson sought the perfection of artistry. Johnson emphasized how an idea was expressed over the idea itself, as he asserts by citing an observation by Nicolas Boileau at the beginning of *Rambler* no. 168: "A mean or common thought expressed in pompous diction, generally pleases more than a new or noble sentiment delivered in low and vulgar language."[34] This may partly explain why he was not so selective when it came to the subject matter of his essays and consequently wrote about such a wide range of topics.

Although Johnson modeled his periodicals after *The Spectator*, his style was quite different from that of Addison or Steele. Rather than adopt a conversational style, his periodicals frequently use difficult, learned words. Indeed, he justifies this use in *The Rambler*, saying, "When common words were less pleasing to the ear, or less distinct in their signification, I have familiarized the terms of philosophy by applying them to popular ideas."[35] Johnson's contemporaries who had been accustomed to the accessible prose of news writers on current affairs, or the lively style of *The Tatler* and *The Spectator*, could not, therefore, easily familiarize themselves with his more pompous tone of *The Rambler*.[36] Horace Walpole referred to the peculiarities of Johnson's diction,[37] and Robert Burrowes noted the many difficult, learned words Johnson used in *The Rambler*, arguing that it was through such use that Johnson's status as its author was easily identified.[38] Burrowes also considered this peculiar style of Johnson's to be unsuitable for periodicals: "if rules for periodical essays are to be drawn from the practice of their great English original, Mr. Addison, . . . nothing can be more opposite to their true character; for as their professed intent is the improvement of general manners, their stile, as well as their subjects, should be levelled to understandings of every description."[39]

The differences between *The Spectator* and *The Rambler* can be also seen in the characterization of their fictitious narrators. Johnson admits in *Rambler* no. 23 that Mr. Rambler, compared with Mr. Spectator, lacks the will to present himself as the reader's equal, instead appearing as a "dictatorial writer, without sprightliness or gaiety."[40] Evidently, Johnson's narrator is not inclined to open a relaxing conversation with the readers.

Ability to Write Quickly as a Qualification for a Hack Writer

The editors of newspapers, periodicals, and magazines had a set number of pages to fill for each edition. One technique employed by popular writers to ensure that they were able to produce sufficient copy, when lacking concrete subjects, was to incorporate (sometimes extensive amounts of) impertinent information into their discussions. In *Tatler* no. 35, for instance, Steele quotes fifty lines from *Hamlet* and attaches a nonsensically long list of names ending with "trix" at the back of the issue; in no. 39, he quotes verbatim a very long dialogue (comprising three-fifths of the whole issue) about his favorite subject, the duel; in no. 42 Addison puts up an unnecessarily detailed inventory of Drury Lane Theatre.[41] Moreover, immediately after this inventory, Addison admits it is filler, which no newspaper can avoid using when a westerly wind blows to prevent the editors from receiving appropriate news from abroad.

The necessity of filling the required number of pages by the deadline also demanded that writers be able to dash off articles about whatever topic was requested; the ability to do so in turn became a key characteristic of hack writers. *The Dunciad* links the facility of writing at length quickly and to a deadline with the bulkiness of a hack writer's output in general. For example, Pope sees the most striking crystallization of this ability in the works of Richard Blackmore, ignoring the difference between hack journalists and a hack writer of epic poetry who wants his works to last, singling out Blackmore as the winner of the noise contest in Book II: "All hail him victor in both gifts of song, / Who sings so loudly, and who sings so long" (Book II, ll. 267–268). Pope says in the annotation, "A just character of Sir *Richard Blackmore*, Kt. who . . . *Writ to the rumbling of his Coach's wheels*, and whose indefatigable Muse produced no less than six Epic poems."[42] The first point to note about Pope's observation is that Blackmore's prolificacy as an author is alluded to metaphorically as the long-windedness of the endless conversation. Second, we should notice that Pope highlights Blackmore's facility, his having mass-produced epics. Epic poems were traditionally considered the highest in the literary hierarchy, as Johnson, among others, points out in the *Life of Milton*.[43] Regardless, Blackmore wrote them without any difficulty "*to the rumbling of his Coach's wheels,*" thus fulfilling unwittingly the Popean qualification for hack writers: having a pen that could easily be deployed whenever required and regardless of topic.[44]

Later, in one of the appendixes to the poem "Of the Poet Laureate," Pope observes, ironically, that one qualification for a poet is that he "must be able to make verses *extempore*, and to pour forth innumerable if requir'd."[45] Pope's allusion to the qualification for laureateship in *The Dunciad* was aimed, in part, at the laureate at the time, Colley Cibber, prince of dullness. Pope's own stance, as Johnson states in his *Life of Pope*, was very different: "his effusions were always voluntary, and his subjects chosen by himself. His independence secured him from drudging at a task, and labouring upon a barren topick . . . He suffered coronations and royal marriages to pass without a song . . . When he could produce nothing new, he was at liberty to be silent."[46]

Behind the attack on Cibber lay a more general swipe at the commercial custom of the day when authors were paid according to the quantity rather than quality of their production. Jonathan Swift jocularly advises poets in general:

Read all the *Prefaces* of *Dryden*,
For these our Criticks much confide in,
(Tho' meerly writ at first for filling
To raise the Volume's Price, a Shilling.)[47]

Considering this, the cumbersome annotations and appendixes attached to the text of *The Dunciad* were designed as mock fillers, parodying the vain efforts of hack writers to inflate the price of their works. The volume of the Twickenham Edition of Pope's works dedicated to *The Dunciad* is the bulkiest of all the edition's volumes. Interestingly, Johnson regards the extensive notes Pope included in his *Iliad* as "undoubtedly written to swell the volumes."[48] He unwittingly evokes the dilemma Pope faced: to earn his living as an "author by profession" while keeping his pride as a self-styled artist.

The situation surrounding hack writers remained unchanged in Johnson's days. The incessant demand for copy by periodicals still necessitated fillers, as Johnson himself observes in *Idler* no. 7: "The compilation of news-papers is often committed to narrow and mercenary minds, not qualified for the task of delighting or instructing; who are content to fill their paper, with whatever matter, without industry to gather, or discernment to select."[49] As in the days of Steele and Addison, this led to the excessive appreciation of a writer's ability to compose extempore as much and as quickly as possible. Johnson, once a Grub Street hack himself, understood well the economic mechanism that determined the monetary value of an author's work according to its size or length. He wrote in a letter to Cave about the publication of *London*, "I do not doubt but you will look over this poem with another eye, and reward it in a different manner, from a mercenary bookseller, who counts the lines he is to purchase, and *considers nothing but the bulk*" (emphasis added).[50] However, given the ubiquity of this system of valuation, Johnson could not help but display the very ability of a hack writer to write much and swiftly. Boswell bears witness to this facility, citing Johnson's own words: "almost all [my] Ramblers were written just as they were wanted for the press; . . . [I] sent a certain portion of the copy of an essay, and wrote the remainder, while the former part of it was printing. When it was wanted, and [I] had fairly sat down to it, [I] was sure it would be done."[51] Johnson was also able to write more substantial works at great speed: he famously wrote *Rasselas* within the space of a week to defray the expense of his mother's funeral. There is also his famous comment: "No man but a blockhead ever wrote, except for money."[52] In short, Johnson understood the plight of the hack writer well, and never completely abandoned his affiliation with that group of writers.

In light of these considerations, what distinguished Johnson as a prose writer from other hack writers and literary drudges? It was partly his exceptional ability for impromptu composition. Boswell bears witness that Johnson's conversation could be printed without correction.[53] Boswell's testimony, though not to be taken at face value, suggests that Johnson's essays, even when composed offhand, were not so clumsy as those of the hack writers Pope attacks in *The Dunciad*. The last issue of *The Rambler*, no. 208, is very informative when we consider how the deadlines that were imposed on periodical writers affected the literary styles they adopted. Johnson explains first that a periodical writer's fate obliges him to "labour on a barren topick, till it is too late to change it" or to "diffuse his thoughts into wild exuberance, which the pressing hour of publication cannot suffer judgment to examine or reduce." Immediately afterwards he claims his own credit of having "refine[d] our language to grammatical purity, and . . . clear[ed] it from colloquial barbarisms."[54] The flow of the argument in *Rambler* no. 208 shows how Johnson, unlike Steele, did not seek to write "in an Air of Common Speech" even when under the same confines of "the pressing hour of publication."

It should furthermore be added that Johnson was surprisingly eager to refine his writings even after publication. While he could write an article on the spot if required, his conviction of the possible artistic merit in prose never allowed him to leave his original articles unpolished. Alexander Chalmers notes that Johnson made more than 6,000 corrections to the second and third editions of *The Rambler*.[55] On the other hand, Johnson alludes in *Rambler* no. 169 to "weekly or diurnal writers" as typical contemporary examples whose "many imperfections are unavoidable"[56] because they do not put in much effort in improving their original productions. Johnson thus draws a distinction between himself and the type of writer whose "productions are seldom intended to remain in the world longer than a week."[57]

Conclusion

The huge potential of an easy, accessible, and conversational style for diffusing information has been most strikingly evidenced in the modern period, for better or worse, by social media sites such as Twitter. The casual tweets of movie stars, politicians, and even people not in the public eye are shared by people of every intellectual level and disseminated all over the world in an instant. It is suggestive of the never-failing efficacy of the conversational style in spreading information that, despite a distance of 300 years, the names of the two media, *The Tatler* and Twitter, both originate in the act of talking.

The early periodical writers like Steele and Addison made the most of this potential and wrote in a style accessible to both the writer and the reader. This strategy, adopted in periodicals imitating Steele and Addison by writers who lacked their literary talents, made such periodicals seem to satirists like Pope to give hack writers ample opportunity to put their writings to the test. His view of the early periodicals is reflected in his derision for the culture of conversation, implied adroitly in his mock annotation and critical apparatus to the text of *The Dunciad*.

However, Johnson assumed a different attitude toward periodicals. The period was over in which the primary function of periodicals was the enlightenment of others by virtue of easy accessibility. In the culture of Johnson's time an exclusive space, represented by the club and restricted to selected members, came to the fore, and displaced the open arena, represented by the coffeehouse, that was accessible to all intellectual levels. Some part of society was no longer satisfied with the mere acquisition of knowledge but was interested in how persuasively knowledge was set forth. From this point of view, Johnson's aim in his periodicals—his use of a loftier style and difficult words, his disrespectful attitudes toward and contrasting indulgence of news writers—can all be regarded as following the larger historical framework and cultural mores in mid-eighteenth-century England.

Notes

1 Samuel Johnson, *The Idler, and The Adventurer*, eds. Walter Bate, Marshall Bullit, and Laurence Fitzroy Powell. *The Yale Edition of the Works of Samuel Johnson* Vol. II. (New Haven, CT: Yale University Press, 1963), 457.

2 Johnson, *Idler and Adventurer*, 458.

3 Johnson, *Idler and Adventurer*, 458.

4 On the difference between newspapers and periodicals, Richmond P. Bond comments, "It lies in the content, in the extent to which the matter is current. The newspaper of course has very much that is timely; the periodical has but little of what we call news of the moment," in *Growth and Change in the Early English Press* (Lawrence: University of Kansas Libraries, 1969), 1–2. Because this chapter is concerned mainly with the stylistic matters of short nonfictional prose, the difference is not important.

5 All quotations from *The Dunciad* are from Alexander Pope, *The Dunciad* (Text B), ed. James Sutherland, vol. 5 of *The Twickenham Edition of the Poems of Alexander Pope* (hereafter cited as *TE*), gen. ed. John Butt, 11 vols. (London: Methuen; New Haven: Yale University Press, 1939–1969).

6 Jeremy Black, *The English Press in the Eighteenth Century* (London: Croom Helm, 1987), 12–13.

7 Roy Porter, *Enlightenment: Britain and the Creation of the Modern World* (London: Allen Lane, 2000), 82.
8 Donald F. Bond, ed., *The Tatler,* 3 vols. (Oxford, UK: Clarendon Press, 1987), 1:51. He also says in no. 204, "We Writers of Diurnals are nearer in our Styles to that of common Talk than any other Writers" (Bond, *Tatler,* 3:87).
9 John Gay, "The Present State of Wit," *Poetry and Prose,* ed. Vinton A. Dearing, 2 vols. (Oxford, UK: Clarendon Press, 1974), 2:451.
10 *The Northern Tatler* (1710); *The Grouler* (1711); *The Grumbler* (1715); *The Prater* (1756).
11 See nos. 225 and 244. He speaks to the same effect in no. 45: "all Desire of Superiority being a Contradiction to that Spirit which makes a just Conversation" (Bond, *Tatler,* 1:326.).
12 Cited in Iona Italia, *The Rise of Literary Journalism in the Eighteenth Century* (Abingdon: Routledge, 2005), 10. As Steele indicates in the first issue of *The Tatler,* he was fully conscious of its female readership.
13 Richard D. Altick, *The English Common Reader: A Social History of the Mass Reading Public 1800–1900* (Chicago: University of Chicago Press, 1957), 35.
14 See *Spectator* no. 10. Donald F. Bond, ed., *The Spectator,* 5 vols. (Oxford, UK: Clarendon Press, 1965), 1:44.
15 James Sutherland, *The Restoration Newspaper and Its Development* (Cambridge: Cambridge University Press, 1986), 228–229. Addison too referred in *Spectator* no. 445 to the serious effect "an approaching Peace," as well as the new Stamp Act, would have on newspapers.
16 Lewis Theobald, ed., preface to *The Censor,* 3 vols. (London: Printed for Jonas Brown, 1717).
17 *TE,* 5:273.
18 See *The Dunciad* Book I, ll. 215–216; Book II, ll. 149, 258, 306–307, 314; Book III, l. 146, and the mock note to Book III, l. 199. Pope even lists the periodicals that attacked him in an appendix to the poem; see *TE,* 5:209–210.
19 Norman Ault lists twenty-six articles Pope contributed to *The Spectator* and *The Guardian*. *The Prose Works of Alexander Pope,* eds. Norman Ault and Rosemary Cowler, 2 vols. (Oxford, UK: Blackwell, 1936–1986), 1:ix–x.
20 His *Essay on Criticism* and *Temple of Fame* were applauded in *Spectator* nos. 253 and 532, respectively, and *The Messiah* was first published anonymously in no. 378.
21 *TE,* 5:267–268.
22 James Sutherland points out "the whole ponderous apparatus is intended to burlesque the labours of learned commentators and textual critics" (*TE,* 5: xii).
23 *TE,* 5:25–26.
24 Catherine N. Parke, "Johnson and the Arts of Conversation," in *The Cambridge Companion to Samuel Johnson,* ed. Greg Clingham (Cambridge: Cambridge University Press, 1997), 22.
25 Samuel Johnson, *The Rambler,* vols. 3–5 of *The Yale Edition of the Works of Samuel Johnson,* eds. W. J. Bate and Albrecht B. Strauss (New Haven, CT: Yale University Press, 1969), 5:169.
26 Johnson, *Idler and Adventurer,* 264.
27 *Boswell's Life of Johnson,* 2:170.
28 Johnson, *Idler and Adventurer,* 23.
29 Johnson, *Idler and Adventurer,* 7.
30 Porter, *Enlightenment,* 76.

31 Robert DeMaria Jr., "The Eighteenth-Century Periodical Essay," in *The Cambridge History of English Literature, 1660–1780*, ed. John Richetti (Cambridge: Cambridge University Press, 2005), 542.
32 Johnson, *Idler and Adventurer*, 217–218.
33 Samuel Johnson, *The Lives of the Most Eminent English Poets*, ed. Roger Lonsdale, 4 vols. (Oxford, UK: Clarendon Press, 2006), 3:37. Johnson also says to the same effect, "he [Addison] therefore presented knowledge in the most alluring form, not lofty and austere, but accessible and familiar."
34 Johnson, *Rambler*, 5:125.
35 Johnson, *Rambler*, 5:319.
36 Nathan Drake, *Essays, Biographical, Critical, and Historical, Illustrative of the Rambler, Adventurer, and Idler, and of the Various Periodical Papers*, 2 vols. (London: Printed for W. Suttaby, 1809–1810), 1:198.
37 Horace Walpole, *The Works of Horatio Walpole, Earl of Orford*, 5 vols. (London: Printed for G. G. and J. Robinson and J. Edwards, 1798), 4:362.
38 "In such writings the hand of the master must be immediately perceived; . . . the Rambler stands convicted of an ineffectual and unnecessary attempt to raise his own consequence by forging letters to himself." Robert Burrowes, "Essays on the Stile of Doctor Samuel Johnson, No. I," in *The Transactions of the Royal Irish Academy, Polite Literature* (Dublin, 1787), 32–33.
39 Burrowes, "Essays," 30.
40 Johnson, *Rambler*, 3:129.
41 Bond, *Tatler*, 1:258–259, 260, 281–287, 303–305.
42 *TE*, 5:308.
43 "By the general consent of criticks, the first praise of genius is due to the writer of an epick poem " (Johnson, *Lives of the Poets*, 1:282). John Dryden too points out marked abilities required of a true epic poet in "A Discourse Concerning the Original and Progress of Satire": see *Essays of John Dryden*, 2 vols., ed. W. P. Ker (Oxford, UK: Clarendon Press, 1926), 2:43. Steele observes, concerning who a poet should take first as a proper theme for his amatory verse, in *Tatler* no. 27, "To do otherwise than so, would be like making an Heroick Poem a Man's first Attempt" (Bond, *Tatler*, 1:209).
44 Blackmore's very first published work was a heroic poem, written "in such occasional uncertain hours as his profession afforded," as he himself confesses (Johnson, *Lives of the Poets*, 3:76).
45 *TE*, 5:416.
46 Johnson, *Lives of the Poets*, 4:63–64.
47 "On Poetry: A Rapsody," 251–254. *The Poems of Jonathan Swift*, 3 vols., ed. Harold Williams (Oxford, UK: Clarendon Press, 1958), 2:648.
48 Johnson, *Lives of the Poets*, 4:74.
49 Johnson, *Idler and Adventurer*, 23.
50 Samuel Johnson, *The Letters of Samuel Johnson*, 5 vols., ed. Bruce Redford (Princeton, NJ: Princeton University Press, 1992–1994), 1:14.
51 *Boswell's Life of Johnson*, 3:42. In *Rambler* no. 21 Johnson also remarks, concerning a plight that writers were facing, "It very often happens that the works of learning or of wit are performed at the direction of those by whom they are to be rewarded; the writer has not always the choice of his subject, but is compelled to accept any task which is thrown before him, without much consideration of his own convenience, and without time to prepare himself by previous studies"

(Johnson, *Rambler*, 3:119). See also Alvin Kernan, *Samuel Johnson and the Impact of Print* (Princeton: Princeton University Press, 1987), 96–97.

52 *Boswell's Life of Johnson*, 3:19.

53 *Boswell's Life of Johnson*, 4:236. Kernan, *Impact of Print,* 17–18, 177–178, explores the influence of printing technology on Johnson's style. This section owes a lot to his discussion.

54 Johnson, *Rambler*, 5:318–319.

55 Alexander Chalmers, "Historical and Biographical Preface to *The Rambler*," in *The British Essayists*, 45 vols. (London, 1802), 19: xxvii.

56 Johnson, *Rambler*, 5:133–134.

57 Johnson, *Rambler*, 5:11.

9

An Analysis of Johnson's View of Knowledge

A Corpus-Stylistic Approach

MASAAKI OGURA

Introduction

The seventeenth and eighteenth centuries in Britain saw the notion of "useful knowledge" increasingly invoked as an ideal and aspiration.[1] This type of knowledge was considered to be "from a vernacular canon, the cultural property of a non-aristocratic gentleman" and was understood to carry universal value.[2] Among the writers who emphasized the importance of useful knowledge in the eighteenth century was Samuel Johnson, who aimed to provide readers—young readers lacking experience in life in particular—with something for them to imitate.[3] Johnson, having "unfailing and intelligent commitment to all forms of truth and civility,"[4] placed importance on learning in a broad sense:

The task of our present writers is very different; it requires, together with that learning which is to be gained from books, that experience which can never be attained by solitary diligence, but must arise from general converse and accurate observation of the living world.[5]

In *A Dictionary of the English Language*,[6] Johnson defines *knowledge* as follows:

1 Certain perception; indubitable apprehension.
2 Learning; illumination of the mind.
3 Skill in anything.
4 Acquaintance with any fact or person.
5 Cognisance; notice.
6 Information; power of knowing.

However, Johnson's perspective on knowledge cannot be comprehensively known from his dictionary entry alone, in which he does not provide an explanation as to what the term meant to him.[7] The following from *Boswell's Life of Johnson* indicates more fully how Johnson thought about the concept of knowledge: "Knowledge is of two kinds. We know a subject ourselves, or we know where we can find information upon it. When we enquire into any subject, the first thing we have to do is to know what books have treated of it. This leads us to look at catalogues, and at the backs of books in libraries."[8]

The first type of knowledge entails the source of information, while the second type is the understanding gained from the information. Regardless of the type, in *Rassalas,* Johnson suggests that knowledge is something that empowers human beings, as indicated by the following passage: "As the prince and Imlac were walking together, the Prince asked Imlac, 'Why art thou so strong, and why is man so weak?' Imlac answers, '[K]nowledge is more than equivalent to force.'"[9]

Here, what Imlac means is that knowledge is more powerful than physical force. The fact that it is useful and has more power than such force, according to Johnson, also makes it a double-edged sword: "Integrity without knowledge is weak and useless, and knowledge without integrity is dangerous and dreadful."[10]

Although these observations suggest, to some extent, how Johnson viewed knowledge, they constitute only a narrow and somewhat arbitrary selection from across his oeuvre: a systematic survey of the term from Johnson's writings as a whole has yet to be conducted. This study examines the term *knowledge* in *The Rambler* (1750–1752), a periodical Johnson described thus: "My other works are wine and water, but my Rambler is pure wine."[11] For Johnson, the duty of a writer is to make a better world. As he states in his *Preface to Shakespeare*: "it is always a writer's duty to make the world better, and justice is a virtue independent on [*sic*] time or place."[12] However, the conception of knowledge represented in *The Rambler* has not been examined, and the present study attempts to address this issue using a corpus-stylistic approach.

Johnson was not the sole contributor to *The Rambler*; other contributors included Samuel Richardson (no. 97), and several authors known as the "Bluestockings"—Hester Mulso (no. 10), Catherine Talbot (no. 30), Elizabeth Carter (no. 44 and no. 100).[13] Though all of these writers shared intellectual interests with Johnson,[14] my analysis in this paper concentrates on essays by Johnson that use the term *knowledge*.

Analysis

Data

To address this research question, I used the text file of *The Rambler* available on *The Oxford Text Archive*. The texts in these files use modern spelling. Here the question arises of whether it is better to use the modern or original spelling. Baron et al. examined the effect that spelling variants can have on research results and reported that data with standardized spellings provide more robust results.[15] Hence, I decided to use the file mentioned. I chose #LancsBox[16] for a concordancer because it has helpful functions such as the extraction of *n*-grams (displaying the distribution of words) as well as the basic functions of word list making or keyword extractions.

For a reference corpus, I use the *Corpus of Later Modern English Text 3.1* (*CLMET*).[17] This corpus comprises three subsections divided in accordance with the time periods 1710–1780, 1780–1850, and 1850–1910, and it consists of approximately 9.8 million words. It is, accordingly, one of the largest historical corpora, with a size far exceeding that of *The Helsinki Corpus of English Texts*, which has traditionally been used for diachronic analyses of English and includes approximately 1.5 million words. Employing *CLMET* rather than the *Helsinki Corpus* increases the validity of the study. Berber-Sardinha, for example, studied the size of the reference corpus when using WordSmith Tools as a concordancer and found that when the size of the reference corpus is more than five times larger than that of the target corpus analyzed, the results of the keyword analysis do not change significantly.[18] Given that *The Rambler* corpus for the present study consists of 316,357 words, I decided that it would be best to use *CLMET*.

Knowledge as a Keyword

The Rambler has been discussed mainly in terms of its moral discourse. Words such as *religion*, *piety*, *fidelity*, and *deed* are often found in the text. However, there is another word that is comparable to these with respect to its significance—*knowledge*. In no. 208, the concluding issue of *The Rambler*, Johnson writes:

> As it has been my principal design to inculcate wisdom or piety, I have allotted few papers to the idle sports of imagination. Some, perhaps, may be found of which the highest excellence is harmless merriment; but scarcely any man is so steadily serious as not to complain, that the severity of dictatorial instruction

> has been too seldom relieved, and that he is driven by the sternness of The Rambler's philosophy to more cheerful and airy companions.[19]

Here, Johnson describes his "principal design" in writing *The Rambler*, which he says was to "inculcate wisdom or piety." This is confirmed by observing the words with which he associates *piety*.

He knows, indeed, that those who value themselves for sense, learning, or piety speak of him with contempt, but he considers them wretches—envious or ignorant—who do not know his happiness or wish to supplant him. He declares to his friends that he is fully satisfied with his own conduct because he has fed every day on twenty dishes, and yet doubled his estate.[20]

A similar pattern can be found in no. 7, where *knowledge* is juxtaposed with *piety* as follows: "There are two persons only whom I cannot charge with having changed their conduct with my change of fortune. One is an old curate that has passed his life in the duties of his profession, with great reputation for his knowledge and piety; the other is a lieutenant of dragoons."[21]

These associations of *piety* with *wisdom, learning,* and *knowledge* suggest that Johnson, as he proposes in no. 208, considers these two concepts to be closely linked. Figure 9.1 shows the frequency of *knowledge* and a selection of other keywords used in *The Rambler*:

The frequency of *knowledge* as compared to other words particularly stands out. Its frequency is far higher than that of the other selected words, indicating that the idea of knowledge holds a prominent position in *The Rambler*. Comparison of the frequency of the use of *knowledge* with the 1710–1780 subsection of *CLMET*, which covers the period in which *The Rambler* was written, provides collateral evidence for this observation.

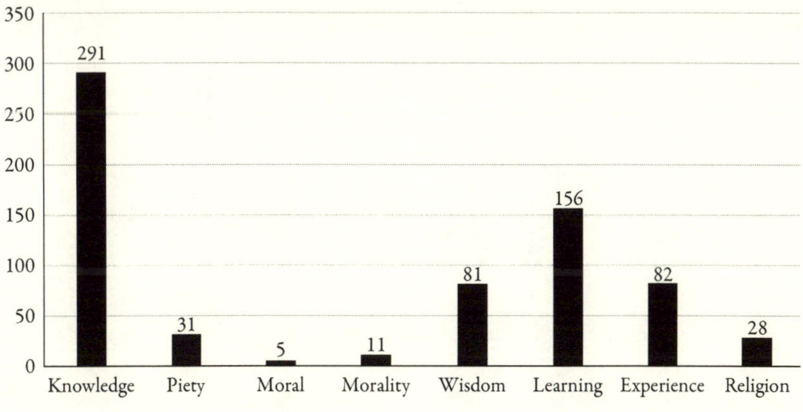

FIG. 9.1 The frequency of knowledge and other keywords in *The Rambler*

As seen in table 9.1, the frequency of the word *knowledge* in *The Rambler* was significantly higher than the overall frequency for all texts during the 1710–1780 time period, with a total raw frequency of 1,942. *Knowledge* is used around 6.6 times more frequently than in the 1710–1780 subsection.

It is interesting to note that *knowledge* also appears in a large number of *The Rambler* issues, as seen in figure 9.2. In fact, among the 208 issues, the word *knowledge* does not appear in only seventy-three. This means that approximately 65 percent of *The Rambler* issues mention *knowledge* in some way. The data pointing along the horizontal axis refers to the issue number and its publication date. For example, "r001_1750_0320" refers to *The Rambler* no. 1, published on March 20, 1750.

One must keep in mind that *The Rambler*, as has already been mentioned, includes authors other than Johnson. This means that one must consider whether the conception of *knowledge* is consistent in all of *The Rambler*'s essays or is held only by Johnson. In fact, although the whole work contains texts by authors other than Johnson, the contributions by others do not

Table 9.1
The Frequency of the Use of the Word *Knowledge* among All Words in *The Rambler*

Texts	Raw frequency	Number of words	Adjusted frequency (per million)
The Rambler	291	316,357	916
1710–1780 *CLMET*	1,942	10,396,571	187.08

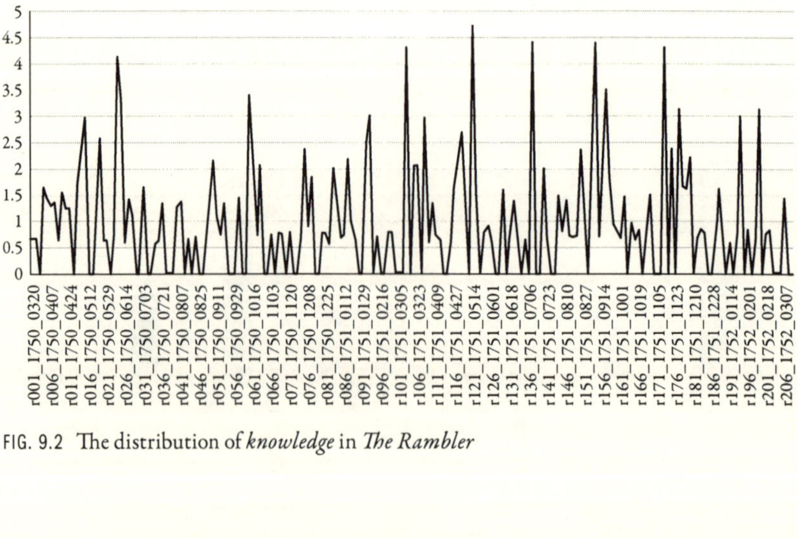

FIG. 9.2 The distribution of *knowledge* in *The Rambler*

include the word *knowledge*; it is only in Johnson's texts where the use of that term is found.

Collocations of the Keyword *Knowledge*

To investigate the typical usage of the word *knowledge* in *The Rambler* in further depth, this section analyzes frequent collocations of other terms with *knowledge*. The present study examines the words appearing within four words of *knowledge*. Table 9.2 is a frequency-based list of collocation that appears in that node.

This table shows us that many of the words that collocate with *knowledge* are functional words such as prepositions (*of*), articles (*the*), conjunctions (*but*), and so on, which do not shed much light on Johnson's understanding of the concept of *knowledge*. However, four content words, nouns, can be found in this list of function words: these four content words, highlighted in table 9.2, are *world*, *extent*, *virtue*, and *life*. These words can be labeled as collocations with *knowledge* in *The Rambler* that stand out from conventional collocations with this word at the time. The top forty collocating words with *knowledge* in the 1710–1780 subsection of *CLMET* are shown in table 9.3.

Table 9.2

Frequency-Based List of Collocations of *Knowledge* in *The Rambler*

Rank	Word	Frequency	Rank	Word	Frequency
1	of	208	21	which	15
2	the	151	22	our	14
3	and	104	23	from	13
4	to	76	24	not	13
5	or	49	25	world	13
6	his	47	26	has	12
7	in	36	27	this	12
8	a	31	28	any	11
9	that	28	29	as	11
10	by	26	30	may	11
11	is	25	31	more	11
12	their	24	32	I	10
13	with	23	33	it	10
14	be	19	34	an	9
15	he	18	35	extent	9
16	have	17	36	virtue	9
17	but	16	37	life	8
18	without	16	38	much	8
19	for	15	39	no	8
20	my	15	40	own	8

Table 9.3
A Frequency-Based List of Collocation of *Knowledge* in the 1710–1780 Subsection of the *CLMET*

Rank	Word	Frequency	Rank	Word	Frequency
1	of	1476	21	for	118
2	the	1195	22	but	105
3	and	721	23	this	105
4	to	399	24	not	97
5	his	289	25	it	96
6	a	279	26	as	95
7	in	273	27	with	95
8	that	203	28	her	92
9	their	148	29	was	85
10	is	146	30	all	84
11	from	142	31	our	83
12	my	141	32	some	75
13	he	140	33	be	73
14	or	135	34	any	72
15	which	130	35	no	58
16	I	129	36	you	58
17	without	124	37	more	55
18	by	120	38	your	55
19	have	120	39	they	54
20	had	119	40	who	51

The next subsections observe the use of these four collocating words and will attempt to examine in more detail the way in which *The Rambler* considers *knowledge*.

World. The term *world* is among the four collocating words with *knowledge*. *World* typically occurs in the form of "knowledge of the world," which occurs seven times. The phrase "knowledge of the world," which appears in a wide range of writing throughout the long eighteenth century, according to Jason D. Solinger,[22] is highly significant in *The Rambler*. When examined in the 1710–1780 subsection of *CLMET*, the phrase appears thirty-seven times, which, considering the size of the corpus, is infrequent compared to *The Rambler*. The first use of this is found in *The Rambler* no. 4, in which Johnson expresses deep admiration for the concept of knowledge and defines it as a form of observation that is sustained by all of humanity. This excerpt has profound examples and metaphors describing the meaning of knowledge, and how it serves a purpose for all of humanity, allowing readers to decode the word's meaning and to realize how this concept has helped them in their lives:

> It is therefore not a sufficient vindication of a character, that it is drawn as it appears; for many characters ought never to be drawn: nor of a narrative, that the train of events is agreeable to observation and experience; for that observation which is called knowledge of the world, will be found much more frequently to make men cunning than good. The purpose of these writings is surely not only to show mankind, but to provide that they may be seen hereafter with less hazard; to teach the means of avoiding the snares which are laid by Treachery for Innocence, without infusing any wish for that superiority with which the betrayer flatters his vanity; to give the power of counteracting fraud, without the temptation to practise it; to initiate youth by mock encounters in the art of necessary defense, and to increase prudence without impairing virtue.[23]

Here, Johnson expresses one purpose of knowledge: to "teach the means of avoiding the snares" that have been laid by the wicked in a bid to trap people with innocent minds. It seems that Johnson is trying to convey the notion that knowledge is composed of lessons we gain by living our lives. Through these lessons, knowledge gained through experience, people are less likely to make the same mistakes and are more likely to improve their decision-making abilities. Johnson's intent for this meaning of knowledge is also demonstrated by the following examples, each of which refers to humankind as having to deal with "less hazard" in life and preparing "mock encounters" in the art of defense in order to protect youth from evil. Johnson points out that knowledge can have adverse effects on humanity as well. Here, he says that knowledge can often make humanity more "cunning than good," or cultivate a sense of supremacy, or potentially use knowledge to exercise forms of "fraud" and evil. In addition to his argument that gaining knowledge is helpful, what we see here is that "knowledge of the world" has both positive and negative sides.

Another way of understanding *knowledge* in relation to *world* is seen in no. 194. Here, Johnson describes the concept of knowledge as varying from individual to individual. This point is exemplified by, for instance, the inclusion in his writing of a "lady" who considers him "wholly unacquainted" and "not qualified" regarding manners, and thus is unable to share his knowledge with the pupil. He moves on to describe the perception of what constitutes the lady's knowledge, stating that it has been established on different things, ranging from fashionable intelligence to appearances in "places of resort":

> The silence with which I was contented to hear my pupil's praises, gave the lady reason to suspect me not much delighted with his acquisitions; but she attributed my discontent to the diminution of my influence, and my fears of losing the patronage of the family; and though she thinks favorably of my learning and morals, she considers me as wholly unacquainted with the customs of the polite

part of mankind; and therefore not qualified to form the manners of a young nobleman, or communicate the knowledge of the world. This knowledge she comprises in the rules of visiting, the history of the present hour, an early intelligence of the change of fashions, an extensive acquaintance with the names and faces of persons of rank, and a frequent appearance in places of resort.[24]

These excerpts show that Johnson regards the idea of knowledge from different points of view that are all intertwined. The central notion of knowledge appears to be a foundation procured from life experiences in combination with life lessons and the history of others who have shared their knowledge with one another. Johnson portrays this idea of knowledge as having both a positive and negative impact on humanity. In fact, Johnson writes:

> Such have been his endeavours, and such his assistances, that every trace of literature was soon obliterated. He has changed his language with his dress, and instead of endeavouring at purity or propriety, has no other care than to catch the reigning phrase and current exclamation, till, by copying whatever is peculiar in the talk of all those whose birth or fortune entitles them to imitation, he has collected every fashionable barbarism of the present winter, and speaks a dialect not to be understood among those who form their style by poring upon authors.[25]

Here, "fashionable barbarism" means shibboleths, the use of an old idea, custom, or principle that is no longer suitable for modern times. Johnson derides the fashionable barbarisms of the present winter as ostensible and derides the man for idealizing them. Johnson is critical of the superficial knowledge of language to decorate the speaker. Rather, he values "endeavoring at purity or propriety," and the purity of manners and propriety, [26] which is the correctness of social or moral behavior. It seems that this knowledge is a part of the "knowledge of the world" that Johnson discusses. How, then, is purity or propriety acquired? The following subsections will investigate this question by considering the other collocations with the term *knowledge* in Johnson's essays, which are *extent*, *virtue*, and *life*.

Extent. Another word that frequently collocates with *knowledge* is *extent*. The typical use of extent with knowledge takes the form of "extent of knowledge," as follows:

> It is never without very melancholy reflections, that we can observe the misconduct, or miscarriage, of those men, who seem, by the force of understanding, or extent of knowledge, exempted from the general frailties of human nature, and privileged from the common infelicities of life. Though the world is

> crowded with scenes of calamity, we look upon the general mass of wretchedness with very little regard, and fix our eyes upon the state of particular persons, whom the eminence of their qualities marks out from the multitude; as in reading an account of a battle, we seldom reflect on the vulgar heaps of slaughter, but follow the hero with our whole attention, through all the varieties of his fortune, without a thought of the thousands that are falling round him.[27]

What Johnson conveys by the phrase "exempted from the general frailties of human nature, and privileged from the common infelicities of life" is the idea of one who seems perfect to the general public. According to Johnson, we tend to feel melancholy when we see an "eminent" man who makes mistakes in his behavior or judgment. It is worth noting the association of "extent of knowledge" with "the force of understanding" in this passage. These two characteristics make a person a "hero." The antithesis of the two phrases shows that understanding and knowledge are viewed by Johnson as very forceful, emphasizing the idea of knowledge as power:

> The danger of early eminence has been extended by some, even to the gifts of nature; and an opinion has been long conceived, that quickness of invention, accuracy of judgment, or extent of knowledge, appearing before the usual time, presage a short life. Even those who are less inclined to form general conclusions, from instances which by their own nature must be rare, have yet been inclined to prognosticate no suitable progress from the first sallies of rapid wits; but have observed, that after a short effort they either loiter or faint, and suffer themselves to be surpassed by the even and regular perseverance of slower understandings.[28]

In this passage, the phrase "extent of knowledge" is aligned with "quickness of invention" and "accuracy of judgement." Johnson says that the emergence of these qualities in one's early years is often considered as presaging a short life. These qualities, summarized as "sallies of rapid wits" in the next sentence, might allow a person to make an impression early on, but are often unsustainable, and thus in the course of time force the person to be overtaken by those with "slow understanding." Thus, Johnson suggests that "quickness of invention" and "accuracy of judgement," if overdeveloped at too early a stage, may be counterproductive and be the cause of unhappiness.

Virtue. Johnson seems to have related the combination of *virtue* and *knowledge* to truth, as in "there is yet more respect to be paid to knowledge, to virtue, and to truth,"[29] and examining the use of *knowledge* with *virtue* offers a way of interpreting Johnson's understanding of knowledge:

> It is, however, impossible that as the attention tends strongly toward one thing, it must retire from another; and he that omits the care of domestic business because he is engrossed by inquiries of more importance to mankind has, at least, the merit of suffering for a good cause. But there are many who can plead no such extenuation of their folly; who shake off the burden of their situation, not that they may soar with less encumbrance to the heights of knowledge or virtue but that they may loiter at ease and sleep in quiet; and who select for friendship and confidence not the faithful and the virtuous, but the soft, the civil, and compliant.[30]

Gaining knowledge is presented here in sharp contrast with "loiter[ing] at ease" and "sleep[ing] in quiet." Johnson does not allow the reader to give the excuse of being foolish instead of trying to reach the heights of knowledge or virtue. The phrase "the heights of knowledge or virtue" indicates that he views knowledge as something to be reached with effort, and he argues that readers should seek knowledge. This is confirmed by the following passage, in which Johnson considers learning as the opposite of loitering. This is consistent with how he looks at learning: "and heat his mind with incredibilities; a book was thus produced without fear of criticism, without the toil of study, without knowledge of nature, or acquaintance with life."[31]

However, these excerpts do not mean that Johnson considers knowledge to be of absolute importance:

> It is apparent, that to excellence in this valuable art, some peculiar qualifications are necessary; for every one's experience will inform him, that the pleasure which men are able to give in conversation, holds no stated proportion to their knowledge or their virtue. Many find their way to the tables and the parties of those who never consider them as of the least importance in any other place; we have all, at one time or other, been content to love those whom we could not esteem, and been persuaded to try the dangerous experiment of admitting him for a companion, whom we knew to be too ignorant for a counsellor, and too treacherous for a friend.[32]

This example shows that Johnson does not necessarily accept knowledge as "holy writ" in every case. Rather, he says that pleasant conversation does not always require knowledge or virtue. This is consistent with the phrase "we have all, at one time or other, been content to love those whom we could not esteem." By this, he means that many enjoy the company of people whom they do not hold in high esteem.

Life. The last collocation to be discussed is *life*, which gives additional insight into Johnson's concept of *knowledge*. Knowledge, which is to be taught, is not always reflected in one's behavior: "Yet since no man has power of acting equal to that of thinking, I know not whether the speculatist may not sometimes incur censures too severe, and by those who form ideas of his life from their knowledge of his books, be considered as worse than others, only because he was expected to be better."[33]

Johnson means here that a thought in the mind is not always represented in behavior. "Those who form ideas of his life from their knowledge" in this context are not likely to have a power of acting equal to the knowledge they get from their books. He indicates that knowledge can be gained from books, but this does not mean that this kind of knowledge always makes a man better in life; knowledge is not only acquired from books but also from life, and knowledge gained from experience is also needed to achieve a better, balanced existence.

> That the world is overrun with vice cannot be denied; but vice, however predominant, has not yet gained an unlimited dominion. Simple and unmingled good is not in our power, but we may generally escape a greater evil by suffering a less; and therefore, those who undertake to initiate the young and ignorant in the knowledge of life should be careful to inculcate the possibility of virtue and happiness, and to encourage endeavors by prospects of success.[34]

Here, Johnson again points out the importance of the knowledge of life. He says that if one tries to teach young and ignorant people knowledge of life, one should be careful to "inculcate" the possibility of virtue and happiness, and to encourage effort by the prospect of success. This phrasing indicates that Johnson associates knowledge with virtue, happiness, and success: "If the wealth of a trader is mentioned, he without hesitation devotes him to bankruptcy; if the beauty and elegance of a lady be commended, he wonders how the town can fall in love with rustic deformity; if a new performance of genius happens to be celebrated, he pronounces the writer a hopeless idiot, without knowledge of books or life, and without the understanding by which it must be acquired."[35]

This part is very clear. Modifying the phrase "a hopeless idiot" with "without knowledge of books or life" suggests that Johnson considers knowledge of both "books and life" to be important, and that the absence of one or the other can make a writer a "hopeless idiot." In *The Rambler*, Johnson seems to put more emphasis on knowledge gained from life than knowledge from books; in *The Rambler*, *life* and *lives* appear 716 times, whereas *book* and *books* appear ninety-four times. Such phrases as "acquaintance with life" (no. 4), "reflection upon life" (no. 29), and "observation upon life" (no. 60) show that Johnson attempts to convey the importance of insights into life, which is consistent with "perspicacity of penetration" in no. 175.

Conclusion and Limitations

In Johnsonian scholarship, *The Rambler* has been discussed mainly in terms of its moral discourse.[36] However, the association of knowledge with virtue in *The Rambler*, and the more frequent use of *knowledge* than words such as *piety* or *religion*, suggests that Johnson places no less importance on knowledge than on moral matters. Johnson argues that knowledge is gained not only from books but also from life experience, in combination with life lessons and the history of others who share their personal experience. This kind of knowledge can be a yardstick by which something is judged. It can also bring fame to its subject or can work as a means of avoiding traps set by the wicked. It is to be learned both from books and from life experience, and striking the right balance between sources of knowledge is important. It is important to note that Johnson indicates knowledge's potential negative effects on humanity. In expressing this idea, he claims that knowledge can often make mankind more "cunning than good," be used to develop a sense of superiority, or can be used to practice fraud and evil.

For Johnson, knowledge is a combination of that gained from books and that gained from conversation and carefully observing the world. It does not cohere as a whole if some of these elements are lacking. An intellectual giant, Johnson was not deflected to any particular aspect of knowledge, but was an advocate of moderation in discussing knowledge.

It should also be noted that the conception of knowledge discussed here is limited to the text of *The Rambler*. This means it would be an overgeneralization to say that Johnson maintained this conception throughout his literary career. In order to obtain a more wide-ranging insight into how Johnson viewed knowledge, it would be necessary to investigate his other works.

Notes

1 Kelly J. Whitmer, "Imagining Uses for Things: Teaching 'Useful Knowledge' in the Early Eighteenth Century." *History of Science* 55, no. 1 (2017): 37–60, 40. https://doi.org/10.1177/0073275316678872.

2 Lauren Jeanne Marsh, *The Rise of Useful Knowledge in Britain* (Minneapolis: University of Minnesota Press, 2003), 118.

3 Yet Johnson's defense of authorship is far from selfish. It represents the strongest obligation he feels, his debt not to any would-be patron of learning but to "the propagators of knowledge" and "teachers of truth." See Lawrence Lipking, *Samuel Johnson* (Cambridge, MA: Harvard University Press, 1998), 27.

4 Greg Clingham, introduction to *The Cambridge Companion to Samuel Johnson*, ed. Greg Clingham (New York: Cambridge University Press, 2002), 3.

5 *The Rambler* no. 4. The excerpts in this paper are from the corpus data compiled by the author based on *The Oxford Text Archive* (http://ota.ox.ac.uk/). In the following notes referring to *The Rambler*, the page numbers of the excerpts are

based on Samuel Johnson, *The Rambler*, in vols. 3–5 of *The Yale Edition of the Works of Samuel Johnson*, eds. W. J. Bate and Albrecht B. Strauss (New Haven, CT: Yale University Press, 1969), III, 20.

6 Samuel Johnson, *A Dictionary of the English Language: In Which the Words Are Deduced from Their Originals, and Illustrated in Their Different Significations by Examples from the Best Writers. To Which Are Prefixed, a History of the Language, and an English Grammar*, vol. 1. London: Printed by W. Strahan, for J. and P. Knapton, et al., 1755.

7 Isamu Hayakawa, discussing the entries included in Johnson's *Dictionary*, argues that the *Dictionary* should be discussed in the context of the Enlightenment. Adopting this perspective, the present research linguistically analyzes Johnson's use of the word "knowledge" itself in his periodical, *The Rambler*, which will help to elucidate how Johnson conceived knowledge. See Hayakawa Isamu, *Keimou shisouka no Johnson jisho: Chi no Shūsei wo mezashite* (*Johnson's Dictionary Under the Enlightenment: For the Purpose of Collecting Knowledge*])(Yokohama, Japan: Shunpūsha. 2013).

8 *Boswell's Life of Johnson*, 2:135.

9 Samuel Johnson, *The History of Rasselas, Prince of Abissinia*, ed. Thomas Keymer (Oxford, UK: Oxford University Press, 2009), 36.

10 Johnson, *The History of Rasselas*, 90.

11 Samuel Rogers, *Recollections of the Table-Talk of Samuel Rogers* (New York: D. Appleton & Company, 1856).

12 Samuel Johnson, *Johnson on Shakespeare*, ed. Arthur Sherbo. Vols. 7 and 8 of *The Yale Edition of the Works of Samuel Johnson* (New Haven, CT: Yale University Press, 1968), xxxiii.

13 No. 15 and no. 107 were written by unidentified correspondents.

14 Alexander Main, *Life and Conversations of Dr. Samuel Johnson* (London: Chapman & Hall, 1874), 154. Both Carter and Talbot contributed to the intellectual growth of their community by writing essays for *The Rambler* by encouraging each another to produce literary works. Afag S. Fazlollahi, "Elizabeth Carter's Legacy: Friendship and Ethics" (PhD diss., Georgia State University, 2011), 163; Johnson believed Carter to be one of the most educated intellectuals of his time, and he recognized in her a talented scholar, a poet and writer, a translator, an essayist, and finally, a friend; Fazlollahi, "Elizabeth Carter's Legacy," 183.

15 Alistair Baron, Paul Rayson, and Dawn Archer, "Word Frequency and Key Word Statistics in Corpus Linguistics," *Anglistik: International Journal of English Studies* 20, no. 1 (2009): 41–67.

16 Vaclav Brezina, Tony McEnery, and Stephen Wattam, "Collocations in Context: A New Perspective on Collocation Networks," *International Journal of Corpus Linguistics* 20, no. 2 (2015): 139–173.

17 Hendrik De Smet, Susanne Flach, Jukka Tyrkkö, and Hans-Jürgen Diller, *The Corpus of Late Modern English (CLMET), version 3.1: Improved Tokenization and Linguistic Annotation*. Katholieke Universiteit Leuven, Freie Universität Berlin, Tampere University, Ruhr-Universität Bochum (2015).

18 Tony Berber-Sardinha, "Comparing Corpora with WordSmith Tools," *Proceedings of the Workshop on Comparing Corpora* 9 (2000): 7–13.

19 *The Rambler* no. 208, V:319.

20 *The Rambler* no. 206, V:309.

21 *The Rambler* no. 75, IV:32.

22 Jason D. Solinger, "Becoming the Gentleman: British Letters and the Gentrification of Ordinary Men. " PhD diss., Brown University, 2004.
23 *The Rambler* no. 4, III: 3:22–23.
24 *The Rambler* no. 194, V:249.
25 *The Rambler* no. 194, V:250.
26 This concept is mentioned in *The Rambler* nos. 37, 157, and 164.
27 *The Rambler* no. 19, III:103–104.
28 *The Rambler* no. 111, IV:228.
29 *The Rambler* no. 60, III:323.
30 *The Rambler* no. 162, V:97.
31 *The Rambler* no. 4, III:20.
32 *The Rambler* no. 188, V:220–221.
33 *The Rambler* no. 77, IV:41.
34 *The Rambler* no. 119, IV:270.
35 *The Rambler* no. 144, V:5.
36 John Converse Dixon, "Politicizing Samuel Johnson: The Moral Essays and the Question of Ideology," *College Literature* 25, no. 3 (1998): 67–90.

10

Johnson's Final Words

With Particular Reference to Boswell's Dirty Deed on Sastres

HITOSHI SUWABE

Introduction

What were Johnson's final words? Johnson's friend, the translator and dramatist John Hoole, has left the most detailed and trustworthy account of events from the day of Johnson's death:

> Monday, Dec. 13. [1784]–Went to Bolt Court at eleven o'clock in the morning; met a young Lady coming down stairs from the Doctor, whom, upon inquiry, I found to be Miss Morris (a sister to Miss Morris, formerly on the stage). Mrs. De Moulins told me that she had seen the Doctor, that by her desire he had been told she came to ask his blessing, and that he said, "God bless you!" I then went up into his chamber, and found him lying very composed in a kind of doze: he spoke to nobody. Sir John Hawkins, Mr. Langton, Mrs. Gardiner, Rev. Mr. Strahan and Mrs. Strahan, Doctors Brocklesby and Butter, Mr. Steevens, and Mr. Nichols the printer, came; but no one chose to disturb him by speaking to him, and he seemed to take no notice of any person. While Mrs. Gardiner and I were there, before the rest came, he took a little warm

> milk in a cup, when he said something upon its not being properly given into his hand: he breathed very regular, though short, and appeared to be mostly in a calm sleep or dozing. I left him in this state, and never more saw him alive.[1]

The most important part of Hoole's account of Johnson's final words center on the remark, he "took a little warm milk in a cup when he said something upon its not being properly given into his hand." Johnson grumbled, doubtless to his servant Frances Barber, about his awkwardness. Since Johnson thereafter fell into a doze and then into an endless silence, it would seem that his grumble were his last words on earth. But are mumbled or grumbled words worthy of the status of a person's final words, let alone Samuel Johnson's? Were these in fact Johnson's last words? This chapter considers the extant versions of Johnson's last words that are recorded in print and manuscript sources, some of which differ markedly from Hoole's account. It pays particular attention to the accounts of Johnson's Italian friend, Francesco Sastres, and discusses why, despite the importance of Sastres's friendship with Johnson in his last years and despite Sastres's presence at Johnson's deathbed, Boswell only refers to him briefly and in passing in the *Life of Johnson*.

Johnson's Final Words

It is generally accepted that there are three possible phrases uttered by Johnson that may have been his final words on his deathbed. The first is, as mentioned, "God bless you," as John Hoole reports. Hoole heard it indirectly from Mrs. "De Moulins" (actually Desmoulins), one of Johnson's household guests. She had been by Johnson's bed when he blessed a Miss Morris. The second version of Johnson's last words is, "God bless you, my dear," as reported by James Boswell. When Johnson died in London, Boswell was far away in Scotland. But, on hearing of Johnson's death, he asked his youngest brother Thomas David Boswell, who was living in London, to go to see Johnson's servant Francis Barber and acquire directly from him the details of Johnson's last days. In the *Life of Johnson* Boswell quotes part of the long letter his brother had sent to him:

> On Monday, the 13th of December, the day on which he died, a Miss Morris, daughter to a particular friend of his, called, and said to Francis, that she begged to be permitted to see the Doctor, that she might earnestly request him to give her his blessing. Francis went into his room, followed by the young lady, and delivered the message. The Doctor turned himself in the bed, and said, "God bless you, my dear!" These were the last words he spoke.—His difficulty of breathing increased till about seven o'clock in the evening, when Mr. Barber and Mrs. Desmoulins, who were sitting in the room, observing that the noise he made in breathing had ceased, went to bed, and found he was dead.[2]

The difference between the two versions is whether Johnson uttered the phrase, "my dear," or not. Both versions are formulaic, words uttered in response to a young girl's request. There is no intention of expressing any personal feeling or emotions. Were they Johnson's final words?

The third version of Johnson's final words are recorded by the lawyer and author Sir John Hawkins and the author and actor Arthur Murphy. They are: "Jam moriturus [Now I am about to die]." This is certainly a fitting Latin phrase for Johnson's final words. Walter Jackson Bate notes that these "words echo the ancient Roman salutation of the dying gladiators to Caesar."[3] Johnson's great respect for the Latin language is proverbial. According to Boswell's *The Journal of the Tour to the Hebrides with Samuel Johnson*, on 5 September 1773, just after arriving on the Isle of Skye, Johnson and Boswell saw a monument of a Macdonald in the church of Armadale. It had an inscription of about fifty lines, written in English. Johnson said, "the inscription should have been in Latin, as every thing intended to be universal and permanent, should be."[4] The next year, when Oliver Goldsmith died, Johnson wrote Goldsmith's epitaph in Latin, despite the strong opposition of his many friends. Johnson's veneration of ancient Greece and Rome as the fountainhead of European culture was ardent and wholehearted, as can be seen in his claim that "A man who has not been in Italy, is always conscious of an inferiority, from his not having seen what it is expected a man should see. The grand object of travelling is to see the shores of the Mediterranean. On those shores were the four great Empires of the world; the Assyrian, the Persian, the Grecian, and the Roman.—All our religion, almost all our arts, almost all that sets us above savages, has come to us from the shores of the Mediterranean."[5]

We must not forget that throughout his life Johnson regarded himself as "a man who has not been in Italy," and that he suffered from a sense of inferiority because of it. Moreover, this fact may explain why Johnson continued to befriend Italians such as Giuseppe Baretti (a friendship that lasted about thirty years) and Francesco Sastres. It is to Sastres, and his status as Hawkins's and Murphy's source for the claim that Johnson's final words were "Jam moriturus," that I now turn.

Sastres, Johnson, and Boswell

Francesco Sastres was an Italian poet, translator, and writer. After publishing *An Introduction to the Italian Grammar* (1775) and *An Introduction to the Italian Language* (1778) in Bristol, Sastres came up to London in 1777, and before long seized a chance to get acquainted with Samuel Johnson. The first reference to Sastres in Boswell's journal is in the entry for 10 April 1779: "I had been at Dr. Johnson's; Paradise and Sastris [*sic*]," and it is possible that Johnson and Sastres had been acquainted for some time before this date.

Sastres attended Johnson regularly during his last days. "Unclubable" Hawkins curtly describes how "word was brought me by Mr. Sastres, to whom, in his last moments, he uttered these words 'Jam moriturus.'"[6] Murphy, however, relates it more vividly and sympathetically: "Mr. Sastres (whom Dr. Johnson esteemed and mentioned in his will) entered the room during his illness. Dr. Johnson, as soon as he saw him, stretched forth his hand, and, in a tone of lamentation, called out, JAM MORITURUS!"[7] Murphy's more evocative account may stem from the fact that he, like Sastres, but unlike Hawkins, was a member of the Essex Head Club. This club, established in December 1783, was the last of several clubs Johnson founded and belonged to during his life. Murphy could easily, therefore, have heard the details of Johnson's final moments from Sastres.

According to Hester Piozzi, Sastres was, "much his [Johnson's] favourite,"[8] and Boswell too initially held Sastres in high regard, as the following letter he wrote on 24 June 1784 to Lord Thurlow clearly shows:

> Dr. Samuel Johnson, though wonderfully recovered from a complication of dangerous illness, is by no means well, and I have reason to think that his valuable life cannot be preserved long, without the benignant influence of a southern climate.
>
> It would therefore be of very great moment were he to go to Italy before winter sets in; and I know he wishes it much. But the objection is that his pension of £300 a year would not be sufficient to defray his expence, and make it convenient for Mr. Sastres, an ingenious and worthy native of that country, and a teacher of Italian here, to accompany him.[9]

Sastres and Boswell continued their acquaintance after Johnson's death, initially on good terms. In February 1786, Boswell, after a long hesitation, came to London to settle down and be called to the English bar. In his journal for 22 February of that year he could write lightheartedly: "Went to the Essex Head Club, where were Barrington, Devaynes, Brocklesby, Poore, Jodrell, Sastres. I eat and drank heartily, and there was good talk, which I enjoyed but do not recollect. Sastres walked home with me. I was now quite tranquillized as to London."[10]

However, Boswell did not include Sastres's name when he listed the members of the Essex Head Club,[11] though he continued to meet Sastres occasionally at the club. Sastres's name may also sound unfamiliar to most readers of Boswell's *Life of Johnson* because Boswell mentioned him only once in the text, as "Mr. Sastres, the Italian master,"[12] and once in a footnote, as a recipient of five pounds from Johnson's legacy.[13] Boswell struck out two sentences from the manuscript draft of the *Life of Johnson* that mentioned Sastres's deep respect for and goodwill to Johnson. Part of the manuscript draft of the *Life of Johnson* that covers 22 June 1784 is as follows (the italics are my own):

> The anxiety of his friends for preserving so valuable a life as long as human means might be supposed to have influence made them plan for him a retreat from the severity of a British winter to the mild climate of Italy. This scheme was at last brought to a very serious resolution at General Paoli's, where some of us had often talked of it. *It was considered that he would be exceedingly helpless and dull were he to go alone, and therefore it was concerted that he should be accompanied by Mr. Sastres the Italian master, who we were persuaded would wait on him with a very affectionate attention, and who very readily agreed to go.* One essential matter however we understood was necessary to be previously settled, which was obtaining from the King such an addition to Johnson's pension as would be sufficient to put him in a situation to defray the expense in a manner becoming the first literary character of a great nation and, independent of all his other merits, the author of the DICTIONARY OF THE ENGLISH LANGUAGE.[14]

With regard to the italicized section, Irma S. Lustig outlines how "This entire sentence is cancelled in the draft and 'Mr. Sastres' and 'master' are heavily scored and written over in a determined effort to make them illegible. Why Boswell wished to conceal Sastres's generous involvement in the scheme is not apparent. Boswell tells us nothing whatever about Sastres, but it is clear that he was a close and valued friend of Johnson's in the latter years of his life. Johnson in his will left him five pounds 'to be laid out in books of piety for his own use.'"[15]

If these passages had not been removed from the draft, Francesco Sastres would have had a more significant presence in the *Life of Johnson*. Why did Boswell eliminate these references to Sastres? Boswell may have removed Sastres's name because he suspected him of a betrayal regarding the publication of some letters Johnson had sent to Sastres. In 1786 Boswell had noted, "Mr. Sastres has eleven letters from Dr. Johnson of which I am to have copies."[16] The contents of these letters clearly showed Johnson's deep affection for Sastres. For example, on 20 October 1784 Johnson wrote as follows from Lichfield:

> You have abundance of naughty tricks; is this your way of writing to a poor sick friend twice a week? Post comes after post, and brings no letter from Mr. Sastres. If you know any thing, write and tell it; if you know nothing, write and say that you know nothing. . . . Mrs. Desmoulines never writes, and I know not how things go on at home; tell me, dear Sir, what you can. . . . I am very weak, and have had bad nights. I am, dear Sir, Your, etc.[17]

Johnson is appealing to Sastres to write to him more often and to give him information about his home in London. Johnson was at that time on his final trip to Lichfield, Ashbourne, Birmingham and Oxford, visiting his old friends and bidding them a final farewell. Despite the significance of these letters, and contrary to Sastres's expectations, Boswell did not use any of Johnson's letters to Sastres in the *Life of Johnson*. A letter Sastres sent to Boswell in February 1788 suggests why this happened:

> Dear Sir, I have very often taken the liberty of calling on you with our Dear great Friend's letters to me in my pocket, but having been always so unfortunate as never to find you at home nor hearing anything from you, I began to think that you considered them of little consequence, and was not very desirous to have them. I have been at the same time earnestly Solicited by Mrs. Piozzi to give the said letters to her, to publish them with the rest of Johnson's to herself. I have been informed, Dear Sir, that your life of Johnson is not yet ready for the press, whereas Mrs. Piozzi's book will be published in a very short time; and considering within my mind that you may make the same use of the said letters from Mrs. Piozzi's publication as from the Manuscript, and trusting on your goodness to excuse me, by considering the many obligations I have to that lady, I have been induced to deliver them into her hands. I hope, Dear Sir, that this will not be interpreted by you as a disregard from me, the reverse of it being the real truth.[18]

Piozzi's *Letters to and from the Late Samuel Johnson* was published on 8 March 1788. Sastres, it seems, sent this letter in advance of the imminent publication of Piozzi's book, hopefully to appease Boswell, and to explain his obligation to Mrs. Piozzi. But Boswell was too irritated to be soothed by such an apology, and felt it discreditable for him to reuse the same letters after Piozzi had published them. At that time his rival, Mrs. Piozzi's *Anecdotes of the Late Samuel Johnson* had gone through four editions since its first publication in 1786, "while Boswell was still floundering"[19] with a tremendous volume of work in front of him, including gathering Johnson's letters to his friends and acquaintances. It is no wonder that Boswell took it as an act of betrayal by Sastres that he had given Johnson's letters to Mrs. Piozzi of all people. This sense of betrayal helps explain why Boswell crossed out the name of Sastres in two places in the manuscript draft of the *Life of Johnson*.

The second place where Boswell cancelled the name of Sastres from the manuscript draft is the page for 28 June 1784 (again, italics are my own):

> On Monday 28 June I had the honour to receive from the Lord Chancellor the following letter. This letter gave me an elevated satisfaction which has been seldom equaled in the course of the events of my life. I next day went and

> showed it to Sir Joshua Reynolds, who was exceedingly pleased with it, *and in the warmth of his friendly joy said that he himself would undertake that Mr. Sastres should have a pension of eighty pounds for his life.* He thought that I should now communicate the negotiation to Dr. Johnson, who might afterwards complain if the success with which it had now been honoured should be too long concealed from him.[20]

In the footnote to the same page Lustig notes, "The name is again heavily scored (not merely struck) out, but this time the last five letters are clearly discernible." In fact, it is not only the names of Sastres that has vanished from the *Life* (1991), but the whole section italicized. Sastres's goodwill to Johnson and the honor of his having received a bequest from Johnson have thus been concealed by Boswell and nearly lost to history. We cannot help attributing jealousy and malice toward Sastres on Boswell's part.

As for the relationship between Boswell and Sastres after the publication of the *Life of Johnson*, we can surmise that it must have been very strained. The only extant record of their acquaintance at this point occurs in Boswell's journal of 28 November 1792: "Punch always hurts me. I was very uneasy this morning and lay long. Dined with my brother T. D., and somewhat soothed by his rational conversation. We went together to the Essex Head Club and met Brocklesby, Reed, Gregory, Calamy and Sastres."[21]

This is Boswell's last reference to Sastres. Three years later in 1795 Boswell died in London, far away from home. As for Sastres, he lived until 1822, having served as consul-general to the Kingdom of the Two Sicilies in his later years.

Sastres and "Jam Moriturus"

The letters Johnson wrote to Sastres include one that may add credence to the account that Johnson's final words were "Jam moriturus." The letter in question was written on 2 September in Ashbourne while Johnson was staying with his friend John Taylor: "My health, by the mercy of God, still improves; and I have hope of standing the English winter, and of seeing you, and reading Petrarch at Bolt-court; but let me not flatter myself too much. I am yet weak, but stronger than I was."[22]

In this letter Johnson looks forward to reading Petrarch with the young Italian in his home at Bolt Court. Johnson had a lifelong interest in Petrarch: he is the poet whose work Johnson as a boy found by chance on an upper shelf in his father's bookshop when he was searching for apples his brother had hidden. Boswell says, "There were no apples; but the large folio proved to be Petrarch, whom he had seen mentioned, in some preface, as one of the restorers of learning. His curiosity having been thus excited, he sat down with avidity, and read a great part of the book."[23] The reference to Petrarch in his 1784 letter to Sastres validates the claim in the Hill-Powell edition of the *Life of Johnson* that "Johnson retained his interest in Italian to the end of his life."[24] Does this letter propose reading the great Italian poet with Sastres or does it propose the resumption of an activity they had already started before Johnson set out on his trip? At any rate, Johnson returned to Bolt Court on 16 November, and the next day he wrote to Sastres, saying, "Mr. Johnson is glad to inform Mr. Sastres that he came home last night."[25] We can reasonably surmise that Sastres hastened to Bolt Court and that they read Petrarch together, Sastres as teacher and Johnson as pupil. While reading Petrarch they may have talked about ancient Rome; for example, about gladiators who fought to the death in front of the emperor and the spectators. It seems only natural that Johnson on his deathbed called out "Jam Moriturus" at the sight of Francesco Sastres. It would have been the concentrated expression of Johnson's cordial friendship, his profound erudition and, above all, his unconquerable mind.

Notes

This essay is based on a paper entitled "Johnson's Final Words," which I read at the Johnson at 300 conference at Pembroke College, Oxford, UK, September 15, 2009.

1 John Hoole, "Narrative of John Hoole," in *Johnsonian Miscellanies*, ed. George Birkbeck Hill, 2 vols. (Oxford, UK: Clarendon Press, 1897), 2:159.
2 *Boswell's Life of Johnson*, 4:417–418. Paul J. Korshin's assertion that Boswell's version is the most trustworthy is not fully convincing. See "Johnson's Last Days: Some Facts and Problems," in *Johnson After Two Hundred Years* (Philadelphia: University of Pennsylvania Press, 1986), 55–76.
3 Walter Jackson Bate, *Samuel Johnson* (New York: Harcourt Brace Jovanovich, 1975), 599.
4 *Boswell's Life of Johnson*, 5:154.
5 *Boswell's Life of Johnson*, 3:36.
6 Hill, *Johnsonian Miscellanies*, 2:134.
7 Hill, *Johnsonian Miscellanies*, 1:447.
8 Hill, *Johnsonian Miscellanies*, 1:292.
9 James Boswell, *Letters of James Boswell*, ed. Chauncey Brewster Tinker, 2 vols. (Oxford, UK: Clarendon Press, 1924), 2:323.
10 Irma S. Lustig and Frederick A. Pottle, eds., *Boswell: The English Experiment, 1785–1789*, (London: Heinemann, 1986), 40. In the footnote of the same page Lustig notes, "Francesco Sastres, Italian teacher and translator, seems to have sent Boswell some interesting Johnsoniana shortly after this meeting."
11 *Boswell's Life of Johnson*, 4:254.
12 *Boswell's Life of Johnson*, 3:22.
13 *Boswell's Life of Johnson*, 4:403.
14 Irma S. Lustig and Frederick A. Pottle, eds., *Boswell: The Applause of the Jury, 1782–1785*, (New York: McGraw-Hill, 1981), 248.
15 Lustig and Pottle, *Boswell: The Applause of the Jury*, n7.

16 Marion S. Pottle, Claude Colleer Abbot, and Frederick A. Pottle, *Catalogue of the Papers of James Boswell at Yale University*, 3 vols. (Edinburgh, UK: Edinburgh University Press, 1993), 3:890.
17 Samuel Johnson, *The Letters of Samuel Johnson,* ed. Bruce Redford, 5 vols. (Prinston University Press, 1992–94), 4:425–426.
18 Marshall Waingrow, ed., *The Correspondence and Other Papers of James Boswell Relating to the Making of the Life of Johnson* (London: Heinemann, 1969), 270–271.
19 Mary Hyde, *The Impossible Friendship* (Cambridge, MA: Harvard University Press, 1972), 114.
20 Hyde, *The Impossible Friendship*, 114.
21 Marlies K. Danziger and Frank Brady, eds., *Boswell: The Great Biographer, 1789–1795*, (London: Heinemann, 1989), 202.
22 *Letters of Johnson*, 4:390.
23 *Boswell's Life of Johnson*, 1:57.
24 *Boswell's Life of Johnson*, 1:116, n2.
25 *Letters of Johnson*, 4:439.

Appendix

Johnson's Translated Works and Criticisms in Japanese

COLLECTED BY HIDEICHI ETO

	Johnson's work (original title)	Japanese translation (title)	Translator (family name, first name)	Publisher	Published year
1	*The History of Rasselas, Prince of Abyssinia*	Oji Rasselas Denki	Takeyama, Koshi	Keibundo	1886
2	*The History of Rasselas, Prince of Abyssinia*	Rasselas den chushaku: Abyssinia kokuo Rasselas keirekishi	Watanabe, Matsushige	Sekizenkwan	1890
3	*The History of Rasselas, Prince of Abyssinia*	Abyssinia-koku Oji Rasselas shi ekigi chokuyakutsuki	Kawata, Kiyohiko	Bunkodo	1893
4	*The History of Rasselas, Prince of Abyssinia*	Oji Rasselas den	Shibano, Rokusuke	Dainippon tosyo	1905
5	*Prayers and Meditations*	Kito to mokuso	Suzuki, Jiro	Ichiryusha	1933
6	*The History of Rasselas, Prince of Abyssinia*	Kofuku no tankyu	Shyumuta, Natsuo	Shisakusha	1948
7	"Proposals for Shakespeare," "Preface of Shakespeare," and "Notes"	Shakespeare ron	Yoshida, Kenichi	Shisakusha	1948
8	"On Wasting Time" and "Dick Minim the Critic" in *Idler*; "Preface to Shakespeare: in *Shakespeare Criticism*, edited by D. Nichol Smith; ""Life of Collins" in *Lives of the Poets*	Eikoku kindai sanbun shu	Fukuhara, Rintaro	Kenkyusha shuppan	1953
9	*The History of Rasselas, Prince of Abyssinia*	Kofuku no tankyu: Abyssinia no oji Rasselas no monogatari	Shumuta, Natsuo	Agatsuma shobo	1962
10	*Rambler* Nos. 59, 60, 61; *Adventurer* No. 115; *Idler* Nos. 14, 31, 35, 40, 97; *Shakespeare Criticism*, edited by D. Nichol Smith; "Life of Cowley" and "Life of Collins" in *Lives of the Poets*; several letters of Johnson	Sekai jinseiron zensyu	Yoshida, Kenichi	Chikuma shobo	1963
11	"Life of Milton" in *Lives of the Poets*	Milton den	Shumuta Natsuo	Chikuma shobo	1974

	Johnson's work (original title)	Japanese translation (title)	Translator (family name, first name)	Publisher	Published year
12	"Proposals for Shakespeare," "Preface of Shakespeare," and "Notes"	Shakespeare ron (A different edition of the translation No. 7)	Yoshida, Kenichi	Sojusha	1975
13	*Life of Savage*	Savage den: aru taihai shijin no shyogai	Suwabe, Hitoshi	Shimbisha	1975
14	"An Extempore Elegy," "Burlesque of Lines by Lope de Vega," and "On Hearing Miss Thrale Deliberate about Her Hat"	Sokkyo tan shi	Izumitani, Yutaka	Shimyakusha	1976
15	"A Short Song of Congratulation" and "To Mrs. Thrale, On her Completing Her Thirty-Fifth Year"	"Seijin shoka," "Thrale fujin he: 35 sai no tanjyo wo shukushite"	Izumitani, Yutaka	Shimyakusha	1977
16	"Proposals for an Edition of Shakespeare," "Preface to Shakespeare," and "Notes on Shakespeare's Plays" in Vol. 12 of *The Yale Edition of the Works of Samuel Johnson*	Shakespeare josetsu	Nakagawa, Makoto	Aratake shuppan	1978
17	*London* and *The Vanity of Human Wishes*	Johnson hakase no shi: London, The Vanity of Human Wishes hyoron to taiyaku	Shibagaki, Shigeru	Kaisosha	1985
18	"Sermon 5," "An Essay on Epitaph," "On Gray's Epitaph," "The Vision of Theodore, Hermit of Teneriffe Found in His Cell," "The Preface to the Preceptor, Containing a General Plan of Education," "Of the Duty of a Journalist," *Rambler* Nos. 170 and 171, "Review of *A Free Inquiry into the Nature and Origin of Evil*"	Tenerihu no inja ・ seodo-noyume: Samuel Johnson zuisousyu	Izumitani, Yutaka	Apolonsha	1991

(continued)

	Johnson's work (original title)	Japanese translation (title)	Translator (family name, first name)	Publisher	Published year
19	*Life of Pope*	Pope den	Nakagawa, Tadashi	Apolonsha	1992
20	Sermons 1–28	Eien no sentaku: Samuel Johnson sekkyo syu	Izumitani, Yutaka	Seikokai shuppan	1997
21	*Life of Swift*	Swift: denki to shihen	Nakagawa, Tadashi	Apolonsha	2005
22	*A Journey to the Western Islands of Scotland*	Scotland seiho shoto no tabi	Suwabe, Hitoshi; Ichikawa, Yasuo; Eto, Hideichi; Shibagaki, Shigeru	Chuo University Press	2006
23	*Life of Dryden*	Dryden den	Nakagawa, Tadashi	Apolonsha	2006
24	*Life of Cowley, Milton, Dryden, Savage, Pope, Swift, Gray*	Igirisu shijin den	Harada, Noriyuki; Engetsu, Katsuhiro; Takeda, Masaaki; Semba, Yutaka; Kobayashi, Akio; Watanabe, Koji; Yoshino, Yuri	Chikuma shobo	2009
25	*A Journey into North Wales in the Year 1774* and *Dr. Johnson's French Journal, 1775*	Johnson hakase to Thrale fujin no tabi nikki: Wales (1774) to France (1775)	Ichikawa, Yasuo; Suwabe, Hitoshi; Inamura, Zenji; Eto, Hideichi	Chuo University Press	2017

	Johnson's works printed in textbooks (anthology)	Japanese title of the textbooks (anthology)	Publisher	Published year
1	*Sanders' Union Fourth Reader*	—	Okamoto, Naokichi	1882
2	*The History of Rasselas, Prince of Abyssinia*	—	Tokyo Domei shuppan shoshi	1885
3	*The History of Rasselas, Prince of Abyssinia*	—	Domei shuppan shoshi	1885
4	*The History of Rasselas, Prince of Abyssinia*	—	Rikugokwan	1886
5	*The History of Rasselas, Prince of Abyssinia*	—	Hobunkwan	1889
6	*The History of Rasselas, Prince of Abyssinia*	—	Sekizenkwan	1889
7	*The History of Rasselas, Prince of Abyssinia*	—	Hakubunsha	1890
8	*The History of Rasselas, Prince of Abyssinia*	—	Ohira &Co.	1892
9	*The History of Rasselas, Prince of Abyssinia*	—	Shoeido and Shokodo	1897
10	*The First Acquaintance with Johnson: The Kobunsha Series of Supplementary English Readers for Middle Schools. No 12*	—	Kobunsha	1900
11	*Johnson's Table Talk by James Boswell No. 1*	—	Kobunsha	1902
12	*Johnson's Table Talk by James Boswell No. 2*	—	Kobunsha	1903
13	*The History of Rasselas, Prince of Abyssinia*	—	Yuhikaku shobo	1904
14	*The Kobunsha Series: Rasselas: Prince of Abyssinia by Samuel Johnson, LL. D. with an introduction by Henry Morley*	—	Kobunsha	1910
15	*Rasselas by Dr. Samuel Johnson*	—	Nichieisha	1912
16	*Lives of the English Poets: Vol. I (Milton)*	—	Kenkyusha	1943, 1949
17	*Lives of the English Poets: Vol. II (Dryden)*	—	Kenkyusha	1943, 1951
18	*Lives of the English Poets: Vol. III (Pope)*	—	Kenkyusha	1943, 1950
19	*Johnson's Essays* (Twelve essays in *Idler* and three essays in *Adventurer*)	—	Apolonsha	1965
20	*The Fountains & Other Stories*	—	Apolonsha	1986
21	"The Plan of an English Dictionary"	Lessons in Language	Kinseido	1986
22	Several persons in Johnson's essays	Characters	Apolonsha	1987
23	*Rambler* Nos. 2, 18, 32, 60, 67, 102 and 196; *Adventurer* Nos. 111 and 120; *Idler* Nos. 27, 31, and 94	Moral Essays: Dream, Hope and Life	New Current International	1988

	Criticism	Author/editor (family name, first name)	Publisher	Published year
1	*Johnson*	Uchida, Mitsugu	Minyusha	1894
2	*Johnson hakase to sono mure*	Ishida, Kenji	Kenkyusha	1933 (Revised, 1949)
3	*Johnson*	Ishida, Kenji and Suzuki, Jiro	Kenkyusha	1934
4	*Igirisu hihyoushi gaisetsu (10): VII. Dr. Johnson*	Narita, Shigehisa	Kobunsha	1936
5	*Johnson dai hakase*	Fukuhara, Rintaro	Kenkyusha	1969
6	*Johnson*	Fukuhara, Rintaro	Kenkyusha	1972
7	*Samuel Johnson* (in English)	Takahashi, Genji	Aiikusha	1978
8	*Doctor Johnson: sono ningen to bungaku*	Shibazaki, Takeo	Aratake shuppan	1980
9	*Johnson no "Eigo jiten": sono rekishiteki igi*	Nagashima, Daisuke	Taisyukan shoten	1983
10	*Doctor Johnson meigen shu*	Nagashima, Daisuke	Taisyukan shoten	1984
11	*Dr. Jonson's Dictionary: Select Comparison between the First Edition and the Fourth* (in English)	Shibagaki, Shigeru	Akashi shoten	1989
12	*Johnson den no keifu*	Nakahara, Akio	Kenkyusha shuppan	1991
13	*Kentou no bungo Johnson: Meijiki "Rasselas" no henei*	Izumitani, Yutaka	Keisuisha	1992
14	*Johnson kenkyu: sono hito to sakuhin*	Izumitani, Yutaka	Keisuisha	1993
15	*Johnson no shi to shinko*	Nagashima, Daisuke	Seikokai shuppan	1995
16	*Dr. Jonson in Boswell's Life and Journals*	Shibagaki, Shigeru	Marujyusha	1997
17	*"Jisyo no Johnson" no seiritsu: Boswell nikki kara denki he*	Nakahara, Akio	Eihosha	1999
18	*Jisyo hensan no dynamism: Johnson, Webster and Japan*	Hayakawa, Isamu	Jiyusha	2001
19	*"Rasselas" jyuyoshi no kenkyu*	—	Keisuisha	2001
20	*Nihon ni okeru Samuel Johnson oyobi James Boswell bunken mokuroku (1871–2005)*	Fujii, Tetsu	Nada shuppan center	2006
21	*Johnson hakase goroku*	Itami, Reiko (ed.)	Parade Books	2007
22	*Jyuhachiseiki no Scotland: Johnson no ryokoki wo megutte*	Eto, Hdeichi	Kaitakusha	2008
23	*Johnson to Boswell: jujitsu no syuhen*	Suwabe, Hitoshi	Chuo University Press	2009

	Criticism	Author/editor (family name, first name)	Publisher	Published year
24	*Eikoku bunka no kyojin: Samuel Johnson*	Eto, Hideichi; Shibagaki, Shigeru: Suwabe, Hitoshi, (eds.)	Minatonohito	2009
25	*Samuel Johnson: sono tayonaru sekai*	Kobayashi, Akio (ed.)	Kinseido	2010
26	*Keimo shisouka no Johnson jisyo: chi no syusei wo mezashite*	Hayakawa, Isamu	Shumpusha	2013
27	*Johnson to "kokugo" jiten no tanjo*	Hayakawa, Isamu	Shumpusha	2014

Acknowledgments

This book began its existence several years ago when Greg Clingham suggested that we needed to publish a book about Johnson scholarship in Japan. As editors of this book, we have been extremely fortunate to have the support of such an inspiring scholar as Greg Clingham. Without his help, we would never have initiated (let alone complete) this Johnson in Japan project. We are deeply grateful for his encouragement and for his practical advice.

We would also like to acknowledge The Johnson Society of Japan for their continuous support of this project. Through the academic activities organized by this society, we have been able to cultivate ideas about this project and to collect feedback from the contributors of this book. We also depended on the wider network of scholars. We would particularly like to thank the following: Ian Calvert, Stephen Clark, Tetsu Fujii, Nicholas Roe, and Laurence Williams. In varying degrees, they have read drafts of this book or parts of it and inspired us to find new ways of thinking about the subject, Johnson in Japan. They have all made working on this book a more rewarding experience.

We would also like to express our thanks to Angela Piliouras, production editor at Westchester Publishing Services, for her kindness and perseverance; Julia Kurtz for her meticulous editing; and the anonymous readers at Bucknell University Press, whose invaluable input have helped bring this book to its present state.

Bibliography

Abe, Masahiko 阿部公彦. *Shijou saiaku no eigo seisaku* 史上最悪の英語政策 (*The Worst-Ever English Policy*). Tokyo: Hitsuji Shobo ひつじ書房, 2017.

Altick, Richard D. *The English Common Reader: A Social History of the Mass Reading Public 1800–1900*. Chicago: University of Chicago Press, 1957.

Anonymous. "Art. IX. *Emma; a Novel.*" *Quarterly Review* (October 1815): 188–201.

Appadurai, Arjun. *Globalization*. Durham, NC: Duke University Press, 2001.

Aravamudam, Srinivas. *Enlightenment Orientalism: Resisting the Rise of the Novel*. Chicago: University of Chicago Press, 2012.

Armstrong, Nancy. *Desire and Domestic Fiction: A Political History of the Novel*. New York: Oxford University Press, 1987.

Austen, Jane. *Pride and Prejudice*. Edited by Pat Rogers. Cambridge: Cambridge University Press, [1813] 2006.

Austen-Leigh, J. E. *A Memoir of Jane Austen and Other Family Recollections*. Oxford, UK: Oxford University Press, [1869] 2002.

Baker, David Erskine, and Isaac Reed, eds. *Biographia Dramatica, or a Companion to the Playhouse*. 2 vols. 1782. 3 vols. London: Longman et al., 1812.

Baldick, Chris. *In Frankenstein's Shadow: Myth, Monstrosity, and Nineteenth-Century Writing*. New York: Oxford University Press, 1987.

Barish, Jonas. *The Antitheatrical Prejudice*. Berkeley: University of California Press, 1985.

Baron, Alistair, Paul Rayson, and Dawn Archer. "Word Frequency and Key Word Statistics in Historical Corpus Linguistics." *Anglistik: International Journal of English Studies* 20, no. 1 (2009): 41–67.

Basker, James G. "Johnson, Boswell, and the Abolition of Slavery." *New Rambler: Journal of the Johnson Society of London* serial no. EVI, 2002–2003 (September 2003).

———. "'The Next Insurrection': Johnson, Race and Rebellion." *The Age of Johnson: A Scholarly Annual* 11, edited by Paul J. Korshin and Jack Lynch, 17–51. New York: AMS 2000.

Bate, Walter Jackson. *Samuel Johnson*. New York: Harcourt Brace, 1975.

Behn, Aphra. *Oroonoko*. Edited by Janet Todd. London: Penguin, 2003.

Berber-Sardinha, Tony. "Comparing Corpora with Wordsmith Tools." *Proceedings of the Workshop on Comparing Corpora* 9 (2000): 7–13, https://doi.org/10.3115/1117729.1117731.

Berry, Helen. "Rethinking Politeness in Eighteenth-Century England: Moll King's Coffee House and the Significance of 'Flash Talk': The Alexander Prize Lecture." *Transactions of the Royal Historical Society* 11 (2001): 65–81.

Black, Jeremy. *The English Press in the Eighteenth Century*. London: Croom Helm, 1987.

Bloom, Harold. "Frankenstein, or the new Prometheus." *Partisan Review* 32 (1965): 611–618.

Boerhaave, Hermann. "Oration on the Usefulness of the Mechanical Method in Medicine." In *Boerhaave's Orations*, translated by E. Kegel-Brinkgreve and A. M. Luyendijk-Elshout. Leiden, Netherlands: E. J. Brill, 1983.

Bohls, Elizabeth. *Women Travel Writers and the Language of Aesthetics, 1716–1818*. Cambridge: Cambridge University Press, 1996.

Bond, Donald F., ed. *The Spectator*. 5 vols. Oxford, UK: Clarendon Press, 1965.

———. *The Tatler*. 3 vols. Oxford, UK: Clarendon Press, 1987.

Bond, Richmond P. *Growth and Change in the Early English Press*. Lawrence: University of Kansas Libraries, 1969.

Boswell, James. *The Journal of a Tour to the Hebrides, with Samuel Johnson, 1773*. Edited by F. A. Pottle and C. H. Bennet. Yale Editions of the Private Papers of James Boswell. London: William Heinemann, 1963.

———. *Letters of James Boswell*. Edited by Chauncey Brewster Tinker. 2 vols. Oxford, UK: Clarendon Press, 1924.

———. *The Life of Johnson: Together with Boswell's Journal of a Tour to the Hebrides and Johnson's Diary of a Journey into North Wales*. Edited by George Birkbeck Hill, revised by L. F. Powell. 6 vols. Oxford, UK: Clarendon Press, 1934–1964.

Boulton, James T., ed. *Samuel Johnson: The Critical Heritage*. London: Routledge, 1971.

Bourdaghs, Michael K., Atsuko Ueda, and Joseph A. Murphy. Introduction to *Theory of Literature and Other Critical Writings* by Sōseki Natsume. New York: Columbia University Press, 2009.

Brack, O. M., Jr., and Thomas Kaminski. "Johnson, James, and the Medicinal Dictionary." *Modern Philology* 81, no. 4 (May 1984): 378–400.

Brezina, Vaclav, Tony McEnery, and Stephen Wattam. "Collocations in Context: A New Perspective on Collocation Networks." *International Journal of Corpus Linguistics* 20, no. 2 (2015): 139–173.

Bruce, James. *Travels to Discover the Source of the Nile, in the Years 1768, 1769, 1770, 1771, 1772, 1773*. London: G. G. J. and J. Robinson, 1790.

Buchan, William. *Domestic Medicine, or a Treatise on the Prevention and Cure of Diseases by Regimen and Simple Medicines*. London: Printed by A. Strahan; T. Cadell Jun. and W. Davies and J. Balfour, and W. Creech, Edinburgh, 1800.

Burns, R. M. *The Great Debate on Miracles: From Joseph Glanvill to David Hume*. Plainsboro, New Jersey: Associated University Press, 1981.

Burrowes, Robert. "Essays on the Stile of Doctor Samuel Johnson, No. I." In *The Transactions of the Royal Irish Academy, Polite Literature*, 27–40. Dublin: Royal Irish Academy, 1787.

Burwick, Frederick. "'The Revolt of Islam': Vegetarian Shelley and the Narrative of Mental Pathology." *Wordsworth Circle* 40, no. 2/3 (Spring–Summer 2009): 87–93.

Cai, Tian Ming. *Limitations of Humanity: Samuel Johnson's Works.* Beijing: International Culture Publishing, 2009.

———. "A Reflection on Johnson's Shakespeare in China." *Johnsonian News Letter* 66, no. 1 (March 2015): 48–52.

Caines, Michael, Paul Goring, Nicola Shaughnessy, Robert Shaughnessy, Gail Marshall, and Tetsuko Kishi, eds. *Lives of Shakespearian Actors I: David Garrick, Charles Macklin and Margaret Woffington by Their Contemporaries.* 3 vols. London: Pickering & Chatto, 2008.

———. *Shakespeare and the Eighteenth Century.* Oxford, UK: Oxford University Press, 2013.

Carlyle, Thomas. "The Hero as Man of Letters: Johnson, Rousseau, Burns." In *On Heroes, Hero-Worship and the Heroic in History*, 154–195. Vol. 5 of *The Works of Thomas Carlyle.* London: Chapman and Hall, 1897.

Carré, Jacques, ed. *The Crisis of Courtesy: Studies in the Conduct-Book in Britain, 1600–1900.* Vol. 51. Leiden, Netherlands: E. J. Brill, 1994.

Carter, Philip. "Polite 'Persons': Character, Biography and the Gentlemen." *Transactions of the Royal Historical Society* 12 (2002): 333–354.

Cass, Jeffrey. "'The Scraps, Patches, and Rags of Daily Life': Gaskell's Oriental Other and the Conservation of Cranford." *Papers on Language and Literature* 35, no. 1 (1999): 417–433.

Cave, Edward, ed. *The Gentleman's Magazine.* 16 vols. London: Pickering & Chatto, 1998.

The Censor. 3 vols. London: The Censor by Lewis Theobald 1717.

Chalmers, Alexander. "Historical and Biographical Preface to *The Rambler.*" In vol. 19 of *The British Essayists*, edited by Alexander Chalmers. 45 vols. London, Robinsons: 1802.

Chatterjee, Kumkum, and Clement Hawes, ed. *Europe Observed: Multiple Gazes in Early Modern Encounters.* Lewisburg, PA: Bucknell University Press, 2008.

Cheyne, George. *The English Malady.* Edited by Roy Porter. London: Tavistock, 1991.

Chilton, Myles. *English Studies Beyond the 'Center': Teaching Literature and the Future of Global English.* New York: Routledge, 2016.

Clingham, Greg, ed. *The Cambridge Companion to Samuel Johnson.* Cambridge : Cambridge University Press, 1997.

———. *James Boswell, the Life of Johnson.* Cambridge: Cambridge University Press, 1992.

———. "Johnson and Borges: Some Reflections." In *Samuel Johnson Among the Modernists*, edited by Anthony W. Lee, 189–212, 272–275. Clemson, SC: Clemson University Press, 2019.

———. "Johnson and China: Culture, Commerce, and the Dream of the Orient in Mid-Eighteenth-Century England." *1650–1850: Ideas, Issues, & Aesthetics in the Early Modern Era* 24 (2019): 178–242.

———. "Johnson, Ends, and the Possibility of Happiness." In *Johnson After 300 Years*, edited by Greg Clingham and Philip Smallwood. Cambridge: Cambridge University Press, 2009.

———. "A Johnsonian in Japan." *Johnsonian News Letter* 60, no. 2 (September 2009): 37–40.

Conder, Josiah. *The Modern Traveller: A Description, Geographical, Historical, and Topographical, of the Various Countries of the Globe.* 30 vols. London: J. Duncan, 1830.

Cowan, Brian. "Café or Coffeehouse? Transnational Histories of Coffee and Sociability." In *Drink in the Eighteenth and Nineteenth Centuries*, Perspectives in Economic and Social History No. 29, edited by Susanne Schmid and Barbara Schmidt-Haberkamp, 35–46. London: Pickering & Chatto, 2014.

———. "Mr. Spectator and the Coffeehouse Public Sphere." *Eighteenth-Century Studies* 37 no. 3 (2004): 345–366.

Cunningham, Vanessa. *Shakespeare and Garrick*. Cambridge: Cambridge University Press, 2008.

Damrosch, Leopold. *Samuel Johnson and the Tragic Sense*. Princeton, NJ: Princeton University Press, 1972.

Danziger, Marlies K., and Frank Brady. *Boswell: The Great Biographer 1789–1795*. London: Heinemann, 1989.

Darwin, Erasmus. *The Temple of Nature; or, The Origin of Society*. Menston, UK: Scholar Press, [1803] 1973.

———. *Zoonomia; or, The Laws of Organic Life*. Vol. 1,Part I. London: J. Johnson, 1794.

Davis, Matthew M. "'Elevated Notions of the Right of Kings': Stuart Sympathies in Johnson's Notes to *Richard II*." In *Samuel Johnson in Historical Context*, edited by Jonathan Clark and Howard Erskine-Hill, 239–264. Houndmills, UK: Palgrave, 2002.

Defoe, Daniel. *The Life, Adventures, and Pyracies, of the Famous Captain Singleton*. Edited by W.R. Owens London: Pickering & Chatto, 2008.

DeMaria, Robert. *The Life of Samuel Johnson: A Critical Biography*. Oxford, UK: Basil Blackwell, 1994.

DeMaria, Robert, Jr., "The Eighteenth-Century Periodical Essay." In *The Cambridge History of English Literature, 1660–1780*, edited by John Richetti, Cambridge: Cambridge University Press, 2005.

Dentith, Simon. "Realist Synthesis in the Nineteenth-Century Novel: 'That Unity Which Lies In the Selection of Our Keenest Consciousness.'" In *A Concise Companion to Realism*, edited by Matthew Beaumont, revised edition, 33–49. Chichester, UK: Wiley-Blackwell, 2010.

Desai, R. W. *Johnson on Shakespeare*. New Delhi, India: Orient Longman, 1979.

De Smet, Hendrik, Susan Flach, Jukka Tyrkkö, and Hans-Jürgen Diller. *The Corpus of Late Modern English (CLMET), version 3.1: In Improved Tokenization and Linguistic Annotation*. Katholieke Universiteit Leuven, Freie Universität Berlin, Tampere University, Ruhr-Universität Bochum, 2015.

Deutsch, Helen. *Loving Dr. Johnson*. Chicago: University of Chicago Press, 2005.

Dobson, Michael. *The Making of the National Poet: Shakespeare, Adaptation and Authorship 1660–1769*. Oxford, UK: Clarendon Press, 1992.

Drake, Nathan. *Essays, Biographical, Critical, and Historical, Illustrative of the Rambler, Adventurer, and Idler, and of the Various Periodical Papers*. 2 vols. London: Printed for W. Suttaby, 1809–1810.

Dryden, John. "Contributions to *Plutarch's Lives*." In vol. 17 of *The Works of John Dryden (Prose 1668–1691)*, edited by Samuel Holt Monk, A. E. Wallace Maurer, and Vinton A. Dearing, 227–288. Berkeley: University of California Press, 1971.

———. "A Discourse Concerning the Original and Progress of Satire." In vol. 2 of *Essays of John Dryden*, edited by W. P. Ker, 15–114. 2 vols. Oxford, UK: Clarendon Press, 1926.

———. *The Poems of John Dryden: Volume Five 1697–1700*, edited by Paul Hammond and David Hopkins. Harlow, UK: Pearson Longman, 2005.

Ellis, Markman. *The Coffee-House: A Cultural History*. London: Weidenfeld & Nicolson, 2004.

Evans, Bergen. Introduction to James Boswell, *The Life of Samuel Johnson*, edited by Bergen Evans. New York: Modern Library, 1952.

Falconer, William. *Dissertation on the Influence of the Passions upon Disorders of the Body*. London: Dilly, 1791.

Fara, Patricia. *Sympathetic Attractions: Magnetic Practices, Beliefs, and Symbolism in Eighteenth-Century England*. Princeton, NJ: Princeton University Press, 1996.

Fazlollahi, Afag S. "Elizabeth Carter's Legacy: Friendship and Ethics." PhD diss., Georgia State University, 2011, 163.

Ferris, Ina. *The Achievement of Literary Authority: Gender, History, and the Waverley Novels*. Ithaca, NY: Cornell University Press, 1991.

Fleeman, J. D. *A Bibliography of the Works of Samuel Johnson*. 2 vols. Oxford, UK: Clarendon Press, 2000.

Folkenflik, Robert. *Samuel Johnson, Biographer*. Ithaca, NY: Cornell University Press, 1978.

French, R. K. *Robert Whytt, the Soul, and Medicine*. London: Wellcome Institute of the History of Medicine, 1969.

Fujii, Tetsu. "Johnson hen" ジョンソン編. In *Sekai bungaku sougou mokuroku* 世界文学総合目録 (*A Catalogue of World Literature*), edited by Michiaki Kawato and Takanori Sakakibara 川戸道昭、榊原貴教. Tokyo: Nada Shuppan Center ナダ出版センター, 2011 .

———. "Nihon de no Johnson jyuyo to kenkyu no rekishi" 日本でのジョンソン受容と研究の歴史 ("A History of Reception and Studies of Johnson in Japan"). In *Eikoku bunkano kyojin Samuel Johnson* 英国文化の巨人: サミュエル・ジョンソン (*Samuel Johnson, a Giant of English Culture*), edited by Hideichi Eto, Shigeru Shibagaki, and Hitoshi Suwabe 江藤秀一、芝垣茂、諏訪部仁. Kamakura, Japan: Minato No Hito 港の人, 2009.

———. "Nihon ni okeru Samuel Johnson kenkyuno nagare" 日本におけるサミュエル・ジョンソン研究の流れ ("A Survey of Johnsonian Studies in Japan"). *Fukuoka Daigaku Kenkyu Ronshu* 福岡大学研究部論集 (*The Bulletin of Central Research Institute*) Series A, 6, no. 4 (2006).

——— 藤井哲. *Nihon ni okeru Samuel Johnson oyobi James Boswell bunken mokuroku (1871–2005)* 日本におけるサミュエル・ジョンソンおよびジェイムズ・ボズウェル文献目録 (*A Bibliography of Johnsonian and Boswellian Studies in Japan (1871–2005)*). Tokyo: Nada Shuppan Center ナダ出版, 2006.

Fujin Club 婦人倶楽部 (*Women's Club*). 11, no. 6 (1930), 12, nos. 1, 2, 4 (1931).

Garrick, David. *The Letters of David Garrick*, edited by David M. Little and George M. Kharl. 3 vols. Oxford, UK: Oxford University Press, 1963.

———. *The Plays of David Garrick*. Edited by H. W. Pedicord and F. L. Bergmann. 7 vols. Carbondale: Southern Illinois University Press, 1980–1982.

Gaskell, Elizabeth. *Cranford*. Edited by Elizabeth Porges Watson. Oxford, UK: Oxford University Press, 2011.

Gay, John. "The Present State of Wit." In vol. 2 of *Poetry and Prose*, edited by Vinton A. Dearing, 449–456. 2 vols. Oxford, UK: Clarendon Press, 1974.

Gilbert, Sandra M., and Susan Gubar. *The Madwoman in the Attic: The Woman Writer and the Nineteenth-Century Literary Imagination*. New Haven, CT: Yale University Press, 1979.

Gillray, James. *Apollo and the Muses, Inflicting Penance on Dr. Pomposo Round Parnassus*. 1783. Etching. National Portrait Gallery, London. NPG D12342.

Godwin, William. *Memoirs of the Author of A Vindication of the Rights of Woman*. In vol. 1 of *Collected Novels and Memoirs of William Godwin*, edited by Mark Philp. London: William Pickering, [1798] 1992.

Goldgar, Anne. *Impolite Learning: Conduct and Community in the Republic of Letters, 1680–1750*. New Haven, CT: Yale University Press, 1995.

Goldsmith, Oliver. *The Bee*. Vol. 1 of *The Collected Works of Oliver Goldsmith*, edited by Arthur Friedman. Oxford, UK: Clarendon Press, 1966.

Gray, James. "'Swear by My Sword': A Note in Johnson's Shakespeare." *Shakespeare Quarterly* 27, no. 2 (1976): 205–208.

Greene, Donald J. *Samuel Johnson*. The Oxford Authors / general editor Frank Kermode. Oxford: Oxford University Press, 1984.

Griffin, Dustin H. *Literary Patronage in England, 1650–1800*. Cambridge: Cambridge University Press, 1996.

Gross, Gloria Sybil. "Dr. Johnson's Practice: The Medical Context for *Rasselas*." In vol. 14 of *Studies in Eighteenth-Century Culture*, edited by O. M. Brack Jr., 378–400. Madison: University of Wisconsin Press, 1985.

———. *In a Fast Coach with a Pretty Woman: Jane Austen and Samuel Johnson*. New York: AMS Press, 2002.

Grundy, Isobel. "Early Women Reading Johnson." In *Samuel Johnson After 300 Years*, edited by Greg Clingham and Philip Smallwood, 207–224. Cambridge: Cambridge University Press, 2009.

———. *Lady Mary Wortley Montague: Comet of the Enlightenment*. Oxford, UK: Oxford University Press, 1999.

———. *Samuel Johnson and the Scale of Greatness*. Athens: University of Georgia Press, 1986.

"Hakase Samuel Johnson ryakuden" 「博士サミュエル、ジヨンソン略伝」 ("A Brief Biography of Dr. Samuel Johnson"). *Shonen en* 少年園 (*Boys' Land*) 7, no. 73 (1891): 23–25.

Hall, John Whitney, ed. *The Cambridge History of Japan*. 6 vols. Cambridge: Cambridge University Press, 1988–1999.

Hanway, Jonas. *A Journal of Eight Days Journey from Portsmouth to Kingston Upon Thames . . . In a Series of Sixty-Four Letters: Addressed to Two Ladies of the Partie. To Which Is Added, an Essay on Tea: Considered as Pernicious to Health: Obstructing Industry and Impoverishing the Nation . . . With Several Political Reflections on Thoughts on Public Love in Twenty-Five Letters to the Same Ladies*. London: H. Woodfall, 1756.

Harada, Noriyuki 原田範行. "Johnson in Japanese Culture." Paper at ISECS conference, UCLA, 6 August 2003.

———. "Johnson in Japanese Culture." *Kyorin University Review* 16 (2004): 113–136.

———. "Johnson to Gaskell" ジョンソンとギャスケル ("Johnson and Gaskell: Diction, Narrative, and Print Culture"). ギャスケル研究 (*Gaskell Studies*) 20 (2016): 1–14.

———. "Literature, London, and Lives of the English Poets." In *London and Literature 1603–1901*, edited by Angela Davenport, Yui Nakatsuma, and Barnaby Ralph, 65–77. Newcastle, UK: Cambridge Scholars, 2017.

———. "Power in Modernization of Language and Literature in Eighteenth-Century Britain and Modern Japan." *IAFOR Journal of Literature and Librarianship* 4, no. 1 (2015): 20–31.

———. "Translation and Transformation: Japanese Reception and Adaptation of Eighteenth-Century English Literature." *Essays and Studies in British and American Literature* 58 (March 2012): 1–22.

Harriman-Smith, James. "The Anti-Performance Prejudice of Shakespeare's Eighteenth-Century Editors." *Restoration and Eighteenth-Century Theatre Research* 29, no. 2 (2014): 47–61.

Hawes, Clement. *The British Eighteenth Century and Global Critique*. New York: Palgrave Macmillan, 2005.

Hawthorne, Nathaniel. *Denki monogatari* 伝記物語 (*Biographical Stories*). Edited by Kiyosi Yoshida 吉田潔. Tokyo: Kanesashi Horyudo 金刺芳流堂, [1842] 1906.

———. *True Stories from History and Biography*, In vol. 6, *Centenary Edition of the Works of Nathaniel Hawthorne*, edited by William Charvat. Columbus: Ohio State University Press, 1972.

Hayakawa, Isamu 早川勇. *Keimou shisouka no Johnson jisho: Chi no shusei wo mezashite* 啓蒙思想下のジョンソン辞書: 知の集成を目指して (*Johnson's Dictionary Under the Enlightenment: For the Purpose of Collecting Knowledge*). Yokohama, Japan: Shunpūsha, 2013.

———. "Meijini okeru seiyo bunkano jyuyo: Samuel Johnson no baai" 明治における西洋文化の受容：サミュエル・ジョンソンの場合 ("The Reception of Western Culture in Meiji-era: A Case of Samuel Johnson"). *Aichi Daigaku Bungaku Ronso* 愛知大学文学論叢 (*Aichi University Departmental Bulletin for Literary Studies*) 148–151 (2013–2015).

Hedgecock, Frank A. *David Garrick and His French Friends*. London: Stanley Paul, 1911.

Henson, Eithne. *The Fictions of Romantick Chivalry: Samuel Johnson and Romance*. Madison, NJ: Fairleigh Dickinson University Press, 1992.

Heydt-Stevenson, Jillian, and Charlotte Sussman, eds. *Recognizing the Romantic Novel: New Histories of British Fiction, 1780–1830*. Liverpool, UK: Liverpool University Press, 2008.

Hill, George Birkbeck, ed. *Johnsonian Miscellanies*. 2 vols, Oxford, UK: Clarendon Press, 1897.

Hirose, Chisato 広瀬千紗子. "Cha no yu to Yedo bungaku" 茶の湯と江戸文学 ("Tea and Literature in the Tokugawa Period"). In *Cha to bungei* 茶と文芸 (*Tea and Arts*). Kyoto, Japan: Tanko 淡交社, 2001.

Hoole, John. "Narrative of John Hoole." In *Johnsonian Miscellanies*, edited by George Birkbeck Hill, 2 vols. Oxford, UK: Clarendon Press, 1897.

Hudson, Nicholas. "Review of John Wiltshire, the Making of Dr. Johnson." In *The Age of Johnson: A Scholarly Annual* 29, New York: AMS, (2010): 331–333.

———. "Three Steps to Perfection; *Rasselas* and the Philosophy of Richard Hooker." *Eighteenth-Century Life* 14, no. 3 (November 1991): 29–39.

Hume, David. *The Letters of David Hume*, edited by Y. T. Greig. 2 vols. Oxford, UK: Oxford University Press, 1932.

Hunter, J. Paul. *Before Novels: Cultural Contexts of Eighteenth-Century English Fiction*. New York: W. W. Norton, 1992.

Hyde, Mary, *The Impossible Friendship*. Cambridge, MA: Harvard University Press, 1972.

Ishida, Kenji 石田憲次. *Johnson hakase to sono mure* ジョンソン博士とその群 (*Dr. Johnson and His Circle*). Tokyo: Kenkyusha 研究社, 1933.

Ishikawa, Tadahisa 石川忠久. *Cha wo utau shi* 茶をうたう詩 詠茶詩録 詳解 (*Tea Poetry in China*). Tokyo: Kenbun Shuppan 研文出版, 2011 .

Italia, Iona. *The Rise of Literary Journalism in the Eighteenth Century*. Abingdon, UK: Routledge, 2005.

Iwama, Machiko 岩間真知子. "Cha no senkusha Tamotsu Morowoka" 茶研究の先駆者・諸岡存 ("Pioneer in Tea Studies"). *Cha* 茶 (January 2008): 56–60; (February 2008): 48–51; (March 2008): 48–51; (April 2008): 50–54; (May 2008): 48–52.

Izumitani, Yutaka. 泉谷寛*Kentou no bungo Johnson:Meijiki Rasselas no henrin* 健闘の文豪ジョンソン (*The Challenge of Johnson, a Man of Literature: A Glimpse of Rasselas in the Meiji Era*). Hiroshima, Japan: Keisuisha 渓水社, 1992 .

———. *Rasselas Juyoshino kenkyu* 『ラセラス』受容史の研究 (*A Study of the Reception of Rasselas in Japan*). Hiroshima, Japan: Keisuisha 渓水社, 2001.

Jitugyo no Nihon 実業の日本 (*Business Magazine of Japan*) 33, nos. 1, 6, 7, 8, 9, 10 (1930); 34, no.1 (1931).

Johnson, Claudia. "'Let Me Make the Novels of a Country': Barbauld's *The British Novelists* (1810/1820)." *Novel: A Forum on Fiction* 34, no. 2 (2001): 163–179.

Johnson, Freya. "Johnson and Austen." In *Samuel Johnson After 300 Years*, edited by Greg Clingham and Philip Smallwood, 225–245. Cambridge: Cambridge University Press, 2009.

Johnson, Samuel. *Diaries, Prayers, and Annals*. Edited by E. L. McAdam Jr., Donald Hyde, and Mary Hyde. Vol.1 of *The Yale Edition of the Works of Samuel Johnson*. New Haven, CT: Yale University Press, 1958.

———. *A Dictionary of the English Language*. 2 vols. London: Printed by W. Strahan, for J. and P. Knapton, et al., 1755–1756.

———. *The History of Rasselas, Prince of Abissinia.* Edited by Thomas Keymer. Oxford, UK: Oxford University Press, 2009.

———. *The History of Rasselas, Prince of Abissinia.* Translated by Tian Ming Cai. Beijing: International Culture Publishing, 2006.

———. *The Idler, and the Adventurer.* Edited by Walter Bate, John Jackson, Marshall Bullitt, and Laurence Fitzroy Powell. Vol. 2 of *The Yale Edition of the Works of Samuel Johnson*. New Haven, CT: Yale University Press, 1963.

———. *Johnson on Shakespeare*. Edited by Arthur Sherbo. Vols. 7 and 8 of *The Yale Edition of the Works of Samuel Johnson*. New Haven, CT: Yale University Press, 1968.

———. *A Journey to the Western Islands of Scotland and The Journal of a Tour to the Hebrides.* London: Penguin Books, 1984.

———. *The Letters of Samuel Johnson*. 5 vols. Edited by Bruce Redford. Princeton, NJ: Princeton University Press, 1992–1994.

———. *Life of Savage*. Edited by Clarence Tracy. Oxford, UK: Clarendon Press, 1971.

———. *Literary Magazine; or, Universal Review*, no. 13 (1757). In *Johnson on Demand: Reviews, Prefaces, and Ghost-Writings,* edited by O. M. Brack Jr. and Robert Demaria Jr., 359–371. Vol. 20 of *The Yale Edition of the Works of Samuel Johnson*. New Haven, CT: Yale University Press, 2018.

———. *The Lives of the Most Eminent English Poets; with Critical Observations on their Works*, 4 vols. Edited by Roger Lonsdale. Oxford, UK: Clarendon Press, 2006.

———. *The Lives of the Poets*. Edited by John H. Middendorf. Vols. 21, 22, and 23 of *The Yale Edition of the Works of Samuel Johnson*. New Haven, CT: Yale University Press, 2010.

———. *The Major Works*. Edited by Donald Greene. Oxford, UK: Oxford University Press, 2008.
———. *The Oxford Authors: Samuel Johnson*. Edited by Donald Greene. Oxford, UK: Oxford University Press, 1984.
———. "Preface to Shakespeare, 1765." In *Johnson on Shakespeare*, 59–113. Vol. 7 of *The Yale Edition of the Works of Samuel Johnson*, edited by Arthur Sherbo. New Haven, CT: Yale University Press, 1967.
———. *The Rambler*. Edited by W. J. Bate and Albrecht B. Strauss. Vols. 3–5 of *The Yale Edition of the Works of Samuel Johnson*. New Haven, CT: Yale University Press, 1969.
———. *Rasselas and Other Tales*. Edited by Gwin J. Kolb. Vol. 16 of *The Yale Edition of the Works of Samuel Johnson*. New Haven, CT: Yale University Press, 1990.
———. "Review of Free Inquiry into the Nature and Origin of Evil." In vol. 2 of *The Works of Samuel Johnson, LL.D. with an Essay on His Life and Genius*, edited by Arthur Murphy. New York: George Dearborn, 1837.
———. *A Voyage to Abyssinia*. New Haven, CT: Yale University Press, 1985.
Jones, Vivien. "Jane Austen's Domestic Realism." In *English and British Fiction 1750–1820*, edited by Peter Garside and Karen O'Brien, 273–295. Vol. 2 of *The Oxford History of the Novel in English*. Oxford, UK: Oxford University Press, 2015.
Jordan, Sarah. "Samuel Johnson and Idleness." In *The Age of Johnson: A Scholarly Annual 11*, edited by Paul J. Korshin and Jack Lynch, 145–176. New York: AMS, 2000.
Kamei, Shunsuke 亀井俊介. *Eibungakusha: Natsume Sōseki* 英文学者夏目漱石 (*Scholar of English: Sōseki Natsume*). Tokyo: Shohakusha 松柏社, 2011.
Karatani, Kojin 柄谷行人. *Nihon kindaibungakuno kigen* 日本近代文学の起源 (*Origins of Modern Japanese Literature*). Tokyo: Kodansha 講談社, 1980. (*Origins of Modern Japanese Literature*. Translated by Brett de Bary et al. Durham, NC: Duke University Press, 1993.)
Kass, Thomas. "Morbid Melancholy, the Imagination, and Samuel Johnson's Sermons." *Logos: A Journal of Catholic Thought and Culture* 8, no. 4 (Fall 2005): 47–63.
Keene, Donald. *Dawn to the West: Japanese Literature in the Modern Era*. New York: Holt, Rinehart and Winston, 1984.
Kernan, Alvin. *Samuel Johnson and the Impact of Print*. Princeton, NJ: Princeton University Press, 1987.
Keymer, Thomas. "*Northanger Abbey* and *Sense and Sensibility*." In *The Cambridge Companion to Jane Austen*, edited by Edward Copeland and Juliet McMaster, 2nd ed. Cambridge: Cambridge University Press, 2011.
King, Lester S. *The Medical World of the Eighteenth Century*. Chicago: University of Chicago Press, 1958.
Kirsten, Peter J., and Robert Markley, eds. *Writing China: Essays on the Amherst Embassy (1816) and Sino-British Relations*. Cambridge, UK: D. S. Brewer, 2016.
Klein, Lawrence E. "Politeness and the Interpretation of the British Eighteenth Century." *Historical Journal* 45, no. 4 (2002): 869–898.
———. *Shaftesbury and the Culture of Politeness: Moral Discourse and Cultural Politics in Early Eighteenth-Century England*. Cambridge: Cambridge University Press, 1994.
Knezevic, Borslav. "An Ethnography of the Provincial: The Social Geography of Gentility in Elizabeth Gaskell's 'Cranford.'" *Victorian Studies* 41, no. 3 (1998): 405–426.

Kobinata, Teijiro 小日向定次郎. *Eibungakushi* 英文学史 (*A History of English Literature*). Tokyo: Bunken-shoin 文献書院, 1924.

Komazawa daigaku bukkyo gakkai nenpo 駒沢大学仏教学会年報 (*Komazawa University Buddhist Studies Bulletin*) 1 (1930).

Korshin, Paul J., ed. *Johnson After Two Hundred Years.* Philadelphia: University of Pennsylvania Press, 1986.

———. "Samuel Johnson's Life Experience with Poverty." In *The Age of Johnson: A Scholarly Annual 11*, edited by Paul J. Korshin and Jack Lynch, 3–20. New York: AMS, 2000.

Lamb, John B. "Mary Shelley's Frankenstein and Milton's Monstrous Myth." *Nineteenth-Century Literature* 47, no. 3 (December 1992): 303–319.

Langford, Paul. *A Polite and Commercial People: England 1727–1783.* Oxford, UK: Oxford University Press, 1992.

———. "The Uses of Eighteenth-Century Politeness." *Transactions of the Royal Historical Society* 12 (2002): 311–331.

Lawrence, William. *Lectures on Physiology, Zoology, and the Natural History of Man.* London: Callow, 1819.

Lee, Anthony W. "Bucknell University Press, 1996–2016: Two Decades of Eighteenth-Century Scholarship." *Eighteenth-Century Life* 42, no. 3 (September 2018): 1–28.

Li, Xiang. *Li Lun Yu Yan Jiu (A Study of Samuel Johnson's Dictionary of the English Language [1755])* (Tian Jin, China: Nankai University Press, 2014).

———. "Qian Zhongshu and Samuel Johnson: Two Literary Figures in Different Times." *Johnsonian News Letter* 64, no. 1 (March 2013): 48–51.

Lipking, Lawrence. *The Ordering of the Arts in Eighteenth-Century England.* Princeton, NJ: Princeton University Press, 1970.

———. *Samuel Johnson.* Cambridge, MA: Harvard University Press, 1998.

Livingston, Robert E. "Global Knowledges: Agency and Place in Literary Studies." *PMLA* 116, no. 1 (January 2001): 145–158.

Locke, John. *An Essay Concerning Human Understanding.* Edited by Roger Woolhouse. Harmondsworth, UK: Penguin, 1997.

Lustig, Irma S., and Frederick A. Pottle, eds. *Boswell: The Applause of the Jury, 1782–1785.* New York: McGraw-Hill, 1981.

———, eds. *Boswell: The English Experiment, 1785–1789.* London: Heinemann, 1986.

Macaulay, Thomas Babington. *Life of Johnson.* Edited by William Schuyler. New York: Macmillan, 1924.

———. "Life of Johnson." In *The Six Chief Lives from Johnson's "Lives of the Poets" with Macaulay's "Life of Johnson,"* edited by Matthew Arnold. London: Macmillan, 1886.

———. *Macaulay's Life of Samuel Johnson.* Edited by Charles Lane Hanson. Boston: Ginn & Company, 1903.

Main, Alexander. *Life and Conversations of Dr. Samuel Johnson.* London: Chapman & Hall, 1874.

Mair, Victor H., and Erling Hoh. *The True History of Tea.* London: Thames & Hudson, 2009.

Mamashi/Mamako/Magamagashi 魔々子. "Bungei sa dan: kodai no shisei to kinsei no kasen (Johnson)" 文芸鎖談第二: 古代の詩聖と近世の歌仙 (ジョンソン) ("On Literature: Bards Classical and Recent—Johnson"). *Doshisha bungakukai zasshi* 同志社文学会雑誌 (*Doshisha University Journal of Literature*) 46 (1891): 26–27.

Marsh, Lauren Jeanne. *The Rise of Useful Knowledge in Britain.* PhD diss., The University of Minnesota, 2003.

Martin, Peter. *Samuel Johnson: A Biography*. Cambridge, MA: Belknap Press of Harvard University Press, 2008.

"Mary Shelley's Reading: Alphabetical List." *Romantic Circles*. Accessed June 21, 2017. https://www.rc.umd.edu/editions/frankenstein/MShelley/readalph.

Matar, Nabil. *Europe through Arab Eyes, 1578–1727*. New York: Columbia University Press, 2009.

Matsui, Sakuko. *Natsume Sōseki as a Critic of English Literature*. Tokyo: Centre for East Asian Cultural Studies, 1975.

Matsumoto, Katusaburo 松本勝三郎. *Eikoku no spy! Kyuseigun wo utsu* 英国のスパイ！救世軍を撃つ (*Attacking the Salvation Army, the Spies from Britain*). Foreword by Tamotsu Morowoka. Tokyo: Shubunkaku 秀文閣, 1940.

———. *Toyo kinshu taikan* 東洋禁酒大観 (*A Survey of Temperance in the Orient*). Osaka, Japan: Kinki Kinshu Association 近畿禁酒聯盟, 1935.

Maxwell, Catherine. "Swinburne and Thackeray's *The Newcomes*." *Victorian Poetry* 47 (2009): 733–746.

Mayhew, Robert J. "Nature and the Choice of Life in 'Rasselas.'" *Studies in English Literature, 1500–1900* 39, no. 3 (Summer 1999): 539–556.

McMaster, R. D. *Thackeray's Cultural Frame of Reference: Allusion in The Newcomes*. Basingstoke, UK: Macmillan, 1991.

Medwin, Thomas. *The Life of Percy Bysshe Shelley*. Edited by H. Buxton Forman. London: Oxford University Press, 1913.

Miles, Robert. *Ann Radcliffe: The Great Enchantress*. Manchester, UK: Manchester University Press, 1995.

Miner, Earl, ed. *English Criticism in Japan: Essays by Younger Japanese Scholars on English and American Literature*. Princeton, NJ: Princeton University Press, 1972.

Miner, Earl R., Odagiri Hiroko, and Robert E. Morrell. *The Princeton Companion to Classical Japanese Literature*. Princeton, NJ: Princeton University Press, 1985.

Misenheimer, James B., and Veva Vonler. "Intellectual Eclecticism: A Ramble through The Rambler." *The New Rambler*, no. 1990–1991 (1991): 16–27, 17.

Miyazaki, Kasumi 宮崎かすみ. *Hyakunengo ni Sōseki wo yomu 100* 年後に漱石を読む (*Reading Sōseki After 100 Years*). Tokyo: Transview トランスビュー, 2009.

Monmosei 文盲生. "Genkon no bungakusha" 現今の文学者 ("Recent Literary Scholars.") *Jogaku zasshi* 女学雑誌 (*Feminist Journal*) 272 (1891): 15–17.

Montagu, Mary Wortley. *The Complete Letters of Lady Mary Wortley Montague*. Edited by Robert Halsband. Oxford, UK: Clarendon Press, 1966–1967.

Morowoka, Tamotsu 諸岡存. *Cha* 茶 (*Tea*). With a short biography of the author by Takako Morowoka and an afterword by Yoichi Ueno. Tokyo: Taikodo 泰光堂, 1949.

———. *Cha: sono kagaku to yakko* 茶–その科学と薬効 (*Tea: Its Science and Medicinal Benefits*). Tokyo: Taikodo 泰光堂, 1943.

———. *Chagyo kokusaku* 茶業国策 (*Tea: National Policy*). Tokyo: Central Tea Association 茶業組合中央会議所, 1938.

———. *Chakyo hyoshaku* 茶経評釈 (*Commentaries on the Classic of Tea*). 2 vols. Tokyo: Shuppan kagaku sogo kenkyujo 出版科学研究所, [1941] 1977.

———. *Chakyo hyoshaku gaihen* 茶経評釈外篇 (*Supplementary Volume to Commentaries on the Classic of Tea*). Tokyo: Shuppan kagaku sogo kenkyujo 出版科学研究所, [1943] 1978.

———. *Cha to sono bunka* 茶とその文化 (*Tea and Its Culture*). Tokyo: Daito Press 大東出版社, 1937.

———. *Gendai josei to nihon cha* 現代女性と日本茶 (*Modern Women and Japanese Tea*). Shizuoka, Japan: Tea Commerce & Industry's Association of Shizuok-shi 静岡市茶業組合, 1938.

———. *Kaishoku Kaimin Kaiben* 快食快眠快便 (*Good Appetite, Sound Sleep, and Regular Motions*). Tokyo: Jitsugyo no nihon sha 実業之日本社, 1939.

———. "Nihonbunka to cha" 日本文化と茶 ("Japanese Culture and Tea"). In *Nihonbunka no seikaku* 日本文化の性格 (*Japanese Culture*), edited by Shiho hoken kyokai Shotoku 司法保健協会《昭徳》. Tokyo: Bunrokusha 文録社, 1941.

———. "Tea Drinking Habit Proved Effective in Health Improvement: Medicinal Properties of Tea Scientifically Ascertained." n.d., n.p.

———. "Zen to Shin-Kokka" 禅と新国家 ("Zen and a New Polity"). In *Man-Mou Koza* 満蒙講座 (*Lectures on Manchuria and Mongolia*), 456–457. Tokyo: Ritsumeikan Press 立命館プレス, 1937.

Nagashima, Daisuke 永嶋大典. "Johnson in Japan: A Fragmentary Sketch." *Transactions of the Johnson Society (Lichfield)* (1993): 14–19.

———. *Johnson no shi to shinko* ジョンソンの死と信仰 (*Johnson's Death and Beliefs*). Tokyo: Seikokai Shuppan 聖公会出版, 1995.

———. "A Short History of Studies on Johnson." In *The Samuel Johnson Encyclopedia*, by Pat Rogers, translated by Daisuke Nagashima, xxix–xliv. Tokyo: Yumani Shobo ゆまに書房, 1999.

Nakahara, Akio 中原章雄. *Johnson den no keifu* ジョンソン伝の系譜 (*Genealogy of the Life of Johnson*). Tokyo: Kenkyusha Shuppan 研究社出版, 1991.

Nakahara, Teishichi 中原貞七, ed. "Dokutoru Samuel Johnson shi no den" どくとる、さみゆうえる、志よんそん氏ノ傳 ("A Life of Dr. Samuel Johnson.") *Goyu shonen* 豪雄少年 (*Brave Boys*) (1891): 314–328.

Nakamura, Masanao 中村正直. *Saigoku-Risshihen* 西国立志編 (*Self-Help*). Tokyo: Kodansha 講談社, [1871] 1981.

Nathan, John. *Sōseki: Modern Japan's Greatest Novelist*. New York: Columbia University Press, 2018.

Natsume, Sōseki. *Bungakuhyoron* 文学評論 (*Literary Criticism*). 2 vols. Tokyo: Iwaniami Shoten 岩波書店, [1909] 1985.

———. *Bungakuron* 文学論 (*Theory of Literature*). 2 vols. Tokyo, Japan: Iwaniami Shoten 岩波書店, [1907] 2007. (*Theory of Literature and Other Critical Writings*. Edited by Michael K. Bourdaghs, Atsuko Ueda, and Joseph A. Murphy. New York: Columbia University Press, 2009.)

Nobuhiro, Shinji 延広真治. "Zekko bungei to cha no yu" 舌耕文芸と茶の湯 ("Oral Arts and Tea"). In *Cha to bungei* 茶と文芸 (*Tea and Arts*). Kyoto: Tankosha 淡交社, 2001.

Novel: A Forum on Fiction. Special Issue, "The Romantic-Era Novel," 34, no. 2 (2001).

Nussbaum, Felicity, ed. *The Global Eighteenth Century*. Baltimore: Johns Hopkins University Press, 2003.

Ogawa, Kimiyo. "Eighteenth-Century Medical Discourse and Sensible Bodies: Sensibility and Selfhood in the Works of William Godwin, Mary Wollstonecraft and Mary Shelley." PhD diss., University of Glasgow, 2005.

Oxford Dictionary of National Biography. https://doi.org/10.1093/ref:odnb/26355.

The Oxford English Dictionary. 2nd ed. 20 vols. Oxford, UK: Clarendon Press, 1989.

Parke, Catherine N. "Johnson and the Arts of Conversation." In *The Cambridge Companion to Samuel Johnson*, edited by Greg Clingham. Cambridge: Cambridge University Press, 1997.

Parker, Fred. *Shakespeare's Johnson.* Oxford, UK: Clarendon Press, 1991.

Pearce, Joseph. *Through Shakespeare's Eyes: Seeing the Catholic Presence in the Plays.* San Francisco: Ignatius Press, 2010.

Pierce, Charles E. *Religious Life of Samuel Johnson*. Hamden, CT: Archon Books, 1983.

Piozzi, Hester Lynch. *Anecdotes of the Late Samuel Johnson, LL.D.* 1786. Reprint, New York: Garland Publishing, 1974.

Ponsonby, Vere Brabazon, ed. *Georgiana. Extracts from the Correspondence of Georgiana, Duchess of Devonshire.* London: John Murray, 1955.

Pope, Alexander. *The Dunciad*. Edited by James Sutherland. In vol. 5 of *The Twickenham Edition of the Poems of Alexander Pope*, edited by John Butt, 11 vols. London: Methuen; New Haven: Yale University Press, 1939–1969.

———. *The Dunciad in Four Books*. Edited by Valerie Rumbold. New York: Longman, 1999.

———. *The Prose Works of Alexander Pope*. Edited by Norman Ault and Rosemary Cowler. Oxford, UK: B. Blackwell, 1936–1986.

———. *The Twickenham Edition of the Poems of Alexander Pope*. eEdited by John Butt. 11 vols. London: Methuen; New Haven: Yale University Press, 1939–1969.

Porter, David. "Sinicizing Early Modernity: The Imperatives of Historical Cosmopolitanism." *Eighteenth-Century Studies* 43, no. 3 (2010): 299–306.

Porter, Roy. *Enlightenment: Britain and the Creation of the Modern World*. London: Allen Lane, 2000.

Pottle, Marion S., Claude Colleer Abbot, and Frederick A. Pottle. *Catalogue of the Papers of James Boswell at Yale University*. 3 vols. Edinburgh, UK: Edinburgh University Press, 1993.

Richetti, John J., ed. *The Cambridge History of English Literature, 1660–1780*. Cambridge: Cambridge University Press, 2005.

Rogers, Samuel. *Recollections of the Table-Talk of Samuel Rogers*. New York: D. Appleton & Company, 1856.

Rumbold, Kate. "Shakespeare and the Stratford Jubilee." In *Shakespeare in the Eighteenth Century*, edited by Fiona Ritchie and Peter Sabor, 254–276. Cambridge: Cambridge University Press, 2014.

Quinlan, Maurice. *Samuel Johnson: A Layman's Religion*. Madison: University of Wisconsin Press, 1964.

Said, Edward W. "Globalizing Literary Study." *PMLA* 116, no. 1 (January 2001): 64–68.

. *Orientalism*. London: Penguin, 2003.

Sangyo Noritsu Daigaku 産業能率大学, ed. *Ueno Yoichi den* 上野陽一伝 (*A Biography of Yoichi Ueno*). Tokyo: Sangyo Noritsu Daigaku Press 産業能率プレス, 1967.

Sano, Mami, and Shigeru Shibagaki. "The Samuel Johnson Club of Japan." *Johnsonian News Letter* 62, no. 2 (September 2012): 36–39.

Santor, Gefen Bar-On. "Shakespeare in the Georgian Theatre." In *The Oxford Handbook of the Georgian Theatre, 1737–1832*, edited by Julia Swindells and David Francis Taylor, 213–228. Oxford, UK: Oxford University Press, 2014.

Schor, Hilary M. *Scheherezade in the Market Place: Elizabeth Gaskell and the Victorian Novel*. Oxford, UK: Oxford University Press, 1992.

Schwartz, Richard B. *Samuel Johnson and the New Science.* Madison: University of Wisconsin Press, 1971.

Scott, Walter. "Journal Entry, 14 March 1826." In *Jane Austen: The Critical Heritage*, 106. Edited by B. C. Southam. London: Routledge & Kegan Paul, 1968.
———. *Lives of the Novelists*. London: Henry Frowde, 1906.
———. "An Unsigned Review of *Emma*, *Quarterly Review*, dated October 1815, issued March 1816, xiv, 188–201." In *Jane Austen: The Critical Heritage*, 67. Edited by B. C. Southam. London: Routledge & Kegan Paul, 1968.
———. *Waverley*. Edited by Claire Lamont and Katherine Sutherland. 2nd ed. Oxford, UK: Oxford University Press, [1814] 2015.
Shakespeare, William. *Hamlet*. Edited by Philip Edwards. New Cambridge Shakespeare. Cambridge: Cambridge University Press, 1985.
———. *Hamlet*. Edited by Ann Thompson and Neil Taylor. Arden Third Series. London: Bloomsbury, 2006.
Shelley, Mary. *Frankenstein; Or, the Modern Prometheus*. In vol. 1 of *The Novels and Selected Works of Mary Shelley*, edited by Nora Crook. London: Routledge, 1996.
Smallwood, Philip. "Johnson's Criticism, the Arts, and the Idea of Art." In *Johnson After 300 Years*, edited by Greg Clingham and Philip Smallwood. Cambridge: Cambridge University Press, 2009.
Smiles, Samuel. *Self-Help: With Illustrations of Character, Conduct, and Perseverance*. Edited by Peter W. Sinnema. Oxford, UK: Oxford University Press, 2002.
Solinger, Jason D. "Becoming the Gentleman: British Letters and the Gentrification of Ordinary Men." PhD diss., Brown University, 2004.
Soupel, Serge. "'The True Culprit Is the Mind Which Can Never Run Away from Itself': Samuel Johnson and Depression." *Studies in the Literary Imagination* 44, no. 1 (2011): 43–62.
Southam, Brian, ed. *Jane Austen: The Critical Heritage*. London: Routledge & Kegan Paul, 1968.
Stephen, Leslie. *English Literature and Society in the Eighteenth Century. Ford Lectures, 1903*. London: Duckworth & Co., 1904
Stone, John. "An Early Spanish Translation of *Rasselas*." *Johnsonian News Letter* 59, no. 2 (September 2008): 24–27.
———. "Johnson on Shakespeare in Spain: A New Document." *Johnsonian News Letter* 65, no. 2 (September 2014): 6–17.
———. "On the Trail of Early Rambler and Idler Translations in France and Spain." *Johnsonian News Letter* 57, no. 1 (2006): 34–41.
———. "Translations." In *Samuel Johnson in Context,* edited by Jack Lynch, 38–44. Cambridge: Cambridge University Press, 2012.
Sturgeon, William. *A Course of Twelve Elementary Lectures on Galvanism*. London: Sherwood, Gilbert, and Piper, 1843.
Sutherland, James. *The Restoration Newspaper and Its Development*. Cambridge: Cambridge University Press, 1986.
Suwabe, Hitoshi. *Johnson and Boswell: jijitsu no shuhen* ジョンソンとボズウェル：事実の周辺. Tokyo: Chuo University Press 中央大学出版部, 2009.
Swift, Jonathan. *The Poems of Jonathan Swift*. Edited by Harold Williams. 3 vols. Oxford, UK: Clarendon Press, 1958.
Taira, Zensuke 平善介. "Nihon Johnson kyokai no sosetu no zengo" 日本ジョンソン協会の創設の前後 （"Reminiscences of the Beginning of the Johnson Society in Japan"）. *Annual Bulletin of the Johnson Society* 31 (May 2007): 1–2.
Takahashi, Genji. 高橋源次. *Samuel Johnson*. Tokyo: Aiikusha 愛育社, 1978.

Takahashi, Masakuma, and Tamotsu Morowoka 高橋正熊, 諸岡存. *Shakaiteki kyoiku saku* 社会的教育策 (*On Society and Education*). Tokyo: Kaihatsusha 開発社, 1902.

Thackeray, William Makepeace. *The Newcomes*. Edited by D. J. Taylor. London: Everyman, [1855] 1994.

———. *Vanity Fair: A Novel without a Hero*. Edited by Helen Small. Oxford, UK: Oxford University Press, 1983.

Theobald, Lewis, ed. *The Censor*. 3 vols. London: Printed for Jonas Brown, 1717.

Tissot, Samuel. *Onanism; or a Treatise upon the Disorders Produced by Masturbations or, the Dangerous Effects of Secret and Excessive Venery*. Translated by A. Hume. London: Thompson, 1781.

Townshend, Dale. "Gothic and the Ghost of *Hamlet*." In *Gothic Shakespeares*, edited by John Drakakis and Dale Townshend, 60–97. London: Routledge, 2008.

Tuite, Clara. *Romantic Austen: Sexual Politics and the Literary Canon*. Cambridge: Cambridge University Press, 2002.

Turner, Katherine. "Critical Reception to 1900." In *Samuel Johnson in Context*, edited by Jack Lynch. Cambridge: Cambridge University Press, 2012.

Uchida, Mitsugi 不知庵主人 [内田貢/魯庵」. *Johnson* (ジョンソン). Tokyo: Minyusha 民友社, 1894.

———. *Junibungo: Johnson* 十二文豪ジョンソン (*Twelve Great Writers: Johnson*). In *Uchida Roan Zenshu* 内田魯庵全集 (*A Complete Works of Roan Uchida*), 2 vols. Tokyo: Yumani Shobo ゆまに書房, 1894.

———. "Rasselas den no sakusha" 『ラセラス傳』の作者 ("The Author of *Rasselas*"). *Kokumin no tomo* 国民之友 (*The Nation's Friend*) 222 (1894): 34–36, 223 (1894): 21–25, 224 (1894): 23–26.

Ueda, Bin. Preface to *The History of Rasselas*. Translated by Rokusaku Shibano. Tokyo: Dainihonntosho 大日本図書, 1905.

Varley, Paul. *Japanese Culture*. Honolulu: University of Hawaii Press, 2000.

Waingrow, Marshall, ed. *The Correspondence and Other Papers of James Boswell Relating to the Making of the Life of Johnson*. London: Heinemann, 1969.

Walpole, Horace. "General Criticism on Dr. Johnson's Writings." In vol. 4 of *The Works of Horatio Walpole, Earl of Orford*, 361–362. 5 vols. London: G. G. and J. Robinson and J. Edwards, 1798.

Watanabe, Shoichi 渡部昇一. "Nakamura Masanao to Samuel Smiles" 中村正直とサミュエル・スマイルズ ("Masanao Nakamura and Samuel Smiles") 西国立志編. In *Saigoku-Risshihen* (*Self-Help*), translated by Masanao Nakamura, 544–556. Tokyo: Kodansha 講談社, 1981.

Whitmer, Kelly J. "Imagining Uses for Things: Teaching 'Useful Knowledge' in the Early Eighteenth Century." *History of Science* 55, no. 1 (2017): 37–60, 40. https://doi.org/10.1177/0073275316678872.

Whytt, Robert. *Observations on the Nature, Causes, and Cure of Those Disorders Which Have Been Commonly Called Nervous, Hypochondriac, or Hysteric*. 2nd ed. Edinburgh, UK: Printed for T. Becket, and P. Du Hondt, London, and J. Balfour, Edinburgh, 1765.

———. *Physiological Essays*. Edinburgh, UK: Hamilton, Balfour and Neill, 1745.

Williams, Anna. *Miscellanies in Prose and Verse*. London: T. Davies, 1746.

Wiltshire, John. *The Making of Dr. Johnson: Icon of Modern Culture*. Icons of Modern Culture Series. Westfield, Hastings, UK: Helm Information, 2009.

———. *Samuel Johnson in the Medical World: The Doctor and the Patient*. Cambridge: Cambridge University Press, 1991.

Wimsatt, W. K. "Images of Samuel Johnson." *ELH* 41, no. 3 (1974): 359–374.
———. *Philosophic Words: A Study of Style and Meaning in the "Rambler" and "Dictionary" of Samuel Johnson*. New Haven, CT: Yale University Press, 1948.
Wollstonecraft, Mary. *Vindication of the Rights of Men (1791)*. In vol. 5 of *The Works of Mary Wollstonecraft*, edited by Janet Todd and Marilyn Butler. London: William Pickering, 1989.
Woolf, Virginia. *A Room of One's Own and Three Guineas*. Oxford, UK: Oxford University Press, [1929] 2015.
Wordsworth, William. *The Prelude: Or, Growth of a Poet's Mind (Text of 1805)*. Oxford, UK: Oxford University Press, 1970.

Notes on Contributors

GREG CLINGHAM is an emeritus professor of English at Bucknell University, where, at different times, he also occupied the NEH Chair in the Humanities and the John P. Crozer Chair in English Literature. He is the author or editor of ten books and dozens of scholarly articles on Johnson, Boswell, Dryden, translation, memory, historiography, Orientalism, archives, the history of the book, and scholarly publishing, including *Johnson, Writing, and Memory*. He is presently writing a cultural history of Lady Anne Barnard at the Cape of Good Hope (1797–1802) while also working on Sir George Macartney's diplomatic papers from China, India, Russia, and the Cape of Good Hope. From 1996 to 2018, Dr. Clingham was the director of Bucknell University Press, which published c. 700 titles during his tenure, including 225 in eighteenth-century studies.

HIDEICHI ETO is a professor of English literature and president at Tokoha University in Shizuoka prefecture. He edited *Eikoku bunka no kyojin Samuel Johnson* (*Samuel Johnson, a Giant of English Culture*) with Hitoshi Suwabe and Shigeru Shibagaki. His translations include Johnson's *Journey to the Western Islands of Scotland* and Boswell's *A Tour to the Hebrides, The Journals of Dr. Johnson, and Mrs. Thrale's Tours in Wales (1774) and France (1775)*. He is a member of the Dr. Johnson Club in Japan and a governor of Dr. Johnson's House.

TADAYUKI FUKUMOTO is a professor in the Department of English Language and English/American Literature at the Faculty of Letters, Ryukoku University. Much of his interest has been in the area concerning the satirical works of Alexander Pope. He has contributed articles to *Juhachi Seiki Igirisu Bungaku Kenkyu* (*Studies of the Eighteenth-Century English Literature*) published by the Johnson Society of Japan.

NORIYUKI HARADA is a professor of English at Keio University and president of the English Literary Society of Japan (ELSJ), specializes in eighteenth-century English literature and comparative literary studies. His recent publications include "Translation and Transformation of Jonathan Swift's Works in Japan" in *"The First Wit of the Age:" Essays on Swift and His Contemporaries in Honour of Hermann J. Real*, *Full Annotation for Gulliver's Travels* (coedited in Japanese), *An Introduction to Gulliver's Travels* (in Japanese), "Literature, London, and Lives of the English Poets" in *London and Literature, 1603–1901*, and "The Rise of the English Novel and the Representations of Japan: Psalmanazar, Defoe, and Swift" in *Studies in Eighteenth-Century English Literature* (in Japanese).

NORIYUKI HATTORI is a professor of English at Osaka University. He is the author of *Fiction as Fabrication: Study of Defoe and Smollett*. He translated Wayne Booth's *The Rhetoric of Fiction*, and George Forster's *A Voyage Round the World* into Japanese.

MIKI IWATA is a professor of English literature at Rikkyo University, Japan. She received her PhD from Tohoku University in 2001 for a thesis on W. B. Yeats and the Irish dramatic movement. Her research interests range from English Renaissance drama to early twentieth-century Irish drama from the viewpoints of postcolonialism and family politics. Her recent publications include "The Disappearance of London from the Early Eighteenth-Century London Stage," "Brothers Lost, Sisters Found: The Verbal Construction of Sisterhood in *Twelfth Night*," and *The Rival Brothers in British and Irish Drama* (in Japanese).

KIMIYO OGAWA is a professor in the Department of English Studies at Sophia University, Japan. She has published essays on Mary Wollstonecraft, Mary Shelley, and Jane Austen. She is currently interested in how advances in medical and physiological science informed representations of mind and human behavior in a range of Gothic texts. Her publications include book chapters on Charlotte Lennox in *British Romanticism in European Perspectives* and on Jane Austen and Yaeko Nogami in *British Romanticism in Asia*.

MASAAKI OGURA is an assistant professor in the Education Department of Osaka Ohtani University, Osaka. His research interests lie in lexicography and stylistics. His research focuses on what linguistic features mark the style of Samuel Johnson's writing and to what extent these features are consistent over the issues of *The Rambler* (1750–1752). His recent publications include "Authors Who Inspired Samuel Johnson's Language Use in *The Rambler*: An Investigation of His Reading Sources Based on a Phraseological Unit 'Of Our Present State,"' *Lexicography*.

HITOSHI SUWABE was a professor of English at Chuo University and Tokyo Institute of Technology. He studied Johnson under J. D. Fleeman at Pembroke College, Oxford, and has written numerous articles on Johnson and Boswell in Japanese and English, which are collected in *Johnson and Boswell.* He has also translated into Japanese Johnson's *Journey to the Western Islands of Scotland* and Boswell's *Journal of a Tour to the Hebrides, with Samuel Johnson, LL.D.* with cotranslators.

MIKA SUZUKI is a professor of English at Shizuoka University, Japan. Her University of London thesis was on Sarah Fielding, on whom she later published a book in Japanese. She has published essays on Jane Austen and Sarah Fielding and has worked on letters and papers left by Margaret Georgiana, Countess Spencer as well as on tea in Britain and Japan.

YURI YOSHINO is a professor in the Department of English Language and Cultures, Gakushuin University, Japan. She received her PhD from the University of London for her dissertation on Maria Edgeworth's narrative strategies for the construction of national identities. She has published essays on Jane Austen, Walter Scott, and Sydney Owenson. Her recent publications include "Maria Edgeworth's Representation of India: The British Empire and 'Sympathy' in 'Lame Jervas' (1804)."

Index